ALL of
THE WOMEN
of THE BIBLE

*

ALL of
THE WOMEN
of THE BIBLE

*

By EDITH DEEN

1817

HARPER & ROW, PUBLISHERS, SAN FRANCISCO

Cambridge, Hagerstown, New York, Philadelphia, Washington
London, Mexico City, São Paulo, Singapore, Sydney

ISBN 0-06-061852-3

Library of Congress catalog card number: 55-8521

88 89 90 91 92 HC 10 9 8 7 6 5 4 3 2 1

To my husband Edgar Deen,
without whose assistance, encouragement,
and faith this book would not have risen
from a dream to a reality

General Contents

*

Contents by Sections

*

[ix]

CONTENTS

[x]

CONTENTS

CONTENTS

SECTION II

ALPHABETICAL LISTING OF
NAMED WOMEN

CONTENTS

CONTENTS

SECTION III

CHRONOLOGICAL LISTINGS OF NAMELESS WOMEN IN THE BACKGROUND

DAUGHTERS

CONTENTS

MOTHERS

CONTENTS

WIDOWS

OTHER UNNAMED WOMEN

CONTENTS

Preface

THE idea for this book sprang from a story I wrote on Lydia, the businesswoman described in Acts. For more than twenty-five years I had edited a woman's department for a metropolitan newspaper and written a daily column, "From a Woman's Corner." One day a prominent layman of the Southwest suggested that I devote a column to Lydia, who, according to the record in Acts, was the first person in Europe to be won to Christianity by the Apostle Paul.

The Lydia story brought letters from readers, who suggested a series on women of the Bible. This idea challenged me. Today the Bible, churches and religion have become big news. In our regional libraries I found many books on women of the Bible, but none was comprehensive. The demand for these books was great, for I saw that many were well-worn; others, though written decades earlier, were still in use. One of these—and one of the best—had been written by Harriet Beecher Stowe, author of *Uncle Tom's Cabin.*

When my articles on twenty-five prominent women of the Bible appeared they were thought to be the first series on this subject to appear in any American newspaper. The interest manifested by our local ministers as well as by other readers encouraged me. Letters came from many areas, suggesting that the articles be published in book form. I realized, however, that the need was not for another book on a few prominent women but for a comprehensive encyclopedia or dictionary including *all of the women of the Bible.*

About this time I read a history of the publishing house of Harper. On the first page of this book, published in 1910, I found the names of Lydia, Phoebe and Rebekah, all Bible names of women in the Harper family prior to the Revolutionary War when James Harper, grandfather of the four brothers who founded the house of Harper, emigrated from England to America.

Remembering that Jesus had said, "If ye have faith as a grain of mustard seed . . . nothing shall be impossible" (Matt. 17:20), I wrote to Harper & Brothers, asking if they would be interested in a book on *all of the women of the Bible*. Their response was immediate and the project received the careful attention of the late John B. Chambers, whose skill and patience lightened my task. While I was preparing the manuscript, William Schoenberg, southwestern sales representative for Harper, visited our home several times and showed real personal interest.

Our task soon became engrossing. My husband helped me, often working in our home library from dinnertime until the early morning hours, searching out all the named and nameless women of the Bible. This was pioneer research for no single source book included them all. Meanwhile, I worked on the Searching Studies of women in the foreground, some fifty of whom were now on my list.

We built an extensive collection of Bible and religious books so that we could do much of our research in our home. Dr. L. R. Elliott, librarian at the Southwestern Baptist Seminary, aided us in many ways. We searched for books on women of the Bible in bookstores and libraries, wherever business took us from the Atlantic to the Pacific Coast, from the north to the south. I worked in the Congressional Library and the New York Public Library as well as libraries in Boston, Los Angeles, San Francisco, Chicago and St. Louis. I found material in the libraries of the Pacific School of Religion and Texas State College for Women, where I am a member of the board of regents.

These women of antiquity became my personal friends and daily companions as I worked month after month from 5:00 A.M. until bedtime writing, rewriting and studying. Often it seemed that such vivid personalities as Sarah, Rebekah, Rachel, Hannah and Mary, the Mother of Jesus, were actually in my sunny yellow study. I discovered their stories are among the most exciting on record. Here in this Bible portrait gallery—the greatest in all literature—are women of our common humanity.

While attempting to re-create these women, so that they might be seen as real human beings, I had one purpose: to try to understand and interpret their spiritual experiences, their faith and their relationship with God. Even with such women as Jezebel, Potiphar's wife or Herodias, their very lack of faith was significant. The lives of the women of the Bible made patterns of light or of darkness. Our friend Dr. Elton Trueblood, the eminent Quaker-philosopher, had said to me, "Watch for the phrase in Kings and Chronicles, 'And his mother was.' " This, he emphasized, was usually followed by the phrase, "And he did that which was good in the sight of the Lord" or "And he did that which was evil in the sight of the Lord." In placing the name of a king's mother and the evaluation of his reign side by side the Hebrews showed how powerful they regarded the role of a mother.

The book divided itself quite naturally into three parts. Section I contains Searching Studies of more than fifty women in the foreground. Section II comprises alphabetically arranged sketches of the more than one hundred and fifty named women in the background. In Section III other sketches, arranged chronologically, describe more than one hundred nameless women in the background, some of whom appear in groups under such headings as daughters, wives, mothers, widows.

In the completion of this book, I owe a debt of gratitude to many people. I wish to thank all of them here though I can mention the names of only a few. First is the late John B. Chambers, whom I mentioned earlier. Next is Alice Parmelee, author of *A Guidebook to the Bible,* who helped me with the final checking and revision. Julia Stair, who styled the manuscript, gave it her training and knowledge. Dr. William L. Reed of Texas Christian University, one of the ablest Old Testament scholars in the United States, read some of the first studies and offered helpful suggestions. The two pastors in our family, my own pastor, Dr. Granville Walker of University Christian Church, and Dr. Guy Moore of Broadway Baptist, have inspired me in my efforts. I am indebted to our skilled typist, Peggy Fleming, who from my scribbled and typed notes produced a beautiful and accurate manuscript.

Our capable home helper Versie Roberts, wife of a minister, created the quiet and order in our home, thus enabling me to work without needless interruptions. Her spiritual insight and knowledge of the Bible brought a sense of calm to my busiest days.

Another who aided me in the early part of these studies is Mamie Walker of the English faculty of Texas State College for Women.

To these and many others I shall be unceasingly grateful for their part in the making of this book.

I look back over almost thirty years of journalism and see them as years of preparation for this task. In 1934 my journey to the Holy Land gave me my first glimpse of the world in which these women of the Bible lived.

Now I send forth these pages, praying that through greater knowledge and understanding of the lives of *all of the women of the Bible* many people will exalt the power of God and turn eagerly to the Bible, the great record of our search for God and His revelation to us.

Fort Worth, Texas   EDITH DEEN
May, 1955

Searching Studies of Women
in the Foreground

CHAPTER I

Women of the Dawn

EVE

GEN. 3:20; 4:1
II COR. 11:3
I TIM. 2:13

God creates her from rib of Adam. She is tempted by serpent. Cain is born, then Abel. Cain kills Abel. Seth is born, also other children. She is mentioned twice in New Testament.

"IN HIS OWN IMAGE"

THE story of the first woman begins with Eve in the Garden of Eden, where she first discovered that she bore a unique relationship to God, the supreme power in the universe. The great reality is not that she came from the rib of Adam but that God created her and brought her womanly nature into being.

The divine purpose relative to woman is found in the first part of the first story of the Creation: "So God created man in his own image, in the image of God created he him; male and female created he them" (Gen. 1:27). Here we have warranty for woman's dominion. The fact that God did not give man dominion until he had woman standing beside him is evidence enough of her exalted place in the Creation.

Various theories regarding the origin of Genesis and of the story concerning Eve, the first woman, have been evolved. Some scholars believe that parts of Genesis are based on myths and fables. Others call it a "legend wrapped around fundamental spiritual truths."

All Bible scholars concede that the story of Creation was conceived by an ancient people, to whom great truths about the spiritual universe in which they lived were becoming known. How these truths became known and why, scholars cannot answer. Nor do they try to answer all the questions concerning the creation of the first woman. The significant fact is that this first woman was set in a pattern of sublime religious truths.

The magnificent theme of the story is that God, seeing the incompleteness of man standing alone, wanted to find a helper for him. Not having found this helper in all created things, such as the birds of the air or the beasts of the field, God was obliged to make for man a helper who was his equal and who shared in the same processes of creation in which he shared. And so God created this helper Eve, whose name means "life," not from the animal kingdom, but from the rib of Adam himself.

The symbolism of the rib is that it was taken from the place nearest to Adam's heart, thus indicating the close relationship of man and woman. The real essence of the story is that man and woman were made for each other, that woman is bone of his bone and flesh of his flesh; therefore they are not all that God intended them to be until they are together.

The oneness of man and woman in true marriage comes into its fullest meaning in Genesis 2:24: "Therefore shall a man leave his father and his mother, and shall cleave unto his wife: and they shall be one flesh." Marriage emerges, not as a civil contract, but as a divine institution. In this union of Adam and Eve all marriages become coeval with Creation, fully demonstrating that the laws of morals and the laws of nature are coincident.

Eve herself, like all of us, came into a universe that was immeasurable and orderly, and her creation takes on the same wonder as that of the stars, the sun, the moon, and all other things which God created and called good.

In the Genesis account Eve is elevated to ethereal beauty and lofty dignity. As a great sculptor might strike a beautiful figure out of Parian marble, Eve arises from the rib of Adam beautiful of form and figure and with Paradise as her birthplace. Milton, in his *Paradise Lost*, has called her Queen of the Universe and Fairest of the Fair. By poet and artist alike she has usually been pictured with gleaming golden hair, with a face celestial in loveliness and a form strong and immortal.

All of the great epochs in a woman's life, her marriage, mating, and motherhood, unfold in all of their completeness in the Genesis account of Eve. The family, too, with all its joys and heartaches comes into being, with Eve as the center of it. In Eve all the elemental questions of life, birth, and death, even sin and temptation, are shown in their human dimension.

When Eve listened to the serpent, representing temptation, she followed, not the will of God, but the path of evil. When she ate the fruit from the Forbidden Tree, she acted independently of God, in whose image she had been created. From God, who watched over her truest interests, she turned to a serpent, which distorted the truth regarding the fruit God had forbidden. The serpent beguiled Eve by telling her that if she would eat of the forbidden fruit she would gain for herself new delights.

After she had partaken of the forbidden fruit, she also gave it to Adam, and he too ate it, thus sharing in her guilt. In this act we have an excellent example of woman's impulsiveness and man's inclination to follow woman wherever she leads, even into sin. Eve with Adam "hid from the presence of God" for they knew they had done wrong. Afterward, when Eve told God that "the serpent beguiled me, and I did eat," she displayed the natural tendency of woman to blame, not herself for her wrongdoings, but those around her.

Though Eve fell far short of the ideal in womanhood, she rose to the dream of her destiny as a wife and mother. Paradise had been lost. She knew that, but something wonderful, maternal care, had been born. In Eve, motherhood became a great sacrifice and a sublime service. The winged creatures and the animals of the Garden of Eden achieved their motherhood lightly, but for Eve, though motherhood often was achieved at the price of anguish, it became her sacred responsibility.

In the birth of her first son Cain and her second son Abel, Eve experienced all the pains of childbirth, never forgetting perhaps what God had said when she ate of the forbidden fruit, "I will multiply your pain in childbirth."

When her first son was born, we know that Eve, like all mothers, also experienced great joy. The whole world had been re-created, and she could exclaim, "I have gotten a man from the Lord." Here are the sublimest words from the lips of Eve, who named her first son Cain, meaning "gotten" or "acquired." Eve realized that her child came not merely from her flesh but from God himself. Her positive assertion of this makes us certain that God, and not the serpent, now ruled over her life.

Later Eve gave birth to a second son, Abel, meaning "breath" or "fading away." The first mother saw her sons grow to be as different in nature as in interests. Early she discerned signs of jealousy between them. Finally Cain, her first son and most beloved, killed his brother Abel. Though the story does not furnish details, we can picture this first mother as experiencing all the anxieties, heartaches, and torments suffered by other mothers of wicked sons down the centuries of time.

Yet Eve knew that God was still in this universe which He had created. In a few years she was to see the fulfillment of His plan in her own life. Cain married and Eve had a grandchild, Enoch, as well as other heirs. A long interval elapsed. Adam, we are told, was 130 years old when Eve, who could not have been much younger, gave birth to Seth, his name meaning "to appoint" or "to establish." And she took new courage in the fact, we know, for she said, "God hath appointed me another seed instead of Abel, whom Cain slew." A great seed this was to be, for the ancestry of Jesus Christ was to be traced back to the line of Seth.

Other sons and daughters were born to Adam of Eve, though the other children's names are not listed. But after her time for childbearing passed, Eve's story merged into that of her children. She lived on in Seth, the strongest of her children, and in the great line of Seth's descendants, who called "upon the name of the Lord."

Twice in the New Testament, both times in the Pauline writings, Eve is mentioned. Paul reminds the Corinthians that they, like Eve, are in danger of being led away from the simplicity of Christ's teaching and can be hurt by the "subtilty of the serpent," which brings disunity (II Cor. 11:3). Paul expresses his position in regard to woman in a letter to his assistant Timothy. He argues that man is superior, "For Adam was first formed, then Eve." Though he recognizes that "woman being deceived was in the transgression," he declares she can be saved in childbearing, if she continues "in faith and charity and holiness with sobriety" (I Tim. 2:13-15).

But let us turn back to the Genesis account where we have the scriptural record that male and female were created in His own image. Despite her later transgressions, Eve still stands forth as a revelation of the Father, and as one who can rise above her transgressions.

SARAH

Wife of Abraham. Goes with him from Ur to Haran and thence to land of Canaan. Sarah is "fair to look upon." God promises to bless her as Mother of Nations. Impatient of divine delays, she gives her maid, Hagar, to husband. Ishmael is born. Finally Sarah gives birth to Isaac. She dies and is buried at Machpelah. Appears among worthies in New Testament.

"MOTHER OF NATIONS"

THE first woman distinctly portrayed in the dramatic history of man's spiritual development is Sarah, beloved wife of Abraham, founder of the House of Israel. The story of the beautiful and distinguished Sarah and her husband, "Father of Faithful," covers more space in the Genesis account than does that of the entire human race from the Creation down to their time.

Sarah's life was one continuous trial of her faith in God's promise that she was to be the Mother of Nations. Through this trial she emerged as a woman of power, one who was a dutiful and beloved wife and who finally became a favored and venerated mother.

In Sarah's period, which was probably sometime in the nineteenth or twentieth century B.C., woman assumed little importance until she

[8]

had given her husband a son, for it was through his son that a man lived on. The tragedy of Sarah's early life was that she was barren, but the miracle of her life was that she gave birth to Isaac, Son of Promise, when, humanly speaking, the time had passed when she could become a mother.

The miracle was achieved through the faith of Abraham and the loyalty of Sarah to her husband. While they still resided at Haran, God said to Abraham, "Get thee out of thy country, and from thy kindred, and from thy father's house, unto a land that I will shew thee: And I will make of thee a great nation" (Gen. 12:1, 2).

Sarah's life became Abraham's. Where he went she went, not as his shadow but as a strong influence. Together they experienced the vicissitudes of nomadic life and found in them great spiritual significance. Abraham, man of God, was willing to forsake home and country for the unknown, with Sarah ever at his side. Her love and loyalty were blessed by Abraham's devotion to her.

Departure from their native land, the only land either of them had ever known, did not divide them in love or purpose. Dangerous were the wastelands and towns through which they traveled, but Sarah never looked back, as Lot's wife did later when she left Sodom. Tenaciously Sarah shared her husband's dangers and heartaches and also his great purposes and dreams.

Early in their wanderings, under the spreading tree of Moreh, in the rich valley of Shechem, Abraham built an altar to the Lord. Later he built an altar near Beth-el, twelve miles north of Jerusalem, and another under an oak at Mamre. It is easy to imagine that Sarah worshiped at these altars with her husband. Though less credulous than he, she had a high conception of wifely duty, for Sarah was obedient, to Abraham. She became what Peter calls an "heir" with Abraham of "the grace of life" (I Pet. 3:7).

The adversity of famine that swept them later into the Valley of the Nile did not divide them, nor did great prosperity, which fol-lowed Abraham through most of the days of his long life. The intensity of their union deepened and became like a mighty force that nothing, not even Hagar, a secondary wife and mother of Abraham's first child, Ishmael, could diminish.

When Sarah and her husband started their wanderings, they both were in their mature years. The Bible says she was sixty-five and he was seventy-five. They had known only one home, Ur, about halfway between the head of the Persian Gulf and Bagdad. From this ancient city of reed and mud huts Sarah traveled with her huband along the level banks of the Euphrates and on around the Fertile Crescent to the trail south along the Mediterranean. The arch of this crescent was flourishing in these times as a place of rich caravan trade.

This couple's caravan was impressive in the beginning; and Abraham increased his wealth as he traveled. Their long entourage consisted of menservants and maidservants as well as sheep, oxen, asses, and other herds and flocks. The extent of their household later may be imagined by the fact that, at Abraham's word, no less than 318 servants, born in his house and trained to arms, accompanied him to the rescue of his nephew, Lot. Those left to attend his flocks and herds, which he possessed in great numbers, must have been in equal proportion. The beautiful confidence and true affection existing between Sarah and Abraham are reflected in the authority she had over this household during his absence. He recognized her as his equal. She never subjected herself to a lesser role, and Abraham never demanded it.

We can picture their long caravan with its riding animals brilliantly attired with wool and bead trappings, as were their riders, forming a cavalcade of color as it moved from the fertile green valley into the parched land where little grew but dry thornbushes and tamarisk trees.

Perhaps the most impressive figure in the caravan was Sarah herself. Though Bible records furnish no further details than the fact that she was "a fair woman to look upon," we can picture her as wearing a flowing robe blending several rich colors, perhaps the warm reds and azure blue made familiar by the old masters. The drapery of her robe extended to a headdress with a veil that partly hid her face. It is easy to imagine she might have had alluring auburn hair, plaited and coiled in halo effect, exquisite olive skin, red lips and cheeks, deep-set eyes that brightened as she smiled, and a figure both commanding and graceful.

Sarah was a princess in bearing and character, as her name signified. From Babylonia, she brought with her the name of Sarai, but fourteen years later, at the time of her approaching motherhood, God changed her name from Sarai to Sarah, and her husband's name from Abram to Abraham (Gen. 17:5, 15).

Sarah was her husband's half-sister on the side of their father Terah, who had journeyed with them from Ur as far as Haran. Such marriages were not uncommon in the early patriarchal era. As Sarah and Abraham journeyed through strange and perilous country, Abraham passed his wife off as his sister, which was a half-truth. Possibly it was because he knew that these ancient monarchs would employ any means, however cruel and violent, to get the radiantly beautiful Sarah into their harems. Early in their wanderings Sarah was taken into King Pharaoh's court, but it is evident from the record that her ardent affection for Abraham was not diminished by the pomp, riches, and power of a great Egyptian king. Josephus informs us that Sarah, courageous and unafraid, admitted to her royal admirer that she was the wife of Abraham; consequently Pharaoh gave many gifts to Abraham because of the beautiful Sarah. Isn't it to Sarah's credit that her own fidelity to Abraham secured her escape?

The same situation recurred when Sarah and Abraham arrived, a decade or more later, at the court of Abimelech in Gerar. This king, too, we are told, desired Sarah for his harem, though these two similar stories may be variant records of the same incident.

Growing impatient for the birth of Abraham's promised son, and not understanding the divine delay, Sarah concluded she was the obstacle. The promise had been made about eleven years before when

Sarah and Abraham had left their homeland. Because she had not yet conceived, Sarah devised the plan of giving her maid Hagar, probably obtained as a gift from Pharaoh, to her husband as a secondary wife, a common custom in patriarchal times. Hagar, who had become the favorite in Sarah's large household of servants, evidently enjoyed her mistress' full confidence.

With wavering faith but with a willingness to forsake her own vanity, Sarah went to Abraham and said, "Behold now, the Lord hath restrained me from bearing: I pray thee, go in unto my maid; it may be that I may obtain children by her. And Abram hearkened to the voice of Sarai" (Gen. 16:2).

Sarah's lack of faith in her ability to give birth to a child of her own was to bring long years of anguish, for this child by the bond-woman Hagar, she later would learn, was not the child God had promised. According to an ancient custom, the child of such a union as Sarah proposed between her maid and her husband would be regarded as Sarah's own child.

After having been admitted to intimacy with Abraham, and after learning she had conceived by him, Hagar became proud and assuming and quickly forgot her mistress' generosity in exalting her from the position of bondwoman to that of concubine. Understandably human, Sarah showed her worst self when she uttered reproach to her husband: "I have given my maid into thy bosom; and when she saw that she had conceived, I was despised in her eyes: the Lord judge between me and thee" (Gen. 16:5).

Sarah, we can be quite certain, still enjoyed the love and confidence of her husband, for when she complained to Abraham about Hagar's insolence and impudence, he answered her saying, "Behold, thy maid is in thy hand; do to her as it pleaseth thee" (Gen. 16:6). That was reassurance enough of Abraham's affection for Sarah and his recognition of her supremacy over a maid, even one who was to bear him a child.

Not one to submit tamely to ingratitude, Sarah took quick steps to reprimand Hagar. In no state of mind to take such reprimands, Hagar fled into the wilderness. "And the angel of the Lord said unto her, Return to thy mistress, and submit thyself under her hands" (Gen. 16:9).

There is no record that further enmity between Sarah and Hagar occurred until about fourteen years later. Sarah doubtless had formed an attachment to Hagar's son Ishmael, her foster son, and may even have regarded him as the Son of Promise. When the boy was thirteen years old, Abraham was circumcized, signifying that he had entered upon a covenant with God. Then God told Abraham that He would not establish His covenant with Ishmael but with a son whom Sarah would bear.

Soon after this three men came toward him as he sat in his tent door. Desiring to offer them his best hospitality, he hastened to Sarah's tent and asked her to make cakes upon the hearth for their guests. In this service Sarah became the first woman in the Bible to extend hospitality to guests.

Her guests turned out to be divine messengers who had come to tell Abraham that Sarah would give birth to a son. Out of curiosity Sarah was listening to their conversation from her own tent. Not knowing who these strangers were, "Sarah laughed within herself, saying, After I am waxed old shall I have pleasure, my lord being old also?" (Gen. 18:12). In a later passage (Gen. 18:15) it is explained that she had laughed because she was afraid. Could it be that her laughter came from a sorrowful heart, that her mirth represented a heaviness of spirit? (Prov. 14:13).

Sarah surely had developed great faith or she could not have become the mother in the Bible's first story of a miracle birth. The ancient writers who recorded her story believed that with God nothing was impossible, not even the birth of a child to a woman long past the age to bear children.

Paul, in his epistle to the Romans, in speaking on salvation that comes not by law but through faith, best expresses the miracle of

Isaac's birth in this manner, "And being not weak in faith, he [Abraham] considered not his own body now dead, when he was about an hundred years old, neither yet the deadness of Sarah's womb" (Rom. 4:19).

Soon Sarah was to know all the bliss of a young mother. She would even nurse her child at her own breast, experiencing the while a visible manifestation of the wonderful power and unchanging love of God. In later years her son Isaac would display tenderhearted qualities, evidence enough of the gentle influence of his mother in these formative years of his life.

On one of Isaac's birthdays, probably his third, his father made a great public feast, celebrating the child's weaning. At this feast, during which throngs of guests rejoiced, Hagar and Ishmael, who was now about seventeen years old, stood aside mocking. Once more Sarah, a woman of positive decision, demanded of Abraham, "Cast out this bondwoman and her son: for the son of this bondwoman shall not be heir with my son, even with Isaac" (Gen. 21:10).

Like any mother of a toddling youngster, Sarah did not look forward to rearing him with a rough half-brother and his jealous mother. Probably there was more wisdom than harshness in the positive stand Sarah took against Hagar and Ishmael, for we have the record that God spoke again to Abraham, saying, "Let it not be grievous in thy sight because of the lad, and because of thy bondwoman; in all that Sarah hath said unto thee, hearken unto her voice; for in Isaac shall thy seed be called" (Gen. 21:12).

Early the next morning Abraham sent away the bondwoman and her son, first placing on her shoulder a skin bottle of water. Though Abraham had been Hagar's legal custodian, he now followed the patriarchal custom when he turned her out, because of her misdemeanors toward his wife. Though in distress when expelled from the household of Abraham and Sarah, Hagar was to find new strength from God, a God who had mercy even upon those who had acted wrongly. He protected Hagar by filling her jug with water and by teaching her son Ishmael to become an expert with the bow.

Now Sarah could instruct her son Isaac in wisdom and piety, without the discord that had been created by these two who had mocked her. Sarah is not to be condoned, of course, for not showing more love, even to those who had mocked her. But in this wasn't she protecting her child rather than herself?

As Isaac reached manhood, Sarah was to come face to face with an even greater trial. At God's command, Abraham set forth with their beloved Son of Promise to sacrifice him upon an altar. As Sarah sorrowfully watched her husband and son depart for the mountains in the land of Moriah, we can imagine her anguish of heart. And yet this woman who had developed great faith could now turn to the same omnipotent God who had miraculously brought forth her child in her old age. He was a God of love and mercy and majesty. She would remain obedient to him.

Anxiety and sorrow were not to overwhelm her for long. She soon would learn that God did not demand the sacrifice of a son. A ram would be offered up instead of Isaac.

We have no record of Sarah in the years that follow her son's and husband's return from Moriah, but we can assume she enjoyed the love and companionship of a devoted husband and a loyal son until her death at the age of one hundred and twenty-seven years. She is the only woman in the Bible whose age at death is recorded. This again signifies the important place that she held in the minds of early Hebrews.

In the Cave of Machpelah, near Abraham's well-loved oak of Mamre, Sarah was buried. In selecting this site for his wife's last resting place, again Abraham demonstrated his great affection for her. Records tell us also that he "mourned" for her (Gen. 23:2). A few years later, on his wedding night, Isaac took his bride Rebekah to his mother's own tent, thus showing how fondly he, too, cherished her memory.

At Hebron, over the cave of Machpelah which Abraham bought from Ephron the Hittite (Gen. 23) there stands today a conservative Moslem mosque. The lower portions of the walls surrounding the enclosure are believed to date from the time of Solomon. Here in the mosque are the cenotaphs of Abraham and Sarah, Isaac and other descendants of their family, erected just above their tombs in the cave below. Sarah, the first matriarch in the Bible, lies there in the honored place.

In Hebrews 11:11, she is mentioned with those whose faith was outstanding. It says of her: "Through faith also Sarah herself received strength to conceive seed, and was delivered of a child when she was past age, because she judged him faithful who had promised." In Galatians 4:23-31, she is the freewoman in what is called the Allegory of Agar or Hagar. The allegory tells that it was the freewoman (Sarah) who gave birth to a child according to the Spirit, while the bondwoman (Hagar) gave birth to a child according to the flesh.

The fact that Sarah is mentioned in three other places in the New Testament, I Peter 3:6 and Romans 4:19 and 9:9, as well as in Isaiah 51:2, is evidence of the revered place she held in Hebrew history. Today this "Mother of Nations" lives on, some four thousand years later, as the woman whose faith helped to achieve one of the miracle births of the Bible.

LOT'S WIFE

GEN. 19:26
LUKE 17:32

Lives at Sodom, enjoying all luxuries ana gaieties that rich husband could provide. When destruction comes upon Sodom, she refuses to leave. Looks back and is turned to pillar of salt.

THE WOMAN WHO LOOKED BACK

FIFTEEN words in the Old Testament tell the story of Lot's wife. This one brief, dramatic record has placed her among the well-known women of the world. The fifteen words are, "But his wife looked back from behind him, and she became a pillar of salt" (Gen. 19:26).

In the New Testament there are three other words about Lot's wife. Jesus held her up as an example, saying, "Remember Lot's wife" (Luke 17:32). This is one of the shortest verses in the Bible. Its terseness probably best explains its urgency. In a previous passage Jesus had been speaking of those in the days of Lot, who "did eat, they drank, they bought, they sold, they planted, they builded," but "out of Sodom it rained fire and brimstone from heaven, and destroyed them all" (Luke 17:28, 29).

The impression is conveyed that Lot's wife was a woman who ate and drank and lived for the things of the world. We do have a scriptural record that her husband was a rich and influential man (Gen. 13:10, 11). We can easily assume that Lot's wife was a worldly, selfish woman, one who spent lavishly and entertained elaborately. Max Eastman, in his movingly realistic poem *Lot's*

Wife says, "Herself, like Sodom's towers, shone blazingly." Here, we imagine, was a woman who wore many jewels and dressed in the richest and most gleaming fabrics.

Rubens, in his "Flight of Lot," painted in 1625 and now in the Louvre, pictures Lot's wife, followed by her daughters; to her one of the angels is speaking a solemn warning. One of the daughters leads an ass loaded with splendid vessels of gold and silver, while the second bears a basket of grapes and other fruits on her head. The wife clasps her hands and looks beseechingly in the face of the angel who warns her of her fate if she should be disobedient. The family procession, accompanied by a spirited little dog, steps forth from the handsome gates of Sodom. Above the towers of the city walls fly frightful demons preparatory to their work of destruction. The air seems full of imps, while an evil spirit, hovering above Lot's wife, glowers at the angel who is trying to save her from destruction.

The fate of Lot's wife has inspired other painters, among them Gozzoli and Lucas Cranach. All depict a woman who had lived under the law, knew its penalties to be swift and immutable, and yet so loved the city on which God was raining fire from heaven that she willingly gave her life for one more look at it.

Can we not conjecture that the fifteen-word Old Testament biography of Lot's wife was written for those who love the things of the world more than the things of the spirit, those who do not possess the pioneering courage to leave a life of ease and comfort and position for a life of sacrifice, hardship, and loneliness? Does not her biography also speak a message to those who are unwilling to flee from iniquity when all efforts to redeem iniquity have failed?

Dr. William B. Riley, in his book on *Wives of the Bible,* makes the apt comment that "When we have read Lot's history we have uncovered Mrs. Lot's character; and when we have studied his affluence, we have seen her influence. . . . The character and con-

duct of children reflect the mother. The marriage of her daughters to Sodomitish men indicated low ethical ideals and low moral
standards." Their later relations with their father were a blot on
their mother's character (Gen. 19:32-35). Lot's earlier actions
toward Abraham indicated the type of wife he had. When he and
his uncle Abraham had become prosperous in herds and flocks,
Abraham offered Lot a choice of territory. And what did he choose?
He chose the most fertile plain of the Jordan. Though we have no
record of his wife in this transaction, we again can visualize her as
a woman sharing in his selfishness, without dissent, and prodding her
husband to greater wealth at any cost to others.

Goethe has said, "Tell me with whom thou dost company and
I will tell thee what thou art." Our best way of describing Lot's
wife is through her husband and her children and her disobedience to the warning of angels. The latter could have saved her,
but she had nothing in common with angels.

When her husband had first come into this fertile plain of
Jordan, he had pitched his tent "toward Sodom," a phrase which
indicates that Lot was not then a part of the wicked Sodom and
Gomorrah. But again, isn't it easy to imagine that his wife wanted
a big stone house in keeping with her husband's great wealth?
Was a tent on the outskirts enough? Wasn't she hoplessly bound
up with all the materialities of Sodom?

When she had to flee, she had to look back. In this she reminds
us of a woman who, after leaving her burning house, rushes back
for treasured material possessions and is burned with the possessions.

Certainly Lot's wife bears none of the qualities of greatness
that we find in the noble women in history—those, for example,
who left England on the *Mayflower* and landed on a desolate
coast in the dead of winter to carve new homes in the wilderness.
These women, too, had to leave all behind, but they were willing

to make the sacrifice in order that they and their families might have religious freedom.

Even though Lot's wife was well out of Sodom with her daughters and husband before the destruction came, she could not be influenced either by the warnings of the angels or by the pleadings of her husband. And as she looked back, she was turned to a pillar of salt.

Tradition has pointed out, however, that a mountain of salt, at the southern extremity of the Dead Sea, was the spot where the event took place. The text described it as a rain of "brimstone and fire from the Lord out of heaven" by which the whole district was overthrown.

Geologists explain that at the south end of the Dead Sea is a burned-out region of oil and asphalt. A great stratum of rock salt lies underneath the Mountain of Sodom on the west shore of the sea. This stratum of salt, they say, is overlaid with a stratum of marl, mingled with free sulphur in a very pure state. Something kindled the gases which accumulate with oil and asphalt, and there was an explosion. Salt and sulphur were carried up into the heavens red hot. Literally it could have rained fire and brimstone. The cities and the whole plain and everything that grew out of the ground were utterly destroyed. This may explain the incrustation of Lot's wife with salt when she turned back.

The differences of opinion regarding the myth and the literal aspect of Lot's wife do not change the great truths of the story. She still stands as a permanent symbol of the woman who looks back and refuses to move forward, the woman who, faced toward salvation, still turns to look longingly on material things she has left behind.

One thing is certain. The story of Lot's wife has not lost its savor in all the thousands of years since Old Testament writers recorded it.

REBEKAH

Meets Abraham's servant as she carries water to well. He is looking for wife for Isaac and is attracted by her courtesy and kindness. She and her damsels journey with him to Canaan where Isaac awaits her. After twenty years she gives birth to twins, Esau and Jacob. Deceives husband in order to win his blessing on Jacob. She is buried at Machpelah.

MOTHER OF TWINS, ESAU AND JACOB

IN a setting of romance and wonder Rebekah is introduced, and from her first sharply etched portrait at the well at Nahor in Mesopotamia she attracts interest. Even in this first scene we seem to sense the kindness in her heart, to hear the music in her voice, and to see the grace in her motions. At the same time we know she is chaste, courteous, helpful, industrious, and trusting.

No young woman in the Bible is so appealing. One of the old masters has depicted Rebekah in a flowing dress of delft blue and a headdress of scarlet and purple. The dress neckline is striped in gold to match the gold in her necklace, ear-screws, and bracelets. The artist has given her a dark, patrician profile, broadly arched eyebrows, gentle but expressive eyes, a slightly aquiline nose, and a firm yet innocent mouth.

At eventide it was that she came to the well, carrying her pitcher on her shoulder. With other women, young and old, who had come to draw water, she took the well-worn trail to the town watering place. Though Rebekah was unaware of it, she was being observed by a meditative old man, a stranger from far away, who stood by with ten thirsty camels.

He had only a little while before concluded a long, tiresome trek from the land of Canaan, home of his master, Abraham. As the latter's steward he faced a grave responsibility, that of choosing a wife for his master's son, Isaac. He had approached his task prayerfully and had asked God for a sign to help him make the right choice. What would be the sign? The young maiden who volunteered to give water to his camels after he asked her for a drink for himself would possess those traits of character he was looking for in a wife for his master's son. How little Rebekah knew of the high destiny that awaited her simply because she volunteered a service that would be only natural to her.

Kneeling in the shadows of the deepening twilight, Abraham's zealous steward, who had been his designated heir before the birth of his sons, spoke to his invisible protector: "O Lord God of my master Abraham, I pray thee, send me good speed this day, and shew kindness unto my master Abraham" (Gen. 24:12).

Eliezer had hardly finished his petition to God when behold there stood before him this lovely maiden Rebekah. The faithful servant hastened to her and said, "Let me, I pray thee, drink a little water of thy pitcher" (Gen. 24:17). She gave him a drink with ready grace and then there came the sign for which the servant had been waiting. "I will draw water for thy camels, also, until they have done drinking," she said (Gen. 24:19).

Rebekah must have had to make several trips down to the well in order to carry enough water in a pitcher for ten thirsty camels. Eliezer gazed in silence, believing all the more in God's goodness. Before asking who her kindred were, he rewarded her with an earring and two bracelets, all of heavy gold.

Then he asked, "Whose daughter art thou? tell me, I pray thee:

is there room in thy father's house for us to lodge in?" (Gen. 24:23).
When Rebekah told him she was the daughter of Bethuel, whom the
servant knew to be his master's nephew, and when she also added
graciously, "We have both straw and provender enough, and room
to lodge in," he humbly thanked God for leading him to the house
of his master's kinsman (Gen. 24:25).

The scene that followed moved fast. After Abraham's steward
explained to Rebekah's family the purpose of his visit, he gave lavish
gifts to her mother and brother Laban and other members of the
family. And Rebekah soon learned that her future husband, Isaac,
who was her second cousin, was heir to his father's flocks and herds,
silver and gold, menservants and maidservants, and many asses. But
of greater significance was the fact that God had established his
covenant with Abraham and his son Isaac, and Rebekah would be
a participant in that covenant.

When Rebekah's family asked her, "Wilt thou go with this man?"
she replied without any hesitancy, "I will go." A woman of positive
direction, Rebekah also had the courage and spirit which would enable her to forsake home and family for a new life in a strange
country.

Apprehensive, however, about giving up their beloved daughter,
her family asked that she remain for a few days, at least ten; but
Abraham's steward was in haste to be on his way. So we picture the
eager-hearted Rebekah departing with her nurse Deborah and her
maids on camels. We can see her family bidding her good-by and
then watching longingly as the caravan disappeared through the
Balikh Valley.

Then it crossed the banks of the Euphrates into the pathless and
sun-bleached sands of the desert on its way to Damascus. It passed
over the Lebanon highlands into the green hills of Galilee and finally
drew near the yellow plains around Beer-sheba. As the caravan came
into the more fertile fields, Rebekah saw an upright man walking
forth in his field, bearing in his measured tread the aspect of one in

holy meditation. He had seen the camels coming and had gone into his fields to pray. As Rebekah drew near, she lowered her veil in the manner of oriental women and alighted from her camel.

After Abraham's steward explained all that had taken place on the journey, Isaac took Rebekah into his mother's tent, a sacred place to him, and she became his wife. "And he loved her: and Isaac was comforted after his mother's death" is the brief but graphic account of the marriage of Isaac and Rebekah (Gen. 24:67). We can imagine that Isaac rejoiced when he saw in Rebekah a reflection of the endearing qualities of his mother, Sarah.

Isaac was now forty, and we can assume that Rebekah was some twenty years younger. Her husband, an agriculturist as well as a cattle raiser, enjoyed great affluence, and we can be sure that these were satisfying years for Rebekah. Though there is little record of her life between her marriage and twenty years later when she gave birth to twins, we can imagine she became a woman of sympathy, foresight, and religious fervor. And we can be certain that she enjoyed peace at home, for her marriage to Isaac is the first monogamous marriage on record.

Only one blessing was lacking in Rebekah's life. She had not conceived, but when she did conceive, she discovered that she was to have twins. We have this record, "And the children struggled together within her; and she said, If it be so, why am I thus? And she went to enquire of the Lord" (Gen. 25:22). This is the first recorded instance of a woman's immediate appeal to God.

God told Rebekah that two nations were in her womb and two manner of people, and that the elder should serve the younger. The struggle is represented as prefiguring the struggle for supremacy between Edom and Israel, descended respectively from Esau and Jacob. And when the first-born Esau came forth, he was red all over like a hairy garment, indicating that he would be material-minded. And then came Jacob, destined to be the more spiritual-minded of the two. Who would be more aware of this than their devout mother?

REBEKAH

Isaac, quiet and retiring, was drawn to the bold, daring, strong, and roaming Esau; and Rebekah, naturally industrious, was drawn to the gentle but impetuous Jacob.

As the sons grew to manhood, their mother began to love wisely but not always too well. And she began to plan how Jacob, the last-born, and not Esau, the first-born, could receive his father's blessing.

Esau had already voluntarily surrendered to Jacob his birthright, and all for bread and a pottage of lentils. The birthright, which Esau's mother knew he had sold so casually to satisfy his hunger, was a very valuable right of an older son. Not only did it assure to its possessor a double share of his father's inheritance, but it carried with it a position of honor as head of the family as well. All this now belonged to Jacob.

All that was lacking was for Jacob to obtain his father's blessing, which would secure to him the birthright of his older brother and all the advantages that birthright entailed. Isaac was now an old man and blind, and his last days seemed near at hand.

Records do not furnish actual historical details, but we can be sure that Rebekah was a mother who pondered deeply over her son's destiny. She recognized the secular bent of the first-born, Esau, and the priestly mold of the last-born, Jacob. Had she not also observed how Esau's associates were the Hittites, known to be a less religious race? (He had even married two Hittite women, Judith and Bashemath, and in that marriage had returned to the polygamous way of life which she and Isaac had abandoned. Had she not observed how Esau spent his time in hunting and other such pleasures while Jacob worshiped at the altar of God? Had she not seen how Esau lived for today and how Jacob, like herself, looked into the future? Had she not seen in Esau's face a love for a mess of pottage and in Jacob's a dream of divine glory?

Yet it was Isaac alone who would ordain his successor. And she had heard him say to Esau, "Bring me venison, and make me savoury

meat, that I may eat, and bless thee before the Lord before my death"
(Gen. 27:7).

This sounded the death knell of a proud mother's hopes. And this
mother was human. She began to plot an act that was deep, dark,
disconcerting. All through her life Rebekah had never wavered in
purpose. Even when she left her homeland for another country, she
proceeded with positive direction.

But now in this crisis in her favorite son's life, she perceived
clearly too, but her faith wavered. She took quick action, guiding her
steps and those of her favorite son by her will, not God's will. One
wonders if she did not fall by the very weight of the burden which
she believed she was carrying for God. She could not picture Esau as
a leader following the great traditions of her people. Only Jacob
could fill that high trust. And so it was her fears overwhelmed her
and she forgot God's part in the affairs of men.

While Esau was bounding over the hills, busy in the chase for
venison for his old and feeble father, Rebekah sent Jacob to bring
back two kids from a pasture near by. And she prepared the savory
dish, probably seasoning the kids' flesh with onion, garlic, salt, and
lemon juice. She also took pieces of goat's skin and bound them on
Jacob's hands and neck; its silken hair would resemble that on the
cheek of a young man. Next she gave him the long white robe, the
vestment of the first-born, which she had kept in a chest with
fragrant herbs and perfumed flowers.

We cannot make any excuses for Rebekah's actions in deceiving
her blind husband and at the same time influencing her son in what
was wrong. But may we not say that, though her actions were
morally indefensible, her motive was pure? Does she not typify the
mother down the ages who, weak in faith, imagines herself to be
carrying out the will of God? And was she not willing to assume all
the responsibility for this deception?

For Jacob had said to his mother, "My father peradventure will feel me, and I shall seem to him as a deceiver; and I shall bring a curse upon me, and not a blessing" (Gen. 27:12).

But his mother hastily replied, "Upon me be thy curse, my son" (Gen. 27:13). What a burden for a mother to assume! And could she assume it alone? Wouldn't they both be guilty of deceiving Isaac and Esau?

But Rebekah did not falter in her purpose. She saw her blind husband prayerfully bestow upon her favorite the blessing which could never be revoked. When her other son learned what had been done by his mother and brother, he threatened to kill his brother. Rebekah must now suffer for her wrong. She must give up what she loved most, her favorite son. Again with positive direction, yet willing to sacrifice herself, she called him forth and sent him to her brother Laban in Mesopotamia.

An old woman now, Rebekah bade her beloved Jacob good-by as he started on his long journey, with his staff in his hand and his bundle of clothes over his shoulder. We can picture her as she took a long, last look before her son's form became lost on the horizon.

The tinkle of goats' bells and the bleating of the sheep would be heard as usual. The sun would rise in splendor and would go down again. When night fell the stars would come out as usual, but Rebekah would never see Jacob again. More than twenty years would pass before he returned.

She would spend her last years with a son who would always remember his mother's part in deceiving him and with a husband who naturally had lost some of the confidence he once had in her. And she and Isaac both would grieve over the actions of Esau's two Hittite wives.

When Jacob did return, his mother would be sleeping by the side of Abraham and Sarah in Machpelah's quiet sepulcher.

RACHEL and LEAH

*

Jacob meets Rachel at well at Haran and makes covenant for her with her father Laban. Is deceived with Leah. Rachel given to Jacob on new pledge. Leah bears Jacob six sons and her maid bears two more. Rachel bears Joseph and her maid bears two more children. Rachel and Leah depart with husband for his homeland. Rachel takes father's gods and conceals them. She bears Benjamin and dies. Buried at Ephrath. Leah buried at Machpelah.

MOTHERS OF TWELVE TRIBES OF ISRAEL

THE Old Testament writer had an eye for the dramatic when he introduced the graceful, gentle, and lovely Rachel against a scene of pastoral beauty. When Jacob first came upon her, she was quietly tending her father's sheep on a low-lying hillside near the city of Haran.

This bright-eyed barefoot maiden, in her brilliantly colored and softly draped dress, must have been a joy to the homesick Jacob's eyes, for he had been on a long journey by foot, a distance of more than 500 miles from the hill country of Palestine to Padan-aram.

And we can imagine he was scorched by the sun, and footsore and weary.

When he inquired of three shepherds about Laban, his mother's brother, he must have been comforted to hear shepherds reply, "Behold, Rachel his daughter cometh with the sheep" (Gen. 29:6). Jacob knew that this comely maiden was his mother's own niece, and not far away from this watering place his grandfather's steward had come upon his mother at the well.

As Rachel made her slow approach, Jacob rolled from the well a large boulder kept there to prevent the water from becoming polluted. And he gave water to Rachel's sheep, just as his mother Rebekah had given water to his grandfather Abraham's camels. Let us suppose that he and Rachel drank from the same dipper and that, from this moment, they were united in spirit.

One of Jacob's first acts was to kiss Rachel's hand as a respectful salutation; and as he did, he "wept," a demonstration of his joy, for he belonged to a demonstrative people, whose emotions ran deep.

After this meeting with Jacob, Rachel ran to her father, who warmly welcomed his nephew. These family ties became meaningful to Jacob, who was now far from home and possibly homesick for his devoted mother. He quickly became attached to his lovely and lovable Cousin Rachel and lost no time in asking her father if he might marry her. And Jacob offered his own labor for the riches he had not brought with him.

For Rachel, he promised to serve as a shepherd for seven years. "And they seemed unto him but a few days, for the love he had to her" (Gen. 29:20). These words are unsurpassed in the whole literature of romantic love. In fact Jacob's service for Rachel marks him as the most devoted lover in the Bible. And his love for Rachel was not a passing fancy. It would last until the end of his life.

When the time for their marriage came, however, confusions and complications arose. Rachel had an older sister Leah.

Leah is described in the King James Version as "tender eyed,

[29]

while Rachel is described as "beautiful and well favoured." That Leah was much less beautiful than her sister is evident from the text, but it does not appear that she was as plain and homely as some commentators conjecture. In one translation she is called weak-eyed, in another sore-eyed. Could it be that she was verging on blindness? And if so, wouldn't her father have sought to marry her off as soon as he could?

There are many varying interpretations on Leah's eyes. The Midrash explains her "tender" eyes as due to her weeping lest she be compelled to marry Esau.

But we need not tarry too long on one word. The implication is that Leah, because of her problems, whatever they might have been, had had to turn within herself and had become more spiritually sensitive than her more "shallow-minded sister." We like to think that Leah's piety had given her eyes a tender quality, but it was the bright-eyed, much gayer Rachel to whom Jacob was attracted.

At the end of the seven years, when the time had been set for the nuptial festivities, Laban sent Leah to Jacob instead of Rachel. This was an easy trick in primitive times, because it was the custom to conduct the bride to the bedchamber of her husband in silence and darkness. According to the laws of the time, the elder daughter should be married first, but it was not according to the agreement Laban had made with Jacob. As Jacob had deceived his father, so had Laban deceived him.

But according to Bible record, Jacob's union with Rachel was celebrated at the close of Leah's marriage festivities, lasting for about a week. Jacob, however, had to serve another seven years as a shepherd, making fourteen altogether, for his beloved Rachel.

It is easy to imagine that problems, many of them not recorded in the Bible text, arose in this polygamous household, where two sisters were married to the same man.

Rachel had Jacob's love, but Leah bore his first four sons. During those years Rachel had to listen to the crying and cooing of her sister's children, while she had none. Though Leah was blessed with children, she it was who hungered for Jacob's love.

Rachel was the more petulant, peevish, and self-willed of the two; Leah was more meek, submissive, and gentle. Because she was not loved, can we not believe that Leah sought peace in God's un-failing tenderness? She learned to demonstrate content in the midst of trial, and happiness in the midst of grief.

When her first son was born, she significantly called him Reuben, saying, "Surely the Lord hath looked upon my affliction; now there-fore my husband will love me" (Gen. 29:32). Then she bore Simeon and Levi and finally Judah. In the birth of three of these sons, she recognized God, finally praising Him fervently.

God had blessed her abundantly. He had turned her mourning into praise and returned her meek, enduring confidence in Him. One wonders if Leah, even in her heavy affliction of being unloved, was not the more content, for she neither envied nor complained.

Rachel, still with empty arms and a heart longing for children, cried out to a doting husband, "Give me children, or else I die" (Gen. 30:1). Jacob, angered, asked her, "Am I in God's stead, who hath withheld from thee the fruit of the womb?" (Gen. 30:2).

What a striking contrast between Rachel's words and the words of her unloved, unsought, undesired, plainer, but more spiritually sensi-tive sister! The two sisters remind us of two plants, one frail and the other strong, and yet both growing in the same soil. Though these sisters stood in one environment most of the days of their lives, there was always this complete difference of character. They did not quar-rel, but wrestled in mind and spirit through all of their lives. When her maid Bilhah bore Jacob a second son, Rachel named him Naphtali, saying, "With great wrestlings have I wrestled with my sister" (Gen. 30:8). The first son by Bilhah was Dan.

And Leah, following the lead of Rachel, took her maid, Zilpah, and gave her to Jacob. And Zilpah bore Jacob two sons, Gad and

Asher, who, according to the traditions of the time, were Leah's sons, now making six in all.

The sisters wrestled again when Reuben, Leah's eldest son, brought mandrakes from the field. This fruit, the size of a large plum and quite round, yellow, and full of soft pulp, was supposed to have a love charm. Both Rachel and Leah cast longing eyes on the mandrakes. Mace in his book on *Hebrew Marriage* states: "From the most ancient time, aphrodisiac virtues have been ascribed to the mandrake, which was therefore supposed to cure barrenness, and it is now known that the root, when eaten, would have the effect of relaxing the womb."

Rachel said to Leah, "Give me, I pray thee, of thy son's mandrakes" (Gen. 30:14).

Leah, perturbed that her sister should want the mandrakes brought from the field by her own son, said to her, "Is it a small matter that thou has taken my husband? and wouldest thou take away my son's mandrakes also?" And Rachel answered, "Therefore he shall lie with thee tonight for thy son's mandrakes" (Gen. 30:15).

And Leah bore Jacob a fifth son, Issachar. Afterward she bore Jacob a sixth son, Zebulun, and then a daughter, Dinah, the first daughter in the Bible whose name is mentioned at birth. It was not until after the birth of all of Leah's children that Rachel bore Joseph, saying, "God hath taken away my reproach" (Gen. 30:23). We infer that prayer and not envy now filled Rachel's life. Later she would have a second son, Benjamin, thus completing the twelve tribes of Israel by two sisters and their two maids. But it would be Rachel's Joseph, often described as the most Christlike character in the Old Testament, who would come from the mystery of such love as Rachel and Jacob bore for each other.

After the birth of his beloved Joseph, Jacob began to long to return to his homeland. He had now been in Mesopotamia about twenty years, but he could not depart easily, for according to the laws of the time, Laban could still claim his children and his two wives. So it was that Jacob began to devise means whereby he might gain for himself large herds of cattle and sheep. In a few years, through his own craftiness, he had become a rich man.

For the first time we find the two wives, Rachel and Leah, united. This time they had aligned themselves unreservedly against their father. Jacob had called them from the field and reviewed to them how Laban had changed his wages ten times, how Laban also had coveted his increasing herds. Jacob related how in a dream he had been told to return to the land of his kindred.

This time one in thought, Rachel and Leah asked him, "Is there yet any portion or inheritance for us in our father's house? Are we not counted of him strangers? for he hath sold us, and hath quite devoured also our money. For all the riches which God hath taken from our father, that is ours, and our children's: now then, whatsoever God hath said unto thee, do" (Gen. 31:14-16).

When Jacob did not make the decision alone, but consulted his wives, he demonstrated that he, like other patriarchs, took no major steps without counseling with his wives. And Rachel and Leah regarded themselves as their husband's equal.

While his father-in-law was off sheep-shearing in a far country, Jacob, with his wives and eleven children and his herds, flocks, and servants, set off for his homeland in Canaan. Onward they trod, back again through many of the same valleys and over the same mountains and through the same endless sands which Jacob's grandfather Abraham and grandmother Sarah and mother Rebekah had trod.

Three days elapsed, and Rachel and Leah's father received word that his family had departed. He set out to follow them and on the seventh day he overtook his daughters and their large family in the hill country of Gilead.

From Jacob Rachel had kept one secret. She had brought with her the household idols worshiped by her father, who did not believe in Jacob's God. Why did she bring them? Possibly Rachel stole them from her father's home to insure the future prosperity of her husband. She doubtless believed that they brought good luck to their possessor. These household gods may even have secured for Jacob the inheritance of his father-in-law's property.

There is quite a contrast here in Rachel's actions. We wonder if Leah was concerned about a material inheritance. Did she not carry with her, wherever she went, not idols but a faith in Jacob's God? Probably she was not in the least perturbed when her father overtook them and cried out loudly over the loss of his gods, almost as loudly as he had cried out at the loss of his daughters and their children. Not knowing that Rachel possessed the gods, Jacob answered his angry father-in-law, "With whomsoever thou findest thy gods, let him not live" (Gen. 31:32).

Laban searched all the tents for his gods, first Leah's, then Rachel's. When he came to Rachel's he found her sitting on the camel's saddle, beneath which she had probably hidden her father's gods. There she sat and did not arise, but explained apologetically to her father, "Let it not displease my lord that I cannot rise up before thee; for the custom of women is upon me" (Gen. 31:35).

"The custom of women" has had many explanations. The *Interpreter's Bible* brings out the thought in its exegesis on this passage that Rachel means "she was ceremonially unclean" (Lev. 15:19-23). "She apologized for not rising when her father entered, pleading her condition. Laban searched in vain. Rachel, in her uncleanness even sat on them and nothing happened to her." That shows how little she feared the power her father believed they had.

Later we learn that Jacob hid all the strange gods that had been brought out of Mesopotamia under the oak at Shechem (Gen. 35:4). This leads us to believe that Rachel, like Jacob, now believed in Jehovah and not the strange gods of Mesopotamia; otherwise, could she have won Jacob's love so wholeheartedly? Rachel's actions, of course, are subject to varying interpretations. But let us not forget that any personality, ancient or modern, has elements that baffle analysis.

Fearing his brother Esau, who had threatened his life when he had left his homeland twenty years earlier, Jacob, as he now neared the edge of Canaan, thought of his family's safety. Because of his great love for Rachel, he assigned to her and to Joseph the place of greatest safety. "And he put the handmaids and their children foremost, and Leah and her children after, and Rachel and Joseph hindermost" (Gen. 33:2). He probably had another reason for this, as Rachel was now with child.

His fears were unwarranted, for Esau ran to meet him, embraced him, and kissed him. Though we can imagine Rachel rejoiced when her husband and his brother were reconciled, we are given every evidence that cares lingered on. For it is recorded that her nurse Deborah, who also had been the nurse to her mother-in-law, Rebekah, died and was buried beneath an oak at Beth-el. Could it be that Deborah had served as a midwife and had delivered most or all of Jacob's children? Now Rachel, as she journeyed into a strange land, must entrust herself to a new nurse.

We know, too, from the record that Leah also had her heartaches. When the caravan had arrived on the edge of Shechem, her daughter Dinah was defiled by Shechem, the son of Hamor.

As the caravan neared Ephrath, the pains of childbirth came upon Rachel, and she gave birth to her second son, Benjamin, in a cave. As she was dying, the first woman in the Bible to die in childbirth, she cried, "Call his name Ben-oni," meaning "child of sorrow." But his father called him Benjamin, meaning "son of happiness." And Rachel's Benjamin completed the number of Jacob's twelve sons, who were to be designated as the twelve tribes of Israel.

Like a refrain we seem to hear again Rachel's earlier cry, "Give me children, or else I die." Could it be that her too impatient cry was heard and answered? Children were bestowed upon Rachel and with them death. How little she knew what she had asked.

"Jacob set a pillar upon her grave" (Gen. 35:20), again showing his great love for her. That grave, still marked just outside of Beth·

lehem, is the oldest single memorial to a woman mentioned in the Bible.

Jacob had loved Rachel at first sight and he loved her until the end. His last poignant reference to Rachel was made some years later when he said, "And I buried her there in the way of Ephrath" (that is, Bethlehem) (Gen. 48:7).

About ten centuries later, as Jeremiah contemplated the desperate plight of the northern exiles, he heard Rachel, their ancient mother, bemoaning them from her grave. More than seventeen centuries after Rachel's death, Matthew in 2:18 wrote, "In Rama was there a voice heard, lamentation, and weeping, and great mourning, Rachel weeping for her children, and would not be comforted, because they are not." Rama was a town on the border between Judah and Israel. It is here that Rachel is represented as raising her head from the tomb and weeping at seeing the whole land depopulated of her sons. In Jeremiah 31:15 we have much the same idea presented. Jeremiah had in mind the Ephraimites going into exile in Babylon.

Rachel's honors and blessing were many, but what of those last years of Leah, the unloved, undesired, and unsought wife? What compensation did she have at the end? Records do not furnish actual historical details, but since she survived Rachel, we know she took her place at last beside Jacob as his chief wife and they shared many long-to-be-cherished memories of their long lives together. Probably now Jacob relied on Leah's counsel, for there was no other to whom he could turn.

From Leah's son Judah came the tribe of Judah, from which came the line of Boaz, Jesse, and David, which produced Jesus (Luke 3:23, 31-33). And from her son Levi sprang the priesthood. Though the latter son committed a great wrong against Shechem, he must later have been visited by God's special favor because he came to represent, in a sense, the priesthood.

In Ruth 4:11, Leah is honored beside Rachel as one which "did build the house of Israel."

DINAH

GEN. 30:21
   34:1, 3, 5, 13, 25, 26
   46:15

Daughter of Leah and Jacob, she sets out for Shechem alone. Is defiled by Shechem, son of prince. Her brothers demand his circumcision and that of other Shechemites. Brothers slay all males in city and wreck it. On dying day Jacob reproves sons for their wrath.

AND HE DISHONORED HER

THE formidable caravan of Dinah's father Jacob had crossed the Jordan only a little while before and was now encamped in the Shechem Valley, set among the rough highlands, in the pivotal pass between Mount Ebal and Mount Gerizim, a pass through which migrants had trekked since the dawn of time.

After their long journey from Padam-aram, with several years spent in Succoth, Dinah and her mother Leah and others in their large family had come to stay for a time in this land of springs and green valleys. A meaningful event had occurred in the lives of this large family of eleven children by four mothers, Leah and Rachel and their maids Zilpah and Bilhah. That was the erection of an altar, El-elohe-Israel (God, the God of Israel). Land had been purchased from Hamor, prince of Shechem. But it is easy to imagine that the strange city of Shechem offered greater fascination to Dinah than did her father's altar; for she was young, and new and unknown places beckoned her onward.

Though we have no warrant in the Scriptures, by either direct word or inference, we can visualize Dinah as a beautiful girl, one who more closely resembled her "well favored" aunt Rachel than she did her mother Leah. We do know that Dinah was now about fourteen or fifteen years old, the marriageable age for orientals.

Like most girls in a large family of brothers, she longed for the company of other girls and "went out to see the daughters of the land" (Gen. 34:1). Josephus relates that she went to attend a festival at Shechem.

Dinah had every blessing, a father both devout and affluent, a spiritually sensitive mother, and ten brothers. But because she was an only daughter, she may have been pampered and spoiled, maybe a bit vain.

Let us imagine it was the spring of the year. The air was cool, and the wind wafted the fragrance of meadow saffron, wild narcissus, and hyacinth, all growing profusely in the Shechem Valley. We can see her wandering off into the picturesque countryside, expecting possibly to go only a short distance. For it is likely she had never been out of sight of her father's tents unaccompanied. Those tents, of black goat's hair woven in narrow strips on a home-made loom, receded into the distance as this simple, inexperienced girl pressed forward into the city of Shechem.

Let us picture her in a graceful tunic-style dress of a soft pastel color, in the tones of the early spring flowers. Perhaps she was also wearing a veil that fell softly across her face, revealing the beauty of innocent eyes which had no fear of the evils of a big city, because they had witnessed none.

If Dinah had listened to the stories of her own family, she should have known better. When her grandfather Isaac had gone down to Gerar with his wife Rebekah, he had passed her off as his sister, in order to keep her from being seized by strange men in the town, for no unprotected woman was safe in these primitive times. And her great grandfather Abraham had offered the same kind of protection to his wife Sarah as they journeyed into Egypt.

But the innocent Dinah went out as unprotected as a common

harlot; and when Shechem, the son of Hamor, from whom her father had bought land, saw this comely, strange girl, he desired her for his own. "He took her, and lay with her, and defiled her" (Gen. 34:2). The Hebrew translation implies that he took her by force.

When Jacob heard what had been done to his only daughter, he held his peace until his sons came in from the field. Hamor, the young man's father, had gone out to call on Jacob. But when Dinah's brothers, Simeon and Levi, heard that their sister had been treated as a common harlot, they came to her defense.

The wrong he committed is the outstanding fact in the story of the young Shechem. However, there is a significant phrase, "And his soul clave unto Dinah the daughter of Jacob, and he loved the damsel, and spake kindly unto the damsel" (Gen. 34:3). And there is another about him: "He was more honourable than all the house of his father" (Gen. 34:19). These two phrases lead us to believe that he had more than a trivial affection for Dinah and that he would try to make amends for the wrong he had done.

His father offered any sum that Jacob might ask as a marriage present, in order that Shechem might marry Dinah. Hamor's cordiality to Dinah's brothers, however, draws a striking contrast to what he told his townsmen: "Shall not their cattle and their substance and every beast of theirs be ours?" (Gen. 35:23). That was what he told them, indicating that he was a man who saw greater riches for his own people in the marriage of his son and Jacob's only daughter.

But Dinah's brothers said, "We cannot do this thing, to give our sister to one that is uncircumcised" (Gen. 34:14). Circumcision was the external rite by which persons were admitted members of the ancient church. It is evident that they did not seek to convert Shechem, but only made a show of religion—a cloak to cover their diabolical act. Shechem and his father were then circumcised, as were all men in the city. But Simeon and Levi, who were still angered, went out the third day and slew Shechem and his father and took their sister out of Shechem's house. And then they slew all the other men in the city, plundering it as they went, and taking with them flocks, herds, asses, children, and wives of the men they had slain.

Angered that his sons had acted in such a treacherous and godless manner, Jacob did not even forgive Simeon and Levi on his death-bed (Gen. 49:5).

The most meaningful phrase in the whole account is "which thing ought not to be done," referring of course to the defilement of Dinah. Those words provide a theme for a whole sermon.

Though Dinah's experience was repulsive and filled with cruelty and immorality, it does point up the high value these early Hebrews placed on chastity among women.

In the next Bible chapter following this one on Dinah we find Jacob and his family—and let us believe Dinah was there, too—going up to Beth-el, about thirty miles from Shechem, to worship. The family had been aroused from its spiritual indolence; it was a period when sudden tragedies, such as the defilement of an only and beloved daughter, could come to a family.

TAMAR

GEN. 38:6, 11, 13, 24
RUTH 4:12
I CHRON. 2:4

Daughter-in-law of Judah and childless widow of two brothers, Er and Onan. By her own craft, she demands her rights to motherhood through levirate law. Becomes mother of twins through her father-in-law.

"SHE HATH BEEN MORE RIGHTEOUS THAN I"

THOUGH events centering around Tamar's life are quite confused and intolerable, according to today's moral standards, her actions were consistent with the standards of morality prevailing in the primitive era in which she lived.

The Genesis account of Tamar serves a dual purpose. First, it is one of the Bible's best examples of the levirate marriage law. This was the ancient custom of marriage between a man and the widow of his brother required by the Mosaic law when there was no male issue and when the two brothers had been residing on the same family property. The law, of course, takes its name from the noun levir, meaning a husband's brother. Second, this Genesis account of Tamar gives us the Bible's most graphic picture of how a quick-witted widow of early Israel protected herself and her family rights.

Tamar, not a wicked woman at all, plays a meaningful role in Old Testament history as the mother of Pharez, ancestor of King David. When she had lost two husbands, both of whom were brothers, and was refused the remaining young brother, she still had the courage to demand her rights to motherhood by law. What did she do? After her mother-in-law's death, she turned to the father of her husband. The legitimacy and courage of her action are implied in every move she makes.

Scripture does not mention Tamar's parentage or place of birth but proceeds to introduce her by saying that her first husband Er "was wicked in the sight of the Lord; and the Lord slew him" (Gen. 38:7). Next she became the wife of his brother Onan, who "displeased the Lord: wherefore he slew him also" (Gen. 38:10).

This union of Tamar with Onan shows the perfect working of the levirate law, devised to retain the ownership of property within the family as well as to prevent the extinction of the family line. After her second husband's death, Judah advised his daughter-in-law Tamar to remain a widow at her father's house until his third son Shelah came of age. But fearing that Tamar possessed a sinister power, and that Shelah might die too, Judah delayed this third son's marriage with Tamar.

A considerable time elapsed and then Judah's wife died. The love of offspring, still deep in the heart of Tamar, caused her to plan how she might seek her rights in motherhood from her father-in-law Judah. Since he had denied her his third son Shelah, she sought a way to force him to accept his responsibility as guaranteed to her by the levirate law.

When Tamar heard that Judah was soon to be in the hills of Timnath with his friend Hirah, the Adullamite, at great personal risk she set upon a plan of her own. It was sheep-shearing season, and many guests would come from the surrounding country. Tamar planned to be there, too, but under a disguise, so that Judah would not recognize her as the widow of his sons.

She removed her garments of widowhood, put on a veil to hide her face, and "wrapped herself," probably in a colorful and becoming festival robe.

Since Tamar's name was the same as that of the stately tropical tree of Bible lands, we can assume that she was a tall, sturdy woman with a graceful carriage, one who would command attention wherever she went. This time she chose to stand by the side of the road where Judah would pass by.

Not recognizing this woman with the veil-covered face as the widow of his two sons and thinking she was a harlot, Judah made advances to her and said, "Go to, I pray thee, let me come in unto thee" (Gen. 38:16).

Clever woman that she was, she said, "What wilt thou give me, that thou mayest come in unto me?" (Gen. 38:16).

"And he said, I will send thee a kid from the flock. And she said, Wilt thou give me a pledge, till thou send it? And he said, What pledge shall I give thee? And she said, Thy signet, and thy bracelets, and thy staff that is in thine hand. And he gave it her, and came in unto her, and she conceived by him" (Gen. 38:17-18).

The unscrupulous actions of Judah, with whom Tamar was here involved, and the noble actions of Joseph, whom Potiphar's wife tried to involve, present a striking contrast. Some commentators conjecture that is why the story of Potiphar's wife immediately follows that of Tamar.

Tamar now turned homeward, carrying with her the signet, bracelet, and staff that had belonged to Judah. Then she removed her veil and put on again the garment of widowhood. A short time afterward Judah sent the kid by his friend Hirah, who had been with him at Timnath for the sheep-shearing. And Judah requested that his more personal possessions be returned when the kid was delivered.

When Hirah entered the town where Tamar lived, carrying with him the kid, he asked for the harlot who had been by the side of the road, but the men told him there was no harlot in the place. This is the best evidence we have that Tamar was not a prostitute but a self-respecting woman, determined to outwit a man and demand her right to children, according to the laws of the time.

About three months later (Gen. 38:24), Judah received word that his daughter-in-law Tamar was "with child by whoredom." This phrase suggests the malicious gossiper who had carried tales to Judah. Angered at this report, he ordered that his daughter-in-law be brought forth and burned, for that would have been the penalty if the report were true (Lev. 20:14). But when Tamar came before Judah, holding his signet, bracelets, and staff, she asked, "Discern, I pray thee, whose are these?" (Gen. 38:25).

Judah could not deny their ownership and admitted, "She hath been more righteous than I; because that I gave her not to Shelah my son. And he knew her again no more" (Gen. 38:26). The last phrase is evidence enough that Tamar was not a promiscuous woman. She had merely acted according to the laws and rather heroically at that; and we can be confident she had exonerated herself, and that Judah had absolved her of all guilt.

Thrice denied a child by a rightful husband, Tamar now gave birth to twins by Judah. Like the twins of Rebekah, there is a detailed account of the appearance of the elder Pharez, who became inheritor of the family birthright. Afterward his brother Zarah was born with the "scarlet thread upon his hand" that the midwife had tied there. The story of the birth of Tamar's sons depicts clearly a woman in travail and the birth of twins.

In the story of Ruth, another widow who also came to motherhood through the levirate law, we find worthy mention made of Tamar, who bore a child to Judah. Other Tamars follow her, one the "fair sister" (II Sam. 13:1) of Absalom and the other the woman of "fair countenance" (II Sam. 14:27) who was the daughter of Absalom. Could it be that they were namesakes of their courageous ancestress, who would not be deprived of her rights of motherhood?

POTIPHAR'S WIFE

GEN. 39:7, 8, 9, 12, 19

Tries to seduce Joseph. He resists her. She seizes his coat, then tells lies on him to her husband and has him cast into prison. Remains silent on her own transgression.

"BECAUSE THOU ART HIS WIFE"

AN ERRING woman remembered only by her wickedness—that was Potiphar's wife. When she attempted infidelity with young Joseph during her husband's absence from home, she disgraced the distinction she might have borne, that of respected wife of the chief of the Egyptian king's bodyguard.

Egyptian sculptures and paintings on the walls of ancient tombs help us to picture her as a woman wearing a dress of exceedingly fine linen, pleated into a chevron pattern in the back. Around her high waistline she wore an ornamental girdle and on her head a gold band set with jewels. Her sensual lips were heavily painted with a purplish pigment, and her slanting eyebrows were made darker with heavy black dye. Around her ankles were gold bands, and she wore other heavy jewelry in her ears and around her neck, and on her long tapering fingers were rings with large jewels.

We know she was a spoiled, selfish woman, probably older than Joseph and certainly more worldly. She knew nothing of Joseph's God and the high standards upheld by those who believed in Him. Her gods were the physical pleasures, and she spent her days trying to satisfy them.

The setting in which she moved was one of elegance and splendor.

Her house, similar to Egyptian royal houses of that period of about 1700 B.C., had a block of high rooms surrounding the main room and inner garden court.

This Egyptian house kept Joseph, the young overseer, busy, for it had stables and harness rooms, shelter for small wooden chariots, servants' quarters, granary courtyards, and conical grain bins, as well as an agricultural center. Even the trees, set in brick tubs containing Nile mud, had to be watered daily. There were slaves to direct, purchases to be made in the market, and distinguished guests who demanded personal attentions.

As supervisor of all this, Joseph, who had been purchased from the Ishmaelites in the slave market, had risen to a place of high trust, for the young Hebrew was faithful, honest, upright, and conscientious. We can be sure, too, that he was beautiful of form and face like his mother Rachel and humble and consecrated like his father Jacob.

It was with dignity that he moved about his master's house, wearing a skirt of fine linen tucked under a colorful belt from which hung a leather tab. On his feet were simple sandals with pointed upturned toes, and his abundant black hair probably hung to his shoulders. But one would be less likely to observe the details of his dress than his quiet demeanor and the noble qualities in his smooth-shaven face.

He was a sturdy, stalwart youth whom evil women would delight to tempt. Potiphar's wife probably was dissatisfied with her own husband. Here in her own house was this handsome young Hebrew with whom she would like to take liberties.

Because Potiphar was one of King Pharaoh's important officials, it is quite natural to suppose he had to be away from home a great deal, and he had entrusted to Joseph not only the safekeeping of his most valuable possessions but also the protection of his family. For a man to feel safe about his family, especially his wife, he had to leave as overseer one who had not only superior ability but also a deep sense of integrity.

Potiphar's wife, however, had no appreciation of good character. After her husband had departed, she sought to become familiar with Joseph. And one day, when no men were about the house, she said to him, "Lie with me" (Gen. 39:7). But he resisted, for he had disciplined himself to do what was right.

He must have startled this evil woman when he answered her invitation by saying, "There is none greater in this house than I; neither hath he kept back anything from me but thee, because thou art his wife: how then can I do this great wickedness, and sin against God?" (Gen. 39:9).

Potiphar's wife had not dealt with such an honorable man before. She was angered, but she was not outdone. Day by day she invited him into her private boudoir, but he always retreated from her advances, because he knew God had great purposes for him to serve, and he must uphold that which was right and good.

Finally, when Potiphar's wife could not entice Joseph, she caught his garment in her hand and held it; but he fled, leaving it with her. This woman who had not received what she asked for determined to hurt Joseph, in order to save face herself. She screamed loudly to other men in the household, saying, "See, he hath brought in an Hebrew unto us to mock us; he came in unto me to lie with me, and I cried with a loud voice" (Gen. 39:14).

She now kept Joseph's garment and showed it to her husband on his return. When Potiphar saw it, he immediately cast Joseph into prison, for his wife had lied, saying, "The Hebrew servant, which thou hast brought unto us, came in unto me to mock me: And it came to pass, as I lifted up my voice and cried, that he left his garment with me, and fled out" (Gen. 39:17-18).

These are the last words of this despicable woman, who has become a symbol of the faithless wife. Her obscurity, except for her wickedness, is final, but the young Joseph rose to noble stature, even within prison walls. Her own silence, in face of the youth's term in prison, is even greater admission to the bad character of Potiphar's wife, who was not only a sensualist but also a coward who could not admit her own guilt.

CHAPTER 2

Women of Israel's Heroic Age

JOCHEBED

EXOD. 6:20
NUM. 26:59

Daughter of Levi and wife of Amram of House of Levi. Mother of Miriam, Aaron, and Moses. Realizes when the latter is a baby that he has a high destiny. Makes an ark and hides him. During his formative years she nurses him in court of King Pharaoh, where he has been adopted by Pharaoh's daughter.

BY FAITH SHE HID HER BABY

FROM her faith in things unseen, Jochebed gained her strength and force. A mother who had learned to trust her Creator and not to doubt, she seemed to be united to the promises of God, absorbed by them and exhilarated by them.

Her whole background speaks of her holiness, the kind that strengthens faith. She was the daughter of Levi (Num. 26:59), born in Egypt, and she became the wife of Amram, grandson of Levi, son of Jacob. From this Levi line, the Levites, charged with the care of the sanctuary, were descended. Jochebed handed down the priestly tradition of her family to her children. Her son Aaron was set apart to be a priest and became the center and founder of the Hebrew priesthood, which he served for almost forty years. Her daughter Miriam led the Israelites in a moment when their faith came alive as they crossed the Sea of Reeds.

But as the mother of Moses, Hebrew lawgiver, statesman, and leader, Jochebed rises up today, some thirty-three centuries later, as one of the immortal mothers of Israel. Interesting it is to note that three times the Scriptures tell us that even when he was a tiny babe there was something special about Moses. In Exodus 2:2 he is called a "goodly child"; in Acts 7:20 he is described as "exceedingly fair" and in Hebrews 11:23 a "proper child." Something, let us be sure, beamed from the features of this child that only a godly mother could understand.

Do we not see in Jochebed some of the qualities of Mary, mother of Jesus, who recognized that her baby was destined by God for some special purpose? Like Mary, Jochebed must also have seen intimations of her child's high destiny and "pondered them in her heart" (Luke 2:19). And Jochebed, again like Mary, was willing to suppress her own maternal love and to dedicate her son to that to which he had been called by God.

It was probably near Memphis in northeast Egypt that Jochebed gave birth to Moses, in the second half of the second millennium B.C. It has been suggested that Levi's daughter Jochebed was more likely an ancestress of Moses rather than his own mother, for many generations must have intervened between the arrival of Jacob's twelve sons in Egypt and the birth of Moses. But like the birthplace and first names of mothers of many great men who rise up out of obscurity, this mother of Moses did not achieve importance until decades, or maybe centuries, later. By this time it was difficult to trace many of the facts centering around her life. But what does a first name matter for this mother of faith?

By name, Jochebed is mentioned only twice in the Bible, but her eminence as a mother in Israel is not thus obscured. Though the meager record we have of her life concerns the first years of Moses' childhood, her greatness rises up like an imperishable monument. And though she is never vividly described, as are many of the great mothers in the Bible, Jochebed lives on because she walked humbly before her God and because she transmitted character to her son Moses, her daughter Miriam, and her older son Aaron. She lives on, too, not by how many big tasks she accomplished, but by how wisely and well she served as a mother.

At the time when Jochebed gave birth to Moses, the Pharaoh had issued an edict to midwives to kill all Hebrew male children at birth. Moses had a natural birth, but the fact that he survived and grew up when all male Hebrew children were being destroyed is noteworthy. Pharaoh's orders were not unlike those of King Herod, who, many centuries later in the time of Jesus, ordered that all male children in Bethlehem two years old or under be destroyed. In spite of this measure, which Pharaoh had taken for the destruction of a people, Israel's deliverance would eventually be accomplished.

How Jochebed managed to save her son from Pharaoh's edict during the first three months of Moses' life is not recorded. We can imagine she might have hidden him in a donkey stable or a storage room where she kept clay jars filled with grain, peppercorns, onions, bread, dates, and other foods. But after he became three months old, she knew she could no longer take the risk of hiding him.

Through these months of anxiety, we can be sure that she lived close to her God. He had endowed her with sufficient wisdom and ingenuity to conceal her boy for three months. Now she knew that her God of infinite compassion would not forsake her. She had faith enough to enter upon a plan fraught with danger, that of leaving her baby in a handmade ark floating at the water's edge close to the dangerous current of the Nile River.

What courage she must have had as she wove by hand the ark of bulrushes out of the long, pliant, tenacious stems of the papyrus plant. This plant itself, she knew, was a protection against crocodiles. What positive faith, too, she must have had that God would protect her child. And yet for Jochebed faith was accompanied by careful planning and work. She not only wove the ark but with her own hands plastered it inside with clay to make it smooth and outside with bitumen to make it watertight. Her faith was not without wisdom.

With the help of her daughter Miriam, she laid her baby amid the flowering flags near the river's bank and left this young girl near by to watch over her little brother. What could have calmed a mother's heart in an hour like this but prayer? And surely she had taught her daughter Miriam to pray also as she watched. Though Miriam deserves great credit, she was the pupil; Jochebed was the teacher. She bore the larger responsibility. She it was who remembered that Pharaoh's daughter was accustomed to come down and bathe at this very spot.

Before she came, the baby Moses may have lain in his handmade ark for several hours. Who knows? We can be sure of one thing. Jochebed was standing near by with a trusting faith that made her know her baby would come to no harm; and her faith was rewarded.

Pharaoh's daughter did appear with her maidens to bathe, right near the spot where the little Moses lay in the reeds. When she came upon the ark partly hidden by the flags, she sent her maid to fetch it (Exod. 2:5). Then she heard the whimpering child, and turning to her maiden she said, "This is one of the Hebrews' children" (Exod. 2:6).

The young Miriam, standing not far away, said, "Shall I go and call to thee a nurse of the Hebrew women, that she may nurse the child for thee?" (Exod. 2:7). "And Pharaoh's daughter said to her, Go" (Exod. 2:8). How much action and exhilaration and triumph resulted from that one word "Go."

So it was that Jochebed, standing not too far away probably, received the joyful news that she could nurse her own child. Though

JOCHEBED

Moses was soon adopted by Pharaoh's daughter, it was his own mother Jochebed who would watch over him until he was seven. Can we not trace in the peculiarly gentle character of Moses the influence of this devout mother? The whole character of Moses displays her holy guidance. She it was who instilled in him a belief in God, Creator of heaven and earth, of man and beast. She it was who imparted to him the sacred traditions of Israel and who told him of the divine promise to Abraham and his descendants that they would become a great nation. She it was who had him alone at night and rocked him to sleep, and during the day she could watch over him as he romped and played inside Pharaoh's palace.

And yet this lowly Levite mother could rejoice that her son Moses, as the adopted son of the princess, would receive the best education available in a king's palace and could later have the privilege of boys of highest rank, probably an education at Heliopolis, the Oxford of ancient Egypt. What other Hebrew son could be so blessed? What other mother could know such inward joy?

In later years, when the priests of Egypt would try to initiate her son into idolatry, he would remember his mother's God and her faith in Him. And he would remain a Hebrew at heart through all the years of his life. We can be quite certain that it was his mother's early influence that enabled Moses to make the decision to leave the court and go out among his own brethren and lift their burden, for from her he had inherited loyalty to his own race.

Whether Jochebed lived to see this or not, we have no record. By the time her son was seven years old, she had disappeared from the record. Probably she went back to the obscurity of her own humble home to watch Moses' progress from afar. We do not know whether she saw him become a great leader, lawgiver, and prophet but we do know she had had the satisfaction of pouring great things into his mind and heart during those most formative years of his life. And we know, too, that this mother of faith had instilled even greater faith in Moses and also in her two other children, Miriam and Aaron.

[53]

ZIPPORAH

EXOD. 2:21
4:25
18:2

Daughter of Jethro, a priest in Midian. Meets Moses when she and her seven sisters are tending their father's sheep. She has two sons by Moses and circumcizes one herself when her husband becomes ill. Spends little time with Moses after he goes into Egypt. Finally has reunion with him after he has become a great leader of Hebrew people.

WIFE OF MOSES, THE GREAT LAWGIVER

THOUGH her husband Moses is one of the greatest leaders of all time, Zipporah herself is an example of one of the Bible's undistinguished wives. In only three passages is she called by name, and these are brief. The seven words spoken by her lead us to believe she was a woman of violent temper who had little sympathy with the religious convictions of her distinguished husband.

Though her name means "bird," not even that gives us any indication of her character. She came from a Midian background (Exod. 2:16). Her father Jethro was a priest. What god Jethro worshiped we can only conjecture. We have reason to believe that he later became a believer in Moses' Jehovah, for Jethro later professed to Moses, "Now I know that the Lord is greater than all gods" (Exod. 18:11). We have no such expression of faith from his daughter Zipporah.

She was one of seven daughters and met Moses in the land of Midian soon after he fled there because he had slain an Egyptian

[54]

who was smiting a Hebrew, one of his own brethren (Exod. 2:11). Zipporah and her sisters, who had been tending their father's sheep, had come with their flocks to draw water at the well. Other shepherds drove the flocks of the seven sisters away, but Moses was a courteous shepherd. He gave water to the sisters' sheep.

And they went and told their father, who offered Moses the hospitality of his house. Zipporah's marriage to Moses after that is recorded briefly in seven words (Exod. 2:21). The romantic element found in the wooing of both Isaac and Jacob is not there. Soon afterward we find Moses engrossed in the woes of his people. His wife does not seem to play a part in either his lofty plans or his tremendous hardships.

From Zipporah's brief record, we know that she had two sons, Gershom and Eliezer. And when Moses started back from Midian to the Land of Egypt, his wife and his sons set forth with him, they on an ass and Moses walking, his rod in his hand. A picture this is of a humble family, whose head was destined to become Israel's great prophet, lawgiver, and leader.

When they halted at an inn for the night, Moses became very ill. The narrative here is obscure, but something was troubling him. He became so ill that his life was in danger. Though records do not furnish actual historical details, again we can only conjecture that he was troubled because his wife, a Midianite, had refused to allow the circumcision of their sons, a symbol of the covenant between God and His people. And Moses, now called by God to the leadership of his people, was troubled because he had neglected the sacred duty of circumcision, which was not practiced by his wife's people.

We can assume that the delay in circumcision was due to Zipporah's prejudices. When she saw her husband so violently ill, she doubtless believed God was angered with him because he had not circumcised his son. She then seized a piece of flint and circumcised her son herself. Which son that was and how old he was, there is no record. Jewish tradition says it was the second son Eliezer.

Though there are difficulties with this primitive story in its present form, one point seems quite clear. Moses and Zipporah were not congenial companions. No doubt their disagreement was due to the fact that she was a Midianite and he a Hebrew, and they had different views.

After the circumcision incident Zipporah becomes a nonentity. What part she played in Moses' life, again, we cannot be sure. She had so little in common with her husband that at the most trying and noble period of his life, on his mission to Pharaoh, he probably had to send her back home. However, it may be that she and her sons did accompany Moses to Egypt and remain with him there, and after the Exodus, when Moses' people were slowly approaching Mount Sinai, Zipporah and her sons may have been sent ahead to visit Jethro and tell of all that God had done for Moses and the Israelites.

Zipporah is mentioned for the last time when she and her sons and father Jethro have joined Moses at Mount Horeb (Exod. 18:5). Jethro acts as spokesman for the entire family. Most of the text centers around him, while Zipporah is only among those present.

Later we find Miriam and Aaron taking issue with their brother Moses because of his Cushite wife. The text of Numbers 12:1 would lead us to believe Zipporah had died and Moses had married a second time. Some scholars, however, believe that Zipporah and the Cushite were the same person. A phrase in Habakkuk 3:7 indicates that this could be true.

Though interpretations regarding incidents of Zipporah's life vary, there is one conclusion we may quite confidently draw from all of them. Zipporah seems to have been a woman who was prejudiced and rebellious. To neither her husband nor her sons did she leave a legacy of spiritual riches.

MIRIAM

EXOD. 15:20, 21
NUM. 12:1, 4, 5, 10, 15
20:1
26:59
DEUT. 24:9
I CHRON. 6:3
MIC. 6:4

Guards brother Moses until Pharaoh's daughter finds him. Leads women of Israel as they sing and dance after safely crossing Sea of Reeds. Later opposes Moses about his wife, also is jealous of Moses. Is stricken with leprosy; Moses heals her. Later she dies at Kadesh.

"SING UNTO THE LORD"

MIRIAM is the first woman in the Bible whose interest was national and whose mission was patriotic. When she led the women of Israel in that oldest of all national anthems, "Sing Unto the Lord," four centuries of bondage in Egypt had been lifted. It was a turning point in Israel's religious development and a woman led in its recognition.

The portrait of Miriam, brilliant, courageous sister of Moses, is drawn in a few graphically real strokes. We have the first picture of her in Exodus 2:4, 7 when she was a little girl. Here she is not named, but is referred to only as Moses' sister. Her courage at this time gives an indication of the kind of woman she was to become.

As she stood guarding her baby brother in the ark made by their mother Jochebed, she exhibited a fearlessness and self-possession unusual in a little girl. She was then probably about seven years old. Though she was awaiting the coming of a powerful princess, the daughter of a hostile tyrant who had decreed that all male babies should be destroyed, Miriam showed poise, intelligence, and finesse. When the daughter of Pharaoh came down with her maidens to the banks of the Nile to bathe and found the little Moses lying there in his ark, Miriam approached her quietly, asking if she would like her to find a Hebrew woman to nurse the baby.

Never disclosing by look or word her own relationship to the child, she brought her mother Jochebed to Pharaoh's daughter. The child Moses was safe at last behind palace walls, with his own mother as his nurse.

Through the years that passed, while Moses was in Pharaoh's house, and during the subsequent period when he had left the scene of courtly splendor to live some forty years in Midian, the Bible gives us no record of Miriam. There is also no record of her during Moses' long pleadings with Pharaoh to release his people, so that they might return to the land of their fathers.

Through the long oppression of the Israelites by hard taskmasters, we can be sure that Miriam was ministering to her people and that she was reverenced as the honored sister of Moses and Aaron, who were to lead the Hebrews out of bondage and form a new nation. The prophet Micah attests to this when he says, "For I brought thee up out of the land of Egypt, and redeemed thee out of the house of servants; and I sent before thee Moses, Aaron, and Miriam" (Mic. 6:4).

The second scene in Miriam's life opens when Israel's deliverance is at hand. Wondrous miracles attesting to the mighty mission of her illustrious brothers had unfolded, and thousands of Hebrew people were departing from Egypt.

Miriam now occupied a unique place among the Hebrew women, that of prophetess. The Hebrew word "prophetess" means a woman who is inspired to teach the will of God. It is also used for wife of a prophet, and is sometimes applied to a singer of hymns. The first meaning must be applied to Miriam because the Bible gives no record that she was ever married. Tradition has it that she became the wife of Hur, who with Aaron held up the hands of Moses, but we have no warrant whatever in Scripture, by direct word or inference, to confirm this tradition.

The next scene depicts Miriam in all her triumph. A strong wind had backed up the waters of the Sea of Reeds, and Miriam led the Hebrew women across the dry sea bottom. Following hard upon them came Pharaoh's detachments of chariots and horsemen. But the sea came flooding back and they were swallowed up in the water. We can see Miriam as a commanding figure, her face radiant in this hour of her people's deliverance. She and the women following behind her moved forward on dry ground through the midst of the sea when the waters were a wall on their right hand and on their left. Miriam played on a timbrel and danced joyfully as she led the song: "Sing ye to the Lord, for he hath triumphed gloriously; the horse and his rider hath he thrown into the sea" (Exod. 15:21).

This Song of Deliverance, sometimes referred to as the Song of Miriam and Moses, is one of the earliest songs in Hebrew literature, and one of the finest. What part Miriam had in the composition of this national anthem, the oldest on record, is not known, but in weaving it into the conscious life of her people she had an equal share with Moses and Aaron.

Miriam is the first woman singer on record. The wonder of it is that she sang unto the Lord, using her great gift for the elevation of her people. With her they exulted over their escape from their enemies. And with freedom came a newly discovered faith and confidence in God. This was Miriam's great hour. She was the new Israel's most renowned woman, and her people held her in high regard. She had filled an important role in the founding of the Hebrew commonwealth.

The third scene in Miriam's life offers a sharp contrast to this one, and occurs some time later. Some chronologists believe it took place only one year after the passage across the Sea of Reeds, but this period seems hardly long enough for Miriam's character to have changed so completely. Miriam has had a spiritual fall—and over what we would least expect. She has spoken against her brother Moses.

The limitations in Miriam's character come into clear focus in this third dramatic scene in her life. No longer does she stand on the summit as she did in her triumphant hour. She is still an exalted person, but no longer a leader in exultation. This time she is a leader in jealousy and bitterness. Probably she had become rebellious because her place was secondary to that of her brother Moses.

With Aaron, we hear her murmuring, "Hath the Lord indeed spoken only by Moses? hath he not spoken also by us? And the Lord heard it" (Num. 12:2). In this delineation of the envious, bitter side of Miriam's character, following so soon after the courageous, inspiring scene of the woman who had sung to God so joyfully, we have one of the most perfect examples in the Bible of woman's mixed nature of good and evil.

Another reason for Miriam's conflict with her brother Moses had arisen. He had married again. His first wife Zipporah, a Midianite, had died. His second wife was a Cushite (Ethiopian), a dark-skinned woman from the African country bordering on Egypt. Opinions vary about this woman. Some scholars think that Moses married only once.

It is probable that Miriam, older than Moses by about seven years, had expressed herself quite freely against her brother's wife from an idolatrous country. That an Ethiopian should be raised above herself, who was a daughter of Israel, was, to one of her evidently proud spirit, unendurable. Because she had such pride in her own race, she may have told Moses that he should have chosen his wife from among his own people. Her great mistake was that she made her complaint public. It tended to break down the authority of Moses and to imperil the hope of the Israelites.

On the other hand, she rang a warning bell to others who might follow Moses' lead. When a man's wife is opposed to the religion of his country, especially the wife of a man occupying the lofty position of Moses, his cause is in peril. And Miriam evidently feared this. She was not alone in her thinking. Aaron was a partner in the complaint, but Miriam's name was placed first. Probably it was she who brought up the matter to Aaron and influenced his thinking. There is a peculiar analogy between Miriam's sin and her punishment. The foul vice of envy had spread over her whole character, like the loathsome disease which had overtaken her. Her sharp words made more real the words James spoke many centuries later: "And the tongue is a fire, . . . it defileth the whole body, and setteth on fire the course of nature" (Jas. 3:6).

Leprosy, the pale plague of Egypt regarded as providential punishment for slander, had smitten Miriam down. She had become a leper "white as snow" (Num. 12:10). "And Moses cried unto the Lord, saying, Heal her now, O God, I beseech thee" (Num. 12:13). Though she had held a grudge against him, Moses acted toward her in a spirit of love. Probably when he saw his sister leprous, he remembered that he had once been stricken with leprosy, too (Exod. 4:6).

We can assume that the heart of Miriam was touched by her brother's love. Though she was shut out of camp for seven days, in accordance with the regulations of the Israelites (Num. 12:15), she was not shut out of the hearts of those she had led in their triumphant hour. Though wearied from their long wanderings and impatient at every delay in reaching the Promised Land, "the people journeyed not till Miriam was brought in again" (Num. 12:15). Doubtless the leprosy of Miriam's mind departed with the leprosy of her body.

The fourth and final scene in Miriam's story takes place at Kadesh, probably in the Wilderness of Zin, some seventy miles south of Hebron. Tradition tells us that after her death her funeral was celebrated in the most solemn manner for thirty days. Like her brothers Aaron and Moses, Miriam did not reach the Promised Land but died in the wilderness; however, her cry of exultation, "Sing unto the Lord," which had signified freedom for the newborn Israel, could not die.

DAUGHTERS OF ZELOPHEHAD

NUM. 26:33
    27:1
    36:11
JOSH. 17:3

Five daughters declare their rights to the property of their father Zelophehad, on his death. Case brought before Moses and fair decision handed down. It is reviewed later and restrictions are put on Israel daughter who marries into another tribe.

THEY DECLARED THEIR RIGHTS

IN THE ancient Near East, up until about 3,500 years ago, women had no property rights. If a father died leaving no sons, his daughters did not inherit what he left.

The first women to declare their rights on the death of their father were the five daughters of Zelophehad: Mahlah, Noah, Hoglah, Milcah, and Tirzah. Their father, a Manassite, had died in the wilderness, and the daughters explained that he was not in the company of Korah, who had rebelled against Moses. Because their father had not died therefore for any cause that doomed their family or their inheritance, they declared they were clearly entitled to what he had left.

This happened at a critical time with Israel. A new census had been made, preparatory to an entrance into the Promised Land. The new land would be distributed according to the census taken before Israel departed from Egypt for the Promised Land.

The daughters of Zelophehad had been numbered among all those in the tribes who either were twenty years of age or would be twenty by the time the land actually was distributed. But they knew that under existing customs they would have no property rights, either now or in the new land. Probably their father had been a man of means. What did they do?

They marched before Moses, the priest Eleazar, and the congregation and stated their case publicly. "Why should the name of our father be done away from among his family, because he hath no son? Give unto us therefore a possession among the brethren of our father" (Num. 27:4).

In order to be fair in the settling of the daughters' case, Moses went before God, a God of justice and right. And the great lawgiver came back and declared, "The daughters of Zelophehad speak right: thou shalt surely give them a possession of an inheritance among their father's brethren; and thou shalt cause the inheritance of their father to pass unto them" (Num. 27:7).

Moses wrote a new law which stated: "If a man die, and have no son, then ye shall cause his inheritance to pass unto his daughter" (Num. 27:8). As a result of this decision, the case was broadened to include other instances, such as when there were no children left and no brothers either to succeed the deceased.

The daughters of Zelophehad had filed one of the earliest reported lawsuits on record. Jurists still turn to it for opinions and have declared it the oldest decided case "that is still cited as an authority." In the American Bar Association *Journal* of February, 1924, there appears an article by Henry C. Clark in which this decision of the daughters of Zelophehad is quoted. It is described as an "early declaratory judgment in which the property rights of women marrying outside of their tribe are clearly set forth."

The decision handed down in this time of Moses was a great victory for these five daughters. At last a woman had rights, because these five had declared theirs and had had the courage to fight their case through with the authorities. Up until now women had had no legal property rights. That is one of the reasons a man always desired a son. Now women were numbered as human beings and legally entitled to the same property rights as men. The judgment which had been passed for the daughters of Zelophehad became law among the twelve tribes of Israel.

Other complications, however, soon arose. The fathers of Israel looked into the future. What if daughters married outside their own tribes? This would seriously threaten the tenure of the land in Israel. The land would go to their children, who on their father's side might belong to another tribe. This would confuse families and complicate interests.

The men of Israel called for a rehearing of the case, stating their point clearly in Numbers 36:3. The case was reviewed. The decision is given in Numbers 36:5-9. The gist of it was that the daughters of Zelophehad could marry whomever they chose, provided they married within the family of their father's tribe, probably some of their cousins. This applied, however, only to daughters who were heiresses. A new, fairer, and broader law had been enacted, and it provided for a balance of power among the tribes.

The five daughters of Zelophehad—Mahlah, Noah, Hoglah, Milcah, and Tirzah—had declared their rights and had won a court decision that legal courts accept as law to this day.

RAHAB

JOSH. 2:1, 3
   6:17, 23, 25
HEB. 11:31
JAS. 2:25

Two spies from Israel's army make their way to harlot's house on city walls of Jericho. She promises to conceal them and aid in approaching battle between her people and Joshua's army, because she believes firmly in their God. She hides spies in flax on her roof-top. She and her family saved when walls of Jericho fall.

WOMAN OF FAITH WHO AIDED JOSHUA'S ARMY

BUILT over the gap between the two walls of Jericho was the house of a woman identified in both the Old and the New Testament as Rahab, the harlot. This ancient "City of Palms," as it was known, was surrounded by two walls. According to recent archaeological findings, there was a space of twelve to fifteen feet between them. Houses of sun-dried brick were built over the gap between the two walls and supported by timbers laid from one wall to the other, or by small cross walls of brick. Rahab's house was in one of these strategic points, and her window looked on the outer wall.

Because of its advantageous location her house attracted the attention of two spies from Shittim. They represented the Israelite army of Joshua, who had succeeded Moses as the leader of Israel on its long journey from Egypt to Canaan. Joshua had made plans to advance on Jericho, which commanded entrance to Palestine from the east.

Down the hills from Shittim, from the eastern edge of the Jordan

Valley, had come these two travelers. It is easy to imagine that they were young and walked with authority, their long, flowing robes swaying as they pressed forward with quick steps. Eager to avoid notice, they mixed with the crowds outside the wall, surreptitiously keeping their gaze on the structure of the massive walls protecting Jericho, key city to the rich Jordan Valley.

The walls represented the city's greatest strength, and not until they were breached or destroyed could the army of Israel move inside the city. The house of the harlot Rahab stood upon the walls and so it was that the spies hastened to it.

Probably city authorities frequently saw unfamiliar characters going in and out of the house of this woman, and they would not question these two strangers. The character of the woman was, of course, of no consequence to spies on a secret mission.

Interpreters differ as to the real character of Rahab. One source brings up the point that Rahab and her household were escorted to safety "without" the camp of Israel (Josh. 6:23). This "without" has special significance, for the camp of Israel was "holy" and no "unclean" person was allowed to enter. This would seem to indicate that Rahab was indeed a harlot.

Rahab and her family, however, finally were received into Israel, apparently by marriage. Jewish tradition makes her the wife of Joshua. Another tradition has it that she became the wife of Prince Salmon, who could have been one of the spies who appealed to her for aid. If so, she became the mother of Boaz, who married Ruth, and their son Obed bore Jesse, the father of King David, through whose line is traced the Christ.

In the genealogy of Christ (Matt. 1:5) we find the name of Rachab, along with names of three other women, Ruth, Thamar (Tamar), and Bath-sheba. There is some question as to whether this was Rahab, the harlot, but most scholars identify Rachab and Rahab as one and the same person.

Josephus and some of the rabbis refer to Rahab not as a harlot but as an innkeeper, to whose house the spies went for lodging (Josh. 2:1). One source stresses the point that persons who kept inns in these early times—this was about the fourteenth century B.C., according to W. F. Albright—were not always the most moral persons. Sometimes they were all called harlots.

The earliest Mosaic laws protested against harlotry. Its social curse was known to Jesus, but when the woman taken in adultery, for example, was brought before him by the scribes and Pharisees, he turned the searchlight upon their own self-righteousness, rather than upon the unfortunate victim of commercialized vice (John 8:1-11). On more than one occasion Christ, in an effort to correct hypocrisy, said that even harlots would enter the kingdom before those whose works appeared more pious than they actually were (Matt. 21:31).

We have evidence that Rahab lied. When her own king ordered her to bring out the men that were seen to enter her house, she answered, "There came men unto me, but I wist not whence they were" (Josh. 2:4). At that moment they were hiding inside her house.

But what Rahab was is not of as much consequence as what she became. The Bible deals with human beings in search of God. Many of them are far from perfect, but among the greatest are those who, like King David, rose above their wrongdoings and became godly despite them. Even though Rahab was called a harlot, she later became a woman of such faith that she could declare to the enemy, "The Lord your God, he is God in heaven above, and in earth beneath" (Josh. 2:11).

The Book of Hebrews enrolls Rahab among the faithful along with Sarah. These are the only two women mentioned by name in the famous roll call of the faithful. The harlot Rahab is commended because by faith she "perished not with them that believed not, when she had received the spies with peace" (Heb. 11:31). James, speaking of how character can be transformed, says, "Likewise also was

[67]

not Rahab the harlot justified by works, when she had received the messengers, and had sent them out another way?" (Jas. 2:25).

Other qualities in Rahab's character are quite evident from the Scripture. She was an industrious woman. She wove fine linen and dried the flax on her roof-top. It was among the stalks of flax drying in the sun that she hid the spies until after nightfall, when the city gates were closed. Then she let them down from the outside wall by a cord from her window, probably a heavy rope of linen she had woven herself.

Rahab, we also know, had a deep devotion to her family and friends. She was clever and alert as well. She had an agreement with the spies whom she was aiding that she would use the same scarlet cord by which they would be let down from the walls of Jericho. During the battle this red cord would designate her house to the army of Joshua and guarantee it protection. It was agreed that all of her family, in order to be safe, must remain indoors with her during the attack.

Rahab also must have been very courageous to be willing to risk her own life in order to protect enemy spies whom she believed to be on a godly mission. She had heard of the Israelite crossing of the Sea of Reeds, when the waters parted before them, also of their victories over the Amorites. So strongly did she believe in the Israelite cause that she could say confidently to enemy spies, "I know that the Lord hath given you the land, and that your terror is fallen upon us, and that all the inhabitants of the land faint because of you" (Josh. 2:9).

Word soon spread among the people of Israel that God would fight for them. A woman living in a house on the city wall had made it possible for Joshua to march forward. And he had led his men, not by might but by strength in the living God, sending the ark of the Covenant and the priests along with the advance guard.

The walls of Jericho fell and the city burned and Joshua declared, 'The city shall be accursed, even it, and all that are therein, to the

Lord: only Rahab the harlot shall live, she and all that are with her in the house, because she hid the messengers that we sent" (Josh. 6:17).

While the city was in flames, Rahab and her family departed from it. They were saved from the total destruction of their city because Rahab the harlot had been willing to prove her faith as well as to declare it.

DEBORAH

JUDG. 4:4, 5, 9, 10, 14
5:1, 7, 12, 15

Wife of the obscure Lapidoth, she becomes a woman of great power. She awakens the people in a period of lethargy. With Barak, she leads them to victory. The martial song celebrating her triumph is one of greatest in history.

"IS NOT THE LORD GONE OUT BEFORE THEE?"

THE only woman in the Bible who was placed at the height of political power by the common consent of the people was Deborah. Though she lived in the time of the "Judges," some thirteen centuries before Christ, there are few women in history who have ever attained the public dignity and supreme authority of Deborah. She was like Joan of Arc, who twenty-seven centuries later rode in front of the French and led them to victory.

Deborah was the wife of an obscure man named Lapidoth. The rabbis say she was a keeper of the tabernacle lamps. If so, what a wonderful yet humble task for this woman who was to become so great in Israel! Later, when her faith in God became the strength of Israel, she would become the keeper of a new spiritual vision that would light all Israel.

In all of her roles, first that of counselor to her people, next as judge in their disputes, and finally as deliverer in time of war, Deborah exhibited womanly excellence. She was indeed "a mother in Israel." She arose to great leadership because she trusted God implicitly and because she could inspire in others that same trust.

For twenty years Jabin, king of Canaan, had oppressed the children of Israel. Their vineyards had been destroyed, their women dishonored, and their children slain. Many had turned to the worship of idols.

Deborah's story comes in the first part of the book of Judges. These men were more than judges in today's meaning of the term, for they were chieftains and heroes as well, and their influence was felt mainly in war. Long before Deborah became a leader in war, she was a homemaker. Her house was on the road between Ramah and Beth-el, in the hill country of Ephraim, where flourished olive and palm trees. It was under one of the most royal of date palms that she would sit and give counsel to the people who came to her.

As a counselor in time of peace, Deborah became known far and near, but her greatest service came in time of war. And she led her people into war. Most of them had stood by fearfully because they were afraid of the enemy's 900 chariots of iron, when they had none. While they paled with fear, Deborah burned with indignation at the oppression of her people. A gifted and an intrepid woman, she felt a call to rise up against such fear and complacency, for she carried in her heart the great hope that God would come to her people's rescue if they would honor Him.

Because the men of Israel had faltered in leadership, Deborah arose to denounce this lack of leadership and to affirm that deliverance from oppression was at hand. Her religious zeal and patriotic fervor armed her with new strength. She became the magnificent personification of the free spirit of the people of Israel.

We can imagine that Deborah looked the part of a great and noble woman. She must have had fire in her eyes, determination in her step, and a positive ring to her voice. We can see her, a tall, handsome woman, wearing a dress of blue crash striped in red and yellow and a yellow turban with a long, pure-white cotton veil, lace edged, reaching to the hem of her dress. A feminine woman, who never had had the ambition to push herself forward, Deborah better personified the homemaker in Israel than a warrior. But as she counseled with her people and began to sense their common danger, she kindled in them an enthusiasm for immediate action against the enemy.

She had the courage to summon one of Israel's most capable military men, Barak, from his home in Kedesh. Together they worked out a plan for action against the enemy. Deborah let Barak know she was not afraid of Sisera, commander of Jabin's army; neither was she afraid of his 900 chariots. She made him feel that the spirit that could animate an army was greater than either weapons or fortifications. Probably she recalled to him that God had led the Israelites through the Sea of Reeds and had broken a mighty oppressor, Pharaoh. And she made Barak realize that God, who had proved Himself to be mightier than Pharaoh, also was mightier than either Jabin or Sisera.

"Go," spoke Deborah positively to the fainthearted Barak, "and draw toward mount Tabor, and take with thee ten thousand men of the children of Naphtali and of the children of Zebulun" (Judg. 4:6). And she convinced Barak that the Lord would deliver Sisera and his chariots and multitudes into their hands.

Barak, sensing the spiritual insight that Deborah possessed and feeling the urgent need for her presence and spiritual counsel, answered, "If thou will go with me, then I will go: but if thou wilt not go with me, then I will not go" (Judg. 4:8). That is one of the most unusual passages in the Bible spoken by a man to a woman. It demonstrates a general's great confidence in a woman, a homebody, too, who had risen to a high place in Israel largely because of one quality, her abiding faith in God.

Without hesitation, the stouthearted Deborah declared triumphantly, "I will surely go with thee; notwithstanding the journey that thou takest shall not be for thine honour; for the Lord shall sell Sisera into the hand of a woman" (Judg. 4:9). In these words Deborah demonstrated more than leadership. Her people were to discover that she was also a prophet.

In Judges 4:9 we learn that "Deborah arose, and went with Barak to Kedesh." That one word "arose" best explains her positive action. She did not sit at home and ponder the matter when the time came for action, but she arose, believing firmly that she was armed with strength from God.

When Barak summoned his tribes of Zebulun and Naphtali to Kedesh, he saw that none was well armed and none rode in chariots. But Deborah's faith carried the Israelites forward unafraid. When she and Barak and their ten thousand men came to the spur of the hills, near where Sisera and his charioteers were, Deborah, looking out from a lofty rock, exclaimed to Barak, "Up; for this is the day in which the Lord hath delivered Sisera into thine hand: is not the Lord gone out before thee?" (Judg. 4:14).

We learn directly from Josephus and indirectly from the song of Deborah that a storm of sleet and hail burst over the plain from the east, driving right into the face of Sisera and his men and charioteers. The slingers and archers were disabled by the beating rain, and the swordsmen were crippled by the biting cold.

Deborah and Barak and their forces had the storm behind them and were not crippled by it. As they saw the storm lash the enemy, they pushed on, believing all the more in providential aid. The flood waters were now racing down the Kishon River. So violent was the rain that Sisera's heavy iron chariots sank deep in the mud, and as they did, many of the charioteers were slain. And the hoofs of the cavalry horses splashed through the mud as a small remnant made its retreat.

Sisera, abandoning his mighty chariot, ran for his life through the blinding rain. He managed to reach the tent of Jael, wife of Heber the Kenite. Because the Kenites had been at peace with Sisera, he thought that here he would be safe, especially since Jael had come forth to offer him her hospitality. Weary from battle and comforted by the warm milk and lodging which Jael had so hospitably given to him, Sisera fell soundly asleep. And as Sisera lay sleeping Jael took a peg which her husband had used to stretch the tents on the ground and with a hammer drove it into Sisera's temples.

Hot in pursuit of Sisera, Barak soon came to the tent of Jael. She went out to meet him and said to him, "Come, and I will shew thee the man whom thou seekest" (Judg. 4:22). And Jael took him into the tent where lay the dead Sisera. It was just as Deborah had prophesied: "For the Lord shall sell Sisera into the hand of a woman" (Judg. 4:9).

To celebrate this great victory the Ode of Deborah, one of the earliest martial songs in history, was composed. It began: "Praise ye the Lord for the avenging of Israel" (Judg. 5:2). Deborah took no credit to herself. She gave all the credit to God, for she knew that only He could cause the earth to tremble, the heavens to drop torrents of water, and the mountains to melt. In the song she is called "a mother in Israel," for she, like a mother, had led the panicky children of Israel to victory. Their cry to her to lead them echoes in the refrain: "Awake, awake, Deborah: awake, awake, utter a song." The tribes of Israel who had stood by her in the conflict were praised.

Tribute is paid to Jael for putting Sisera to death. In every line of the song one senses Deborah's extreme devotion to God and to the well-being of her nation. At the end of the song, which runs through thirty-one verses of Judges 5, her courageous voice sounds forth like the clear notes of a trumpet of freedom. Her people were no longer enslaved. Now with her they could declare, "So let all thine enemies perish, O Lord: but let them that love him be as the sun when he goeth forth in his might." Such fire as Deborah possessed literally never died out of Israel.

Her glorious victory is best recorded in these concluding but meaningful lines of her Bible biography: "And the land had rest forty years" (Judg. 5:31).

JEPHTHAH'S DAUGHTER

JUDG. 11:34, 35, 40

Jephthah, ninth judge of Israel, makes public vow to offer a burnt offering in case of victory. He is victorious, but learns his daughter must be his offering. She accepts her father's pledge with meekness and patience.

EXAMPLE OF NOBLE SUBMISSION

SCARCELY a century had elapsed since Deborah's great victory. The people freed by her were now plunged into idolatry and threatened by foreign domination again. In the darkness of this era the figures of a father and daughter, his only child, emerge as the providential agents of restoration.

The daughter had such a sublime reverence for a promise made to God that she was even willing to lay down her life for it. The father, Jephthah, described as "a mighty man of valour" (Judg. 11:1), was the son of a distinguished Hebrew named Gilead, who lived in a territory of that name. His mother was a stranger to the tribe, an inferior woman described as a harlot (Judg. 11:1, 2). Despite his mother's foreign blood and the heathen qualities of many of his tribesmen, Jephthah became a great commander and a believer in the one God.

In the early part of his life, because of his illegitimacy, he had been banished from his father's house and had taken up his residence in Tob, not far from Gilead. Here he became head of a warring tribe of freebooters who went raiding with him. When war broke out between the Ammonites and the Gileadites, the latter sought Jephthah as their commander. He consented only after a solemn covenant, ratified on both sides at Mizpeh, a strongly fortified frontier town of Gilead.

Here he established his residence temporarily and brought his daughter. After a fruitless appeal for peace to their leaders and for aid to the adjacent tribe of Ephraim, Jephthah, urged by the "spirit of the Lord," sped through the territories of Manasseh and his own Gilead, summoning the Israelites to arms.

It seems that his army represented a small minority compared to that of the enemy. In his perplexity to give fresh courage to his troops and to sustain his own confidence against such fearful odds, he made a vow publicly to the Lord. In that reckless vow he exhibited a rude and unenlightened piety typical of the wild mountaineer fighter that he was when he declared, "If thou shalt without fail deliver the children of Ammon into mine hands, then shall it be, that whatsoever cometh forth of the doors of my house to meet me, when I return in peace from the children of Ammon, shall surely be the Lord's, and I will offer it up for a burnt offering" (Judg. 11:30-31).

What a contrast between Jephthah's vow and that of Hannah who had pledged to lend her child to God as long as he lived. What a contrast, also, to the simple and sublime trust of Deborah, who went against a fearful enemy strongly armed with faith in God. Not so strongly armed, Jephthah was willing to make any kind of promise to insure victory.

Jephthah routed the Ammonites, and twenty of their cities fell before him. Elated with his unexpected success, he hurried to Mizpeh, where he had left his daughter. The women and maidens had assembled to greet this victorious warrior with songs and dances. Who should be the first to come out from Jephthah's own doorway but his beloved daughter! Probably he had thought a servant or hound dog would precede her. Or maybe not until this moment had he stopped to realize how rash and cruel had been his vow. But now his shock was great and his distress poignant as he looked and saw his beautiful daughter standing there in front of his own doorway.

Let us visualize her in all the freshness of youth, with her luxuriant hair falling loosely over her shoulders, and with the wind blowing her hair and at the same time swaying her full-skirted and brightly colored dress. Her red lips were probably parted in a radiant smile and her eyes were filled with joy as she beat a timbrel and sang. Her country was free again. The enemy had been annihilated, and her own father had been in command. Now he would be first in Israel.

She ran to embrace him. Had he not been all in all to her? Born in exile, reared amid the wild scenes of desert life, she had known no other protection but her father's tent, no greater love than his. And we can be sure that, mighty warrior though he was, whose name had spread panic throughout all neighboring lands, he had been to his beloved daughter the tenderest kind of parent.

While the whole land echoed the triumphant shouts of freedom, all the glory died out for Jephthah as he embraced his daughter, only to cry loudly, "Alas, my daughter! thou has brought me very low, and thou art one of them that trouble me: for I have opened my mouth unto the Lord, and I cannot go back" (Judg. 11:35).

With heroic courage Jephthah's daughter gave the answer that has become a classic: "My father, if thou hast opened thy mouth unto the Lord, do to me according to that which hath proceeded out of thy mouth; forasmuch as the Lord hath taken vengeance for thee of thine enemies, even of the children of Ammon" (Judg. 11:36). His daughter's noble submission to his vow now made the consequence of it even harder for Jephthah to bear.

Pure of heart and unmindful of tragedy, Jephthah's daughter probably did not at first grasp her father's distressing predicament. Then she began to know that the life she had envisioned as a wife and mother, the hope of every woman in Israel, was gone. Let us imagine she needed spiritual strength to face such a crisis and so she asked her father for two months, so that she might go to the mountains with young friends and "bewail her virginity" (Judg. 11:38).

Then it was she returned calmly and obediently to her father, who, the Scriptures say, "did with her according to his vow" (Judg. 11:39). A great many Bible commentators take this story literally, saying Jephthah did go forth and offer his daughter for a burnt offering. There is little argument for a different interpretation except in that earlier phrase, "shall surely be the Lord's" (Judg. 11:31), indicating he could have meant to offer her to the service of the sanctuary.

Some commentators make the point that while Jephthah's daughter was in the mountains for two months her father had time to weigh with himself the rashness of his promise. And, despite the turbulent times, there were in Israel many noble, God-fearing men and women who intelligently understood and practiced the wise and merciful system of Moses, that of not offering human beings as burnt sacrifices. If so, Jephthah's daughter gave her life to service in the tabernacle. The phrase "she knew no man" (Judg. 11:39) conveys the thought that she became a celibate. It has been suggested that what the daughters of Israel bewailed was not her death but her celibacy.

We are positive that she did not marry and bear children, and for an only child of a mighty warrior to die unmarried and leave a name in Israel extinguished was indeed a heavy judgment. But despite the seeming tragedy of this daughter of Israel, she lives on, even now, almost thirty-one centuries later, as the embodiment of a courageous young woman who was both meek in spirit and patient in suffering.

DELILAH

JUDG. 16:4, 6, 10, 12, 13, 18

A woman representing the Philistines, enemies to Samson's Hebrew race, inveigles and betrays him for money paid by enemy. Learning that his strength is in his hair, she has it shaved off. He awakens to find strength gone.

"ENTICE HIM AND SEE WHERE HIS STRENGTH LIES"

DELILAH typifies the terrible energy of evil in a woman just as Samson typifies the preternatural strength in a man. She has come down through these thirty-one centuries as the woman who, in an insidious manner, sought to destroy a man who seemed to be unconquerable.

The rabbis generally concede that Delilah was a Philistine, and Josephus declares her to have been one. Samson, one of the most eminent Hebrew "Judges," had to his credit many heroic achievements against the Philistines. They hated him and sought to work his ruin through Delilah.

She lived, we are told, in the Valley of Sorek, a brook valley which cut through the foothills between the Philistine plains and the highlands of Judah. When Samson went down to see Delilah, he had already demonstrated that he was a giant in physical strength but that when it came to women he was a dwarf in willpower and moral resistance.

Shortly before going down to see Delilah he had visited a harlot. The Bible text relates this quite casually in Judges 16:1, as if Samson had a low sense of morals. Earlier than this, he had been married to a woman living at Timnath, a daughter of the Philistines. She turned out to be a weeping and inconstant wife (Judg. 14:17, 20). While Samson was away, she was courted by his friend. Samson's mother and father Manoah, a godly pair, had objected to the marriage of their son, who from the womb had been consecrated to God (Judg. 13:5). His wife did not believe in the one God. But when Samson's parents expressed their objection to her, he answered them saying, "She pleaseth me well" (Judg. 14:3).

Though victimized by these two seductive women, Samson started courting Delilah, who turned out to be the worst of the three. When he came into her presence, he became a slave to passion. And he let himself forget that his paramour was a Philistine in sympathy, while he had consecrated his life to deliver Israel out of the hands of the Philistines. He was blind to the fact that Delilah was a woman who finally would lure him to his ruin, and all for 1,100 pieces of silver from each of the lords of the Philistines.

We can be sure that Delilah possessed a fascinating quality and had an exotic kind of beauty. Though the Bible gives us no exact details of this or of what she wore, she undoubtedly decked herself in her finest clothes when an eminent man like Samson called. Probably she wore a dress embroidered with gold threads from Ophir and colored threads dyed with Tyrian dyes. In her ears and on her ankles, fingers, and toes she wore gold jewelry.

It is likely that she also used perfumes from India, and she made of her home a charming and restful place. We can imagine that she had musicians playing the dulcimer and lyre on the garden terrace, where a fountain sprayed, cooling the area. Her home probably had become a frequent retreat for the eminent and mighty Samson.

He was completely blind to the fact that Delilah was a deceitful woman, determined to find out the secret of his great strength so that his enemies could conquer him. One day while she was alone with Samson, she boldly asked him, "Tell me, I pray thee, wherein thy great strength lieth, and wherewith thou mightest be bound to afflict thee" (Judg. 16:6). She spoke in jest, as if to make him believe that no man could bind him. He replied, pretending to reveal the means by which she might test his invincible strength. But each time he tricked her. This became a game to them, she coaxing him to tell her the source of his strength, and he giving her a series of wrong explanations.

Day after day, during their lovemaking, she pressed him hard for the answer. Finally one day Samson confessed to her the secret of his strength, which, he said, was in the locks of his hair. If they were shaved, he told her, his strength would leave him and he would be like any other man. He revealed to her that even before his birth he had been consecrated to God and he had kept the Nazarite vows, one of which was that his hair would not be cut.

When he told Delilah all that was in his heart, she made him fall asleep on her knee. And as he slept, she called for a man to shave the seven locks from his head.

When he awoke, he discovered too late that Delilah had deceived him. She was not a tender lover but a cruel enemy. "The Philistines be upon thee, Samson" (Judg. 16:20), she said as she awoke him. And Samson knew that his strength had gone from him.

We wonder where Delilah was as the Philistines came forth and seized Samson, gouging out his eyes and binding him with bronze fetters. Did she know that the eyes which had gazed on her in delighted love had now been cruelly mutilated? Had she gone to collect and to spend those 1,100 pieces of silver from each of the lords of the Philistines?

And where was Delilah when the lords of the Philistines and throngs of other Philistines gathered at a great festival and public sacrifice to their god Dagon? Was Delilah again with them? Did she see Samson stand between the pillars in the great assembly hall and pull them down? If so, she probably perished along with hundreds of others upon whom the building fell.

Milton, in his dramatic poem *Samson Agonistes* (1671), represents Delilah as coming to the prison while Samson was there and offering to atone for her faithlessness. But there is no Biblical authority for this. The three-act grand opera *Samson et Dalila*, by Saint-Saëns, first performed at Weimar December 2, 1877, also follows the Bible theme. So does Handel's oratorio *Samson*, first performed at Covent Garden, London, during the Lenten season in 1742.

Could it be that Delilah also was the woman who prompted the words in Proverbs: "For the lips of a strange woman drop as an honeycomb, and her mouth is smoother than oil" (Prov. 5:3)?

RUTH

RUTH 1:4, 14, 16, 22
    2:2, 8, 21, 22
    3:9
    4:5, 10, 13
MATT. 1:5

Leaves her own land of Moab and goes with her mother-in-law Naomi to Bethlehem. Supports both of them with her gleanings from barley in field of Boaz, whom she later marries. Their son Obed is grandfather of King David.

THE FAITHFUL DAUGHTER-IN-LAW

RUTH, the central figure in the Book of Ruth, is one of the most lovable women in the Bible. And her abiding love embraces the person you would least expect it to, her mother-in-law, Naomi. The latter was a Hebrew from Bethlehem-Judah, while Ruth was a foreigner from Moab, a lofty tableland to the east of the Dead Sea. Ruth's alien background is repeatedly stressed. In the short book, five times she is "Ruth the Moabitess," also "the woman of Moab," the "Moabitish damsel," and a "stranger."

Though of a neighboring people, hated by early Israel, Ruth finally won her way into their hearts as the ideal daughter-in-law, wife, and mother. The people of the little town of Bethlehem admired her, not because of her genius or her foresight or her great beauty, but because of her womanly sweetness. Her story, which finally culminates in her marriage to Boaz, a man of influence, is one of the most beautiful romances in the Bible.

Modest, meek, courteous, loyal, responsible, gentle yet decisive, Ruth always seems to do the right thing at the right time. Though the Bible gives no clear-cut description of her appearance, literature and art have depicted her as extremely lovely. In his book on *Ruth* Irving Fineman describes her as a woman "whose radiant beauty of face and form neither the shadows nor the sad state of her raiment could obscure." He further depicts her as having gleaming golden hair and dark eyes. Frank Slaughter's *Song of Ruth* pictures her as "startlingly beautiful, with dark red hair, high cheekbones, and warm eyes" and as a woman who dressed in the "clinging robe of a temple priestess."

At the opening of the story Ruth as the young widow of Mahlon faces an uncertain future, along with her mother-in-law Naomi and her sister-in-law Orpah, widow of Chilion. From this point on Ruth herself becomes the embodiment of all that is fine in a young widow. We do not hear her crying out at the loss of her husband, but expressing her affection for him in her loyalty to his mother, his people, his country, and his God. Nor do we find her pitying herself, though she and her mother-in-law are destitute. Instead she chooses to follow her mother-in-law wherever she leads, and she does so in a spirit of love.

Ruth's husband and his father Elimelech and mother Naomi and brother Chilion had left Bethlehem ten years before because of famine. Recent explorations of the land of Moab have given confirmation of the fertility of the plains of ancient Moab, a fact which is implied in the statement that Naomi's family went there to escape the famine of Judah. Dr. William L. Reed, professor of Old Testament at Texas Christian University and a well-known archaeologist of the Holy Land, reports that explorations and excavations point toward a close association among Hebrews and Moabites, as is implied in the story of Ruth.

Naomi and her family had gone into the fertile, well-watered highlands of Moab east of the Dead Sea, but there her husband and her two sons had died.

Old and weary, Naomi longed to return to the land of her birth. All three women wept as they stood to say good-by. Naomi pleaded with her two daughters-in-law to turn back to their mother's house. Orpah did turn back, but Ruth clung lovingly to her mother-in-law, and as she did she made this most wonderful confession of love ever spoken by a daughter-in-law, "Intreat me not to leave thee, or to return from following after thee: for whither thou goest, I will go; and where thou lodgest, I will lodge: thy people shall be my people, and thy God my God: Where thou diest, will I die, and there will I be buried" (Ruth 1:16).

Like so many young widows, she might have said, "Somebody else must take care of this forlorn old woman. I'm still young. I want to marry again. The mother of my first husband is in my way." But Ruth made this other choice, and she made it gracefully.

She never swerved from her unselfish purpose during the many trials that followed. Nor did she ever complain because she had given up everything, her country, her relationships with young friends, or her chance to marry a man of her own country. She had given them all up with a resolution fierce in its quietness.

The young and beautiful daughter-in-law and the old and wise mother-in-law now turned their faces resolutely toward Palestine.

The journey was less than 120 miles, but this distance represented a long, fatiguing, and dangerous trek in this period thirteen centuries before Christ, especially for two lone women who had neither money beyond their barest needs nor protector. They crossed the Arnon and the Jordan, ascending mountains and descending into deep valleys, partly on foot, let us suppose, and partly on donkeys. This journey through desolate places caused them to cling more closely together.

When they reached Bethlehem, in order to support herself and her mother-in-law Ruth performed the lowliest of tasks, that of following the reapers and gathering up the fragments of grain which fell and were left behind for the poor. Without the least feeling of self-pity or dread of a difficult task, Ruth gleaned all day in the hot sun, returning to Naomi joyfully at the end of the day with her small harvest.

One day, as Ruth gleaned, she came into a field belonging to Boaz, a large landowner, who was a distant kinsman of Naomi's husband. For a time Ruth worked with the other poor gleaners and was unknown to Boaz. She performed her work well, from the hour that the sun first rose over the fields of swaying barley until it dipped gently behind the low-lying hills of Judah.

Humble woman that Ruth was, she did not rush to Boaz, her husband's rich kinsman, and introduce herself, but worked quietly at her task. Her good work was rewarded. When Boaz came into his fields and saw this pretty young woman, he inquired of his servants who she was, and they told him she was the Moabitess who had come back with Naomi from the country of Moab. Immediately offering her his protection, he asked her not to glean in any field except his own, ordered his young men not to touch her, and invited her to drink of the water which they had drawn.

Later he returned his admiration for her in little kindnesses, for he knew not only that she had to support her mother-in-law but that she was a woman with a gentle disposition. "The Lord recompense thy work, and a full reward be given thee of the Lord God of Israel, under whose wings thou art come to trust" (Ruth 2:12).

Boaz, who was a man of God, also a man of intelligence and with a high code of morals, could appreciate Ruth's quiet loveliness, her inborn purity and generosity of soul. And he began to shower small favors upon her. He asked her to come and eat bread and to dip her morsel in wine. As she sat among the reapers, he passed parched grain to her and instructed his helpers to pull out some stalks from their bundles and leave them for her so as to make her gleanings easier and more productive.

When Ruth returned to Naomi at the end of each day with about an ephah (or a bushel) of barley, Naomi would always question her about the day's happenings. Once when Ruth told her she had gleaned in the field of Boaz that day, Naomi said, "Blessed be he of the Lord, who hath not left off his kindness to the living and to the dead." And Naomi added, "The man is near of kin unto us, one of our next kinsmen" (Ruth 2:20).

The entire scene was now set for the culmination of a beautiful romance. We know why Goethe has called the Book of Ruth "the loveliest little idyll that tradition has transmitted to us."

Naomi, an honored matron of Judah, made the next step on behalf of a brighter future for her beloved daughter-in-law. With bold tenderness she directed Ruth to the threshing floor at night, where Boaz would be winnowing his grain. She instructed her to wash, anoint herself, and put on her best raiment, and to go where Boaz was after he had finished eating and drinking. This wise mother-in-law advised Ruth one step further.

"And it shall be, when he lieth down, that thou shalt mark the place where he shall lie, and thou shalt go in, and uncover his feet, and lay thee down; and he will tell thee what thou shalt do" (Ruth 3:4). Ruth, knowing that her mother-in-law would command her to do nothing that was not considered proper, replied, "All that thou sayest unto me I will do" (Ruth 3:5).

The bold yet humble advance of Ruth was accepted by Boaz with a tender dignity and a chivalrous delicacy. He treated this act by which she threw herself upon his protection as an honor due him, for which he was bound to be grateful. And he hastened to assure her that he was her debtor for the preference she had shown for him. He became as careful for her reputation and chastity as if she had been his daughter.

The measure recommended by Naomi and adopted by Ruth was equivalent to a legal call on Boaz, as the supposed nearest kinsman of the family, to fulfill the duty of that relationship. An archaic custom this was, and one which subjected Ruth to a severe moral test, but she had confidence in her mother-in-law's judgment and she also knew that Boaz had proved himself to be meticulously upright.

This part of the story is handled in the Bible with great delicacy and restraint. First Boaz told his servant not to let it be known that Ruth had come to the threshing floor. There might be idle gossip. He also knew there was a nearer kinsman than himself, one who would have a prior claim to Ruth.

He immediately sent word to Naomi that he gladly accepted the legal protection of her daughter-in-law. Now he summoned the next of kin. This man waived his right to the young widow, admitting that he did not care to redeem Elimelech's portion of the land, a necessary part of a levirate matrimonial transaction, which assured the continuation of family life, the preservation of property, and the welfare of widows.

Boaz had shown his honorable and businesslike traits of character in going to the gates of the city before the elders. Then he went forth publicly to tell that he had brought Ruth the Moabitess, the widow of Mahlon, to be his wife. And the lovely stranger in Judah became the wife of the rich land proprietor Boaz. By her perseverance and faithfulness, she had achieved the seemingly impossible. She had been lifted out of obscurity and poverty to influence and plenty.

From this marriage of Ruth and Boaz sprang an auspicious lineage, the House of David (Matt. 1:5). Before the birth of her son Obed, Ruth was assured that her child's name would be "famous in Israel"

(Ruth 4:14). And Naomi was told that the child would be a nourisher of her old age. Her neighbors, rejoicing with her, said, "Thy daughter in law, which loveth thee, which is better to thee than seven sons, hath born him" (Ruth 4:15). And Naomi joyfully took over the duties of nurse to her grandchild.

Love had worked the miracle in Ruth's life. She was beloved by all because she was so lovable. She had proved that love can lift one out of poverty and obscurity, love can bring forth a wonderful child, love can shed its rays, like sunlight, on all whom it touches, even a forlorn and weary mother-in-law. Ruth's love had even penetrated the barriers of race.

HANNAH

I SAM. I:2, 5, 8, 9, 13, 15, 19, 20, 22

I SAM. 2:I, 2I

Consecrated mother prays for a son. Samuel is born. She lovingly tends him in his formative years as she prepares him for temple service. Utters famous prayer of dedication in temple. Makes a coat for Samuel each year when she goes to visit him.

THE PRAYERFUL MOTHER

THE woman who personifies the ideal in motherhood in the Old Testament is Hannah, mother of Samuel, the earliest of the great Hebrew prophets after Moses and the last of the "Judges." Hannah's story, told in the first two chapters of the first Bible book bearing her son's name, breathes of her love and care of her first-born, the worthy son of a worthy mother.

In her consecration as a mother Hannah probably inspired Mary, Mother of Jesus, who lived almost twelve centuries later. One wonders if Hannah's Song of Triumph (I Sam. 2:2-10) was not known by Mary. It could have inspired her Magnificat (Luke 1:46-55), because there is certainly a similarity between these two songs of exultation.

Hannah's environment was not conducive to prayer, for the people of Israel had lapsed from the high standards of morality and spirituality set up by Moses. She had to break away from old traditions and find a new path. Her home environment was not conducive to great dreams either. Her husband Elkanah was a good but easygoing, undistinguished priest; and in these polygamous times he and his other wife, Peninnah, had children, while Hannah had none.

But she believed with all her heart that God was the creator of children and that only God could convert a woman into a mother. Every year she went from her home at Ramah to the temple at Shiloh, and her most ardent prayer was for a child.

It is easy to imagine that Hannah was a young woman whose face bore the radiance of her own spirituality, and that she dressed in a brightly colored, loosely flowing dress of muslin. We can be quite sure that she had stitched it herself and embroidered it with bright colors, for Hannah was gifted with the needle. Later these same gifted hands would lovingly stitch garments for her little son to wear as he served in the temple at Shiloh.

A much anticipated occasion this was when Hannah, Elkanah, and other members of the family saddled their asses and climbed the autumn-tinted hills to Shiloh. Though she was her husband's favorite wife, these journeys to Shiloh, at the vintage season when fall was folding in over the Palestine hills, were trying ones for Hannah. As she saw parents and children coming together, probably she grieved all the more because she had no part in the coming generation. As her husband made his sacrifices in the tabernacle, he would give portions to his other wife Peninnah and to her sons and daughters. Though he gave Hannah a "worthy portion," it was much smaller because she had no children.

Peninnah, jealous because Hannah was the favorite wife, made light of Hannah because "the Lord had shut up her womb" (I Sam. 1:6). But it is greatly to Hannah's credit that this bad treatment caused no outward conflict on her part. Though grieved in spirit, we hear no railing or furious revenge on her part.

Each year, though, it became a hard experience emotionally for Hannah to make the journey to Shiloh. Finally on one trip she wept and would not eat. Her husband, a sensitive man, asked, "Why weepest thou? and why eatest thou not? and why is thy heart grieved? am I not better to thee than ten sons?" (I Sam. 1:8).

We have no answer from Hannah, but we do know she arose and went into the tabernacle to pour out her anguish of soul. And the prayer that she prayed has become one of the great petitions of a mother. "O Lord of hosts," she prayed fervently, "if thou wilt indeed look on the affliction of thine handmaid, and remember me, and not forget thine handmaid, but wilt give unto thine handmaid a man child, then I will give him unto the Lord all the days of his life, and there shall no razor come upon his head" (I Sam. 1:11). In that last phrase she vowed that she would consecrate her child to God, just as Samson's mother had consecrated him and John the Baptist's mother later would consecrate him. The uncut hair of Hannah's child would be a sign that he was consecrated to God.

Hannah was the fourth great woman in sacred history who grieved because she had not conceived, and among the four she was the most prayerful. Sarah had laughed when she learned a child would be born to her in old age. Rebekah bore her trial with listlessness and indifference. Rachel, irritated at her long wait for a child, exclaimed, "Give me children, or else I die." Hannah sought her call as a mother in the power of God, for she desired a son as a poet desires a song.

Her repetition of the word "handmaid" three times expressed her humility, submission, and sense of dependence on God. From such humility Hannah received new strength.

Eli, the priest, seeing her lips move, but not understanding her silence, asked if she were drunk. But Hannah asserted, "No, my lord, I am a woman of a sorrowful spirit: I have drunk neither wine nor strong drink, but have poured out my soul before the Lord" (I Sam. 1:15).

This defense of Hannah is almost as wonderful as her prayer. It argues her conscious integrity, innocence, and serenity of spirit, even in an hour of great trial and unjustified criticism. When Eli saw how eager she was for a child, he joined her in prayer, asking that the God of Israel grant her petition. And Hannah went her way firm in her conviction that God would answer her prayer for a son. She worshiped with her husband again the next morning.

This continued reverence was significant. It showed she was not one to pray once and be satisfied, but was willing to pray again and again. When her prayer was answered and there was born to her a son, she named him Samuel, meaning "asked of the Lord" (I Sam. 1:20). In her loving care of Samuel, Hannah becomes the prototype of the good mother everywhere, setting a stirring example of high morality and spirituality, which could bring a new order into the world.

Let us picture this early mother of Israel, if we may, as she nursed and tended the little Samuel, bestowing upon him all the love that a devoted mother would have for her first-born. When he was little, she never left him with others, but gently tended him herself. She even declined a trip with her husband to the tabernacle at Shiloh because her baby had not yet been weaned. In that decision alone she placed upon motherhood a high obligation and responsibility.

Finally, when the child was weaned, Hannah dressed him for his first trip to the tabernacle, where she was to leave him. The atmosphere around this place of worship sometimes became polluted. Eli, the priest, though a good man himself, had sons who "lay with the women that assembled at the door of the tabernacle of the congregation" (I Sam. 2:22). But Hannah had no fears for her son. She had placed him in the hands of God, and she believed strongly in her heart that God would answer the petition she had made before his birth.

Loving him as she did, it was a sacrifice for her to return to Ramah without him. But Hannah was a wise and prudent mother as well as a devoted one, a mother who possessed fortitude as well as vision. Practical, too, she did not discommode the whole family, sacrifice the good of her husband, and move to Shiloh simply because she desired in her heart to be near Samuel day and night. While he was a little fellow, for his own good she weaned him in spirit just as she had weaned him from her breast.

Before she left Samuel in the tabernacle with Eli, however, she prayed to God a triumphant prayer that has been called the forerunner of Mary's Magnificat. In it Hannah exhibited the fervency, depth, and fire of a woman who was happy and who sang her happiness and belief in God. She loved her God, not mainly because He had delivered to her a son, but for what He was to all, a God of knowledge and of power.

She prayed for those who stumbled, but were girded with strength, those who had been hungry, but were fed, those also who were barren, as she had been barren. She sang also to the Lord who bringeth low and lifteth up, who raiseth up the poor out of the dust and lifteth up the beggar from the dunghill, to set them among princes.

Hannah affirmed also that God would keep the feet of his saints on the right road and the wicked should be cut off in darkness. She spoke with positive devotion, saying, "For by strength shall no man prevail" (I Sam. 2:9). She was certain that the Lord would judge the ends of the earth and exalt His anointed.

One of the remarkable things about Hannah's prayer was that she prayed it after she had become the mother of a wonderful son, making us know she was a woman who prayed in good times and bad, in joy and affliction. She was grateful that her son, young though he was, could learn to perform many little duties in the tabernacle—light a candle or hold a dish or run an errand or shut a door. And because he would learn to do these menial tasks joyfully, he would rise in a greater ministry to the Lord.

After a while the boy Samuel did his work so well in the temple that Eli appointed him to wear the simple linen vest worn by the priests and called an ephod. Hannah made him a coat or robe of blue fabric to wear under the ephod. We can be sure Hannah put love into every stitch of the coat, which reached to the boy's feet. As Samuel outgrew one coat each year, she would make him another and take it with her when the family went to Shiloh for the yearly sacrifices.

The priest, Eli, witnessing the unselfishness of Hannah, asked that God visit her, and she conceived and bore three sons and two daughters. The last of Hannah's biography confirms that the child Samuel grew before the Lord (I Sam. 2:21). This links the boyhood of Samuel with that of Jesus. It is recorded that when Jesus was twelve He went to the temple at Jerusalem and tarried there. He, too, "increased in wisdom and stature, and in favour with God and man" (Luke 2:52).

Hannah, like Mary, gave her child to God, and after she did, slipped into the background and became immortal through her son.

ICHABOD'S MOTHER

I SAM. 4:19-22   *Husband killed in battle. She gives birth to son after husband's death and other family tragedies, then dies.*

A MOTHER WITHOUT HOPE

IN that gallery of Bible women where we find mirrored every type of woman living today stands Ichabod's mother, symbolizing the woman who gives birth to a child after she has received word of her husband's death in battle. Then she dies herself. More particularly she symbolizes the mother who succumbs to dark, despairing hopelessness.

Her husband, Phinehas, was immoral and greedy. Since she made no record of any kind herself, it is easy to imagine her as a careworn, sorrowful woman. Her first name is not recorded, and the only words from her lips are "The glory is departed from Israel: because the ark of God was taken" (I Sam. 4:21).

This leads one to believe that she was a sincerely devout woman but one who believed more in the ark, a symbol of God, than in God himself. She probably held to the superstitious belief that the ark of the Covenant, and not God, had helped her people in the crossing of the Jordan by causing the waters to part, and had delivered Jericho to them on the solemn march around the city by causing the walls to fall.

Her religion probably represented an emotionalism and not a true devotion to God. And it could not sustain her in her many family tragedies, beginning with the death of her husband and his brother in battle. She probably realized, too, that her husband did not hand down a good heritage to her son, for he and his brother, it is recorded, "lay with the women that assembled at the door of the tabernacle of the congregation" (I Sam. 2:22). And he and his brother, it was later learned, had been guardians of the ark when it fell into the hands of the enemy.

She faced another tragedy, too, just before the birth of her son. Her aged father-in-law, Eli, priest at the temple at Shiloh, had fallen and broken his neck when he received the shocking news that his two sons had been killed in battle and that the ark of the Covenant, so long in his temple at Shiloh, had been taken by the Philistines.

The loss of the ark seemed to bring almost as great a shock to Ichabod's mother as it did to Eli. And when this was added to other family tragedies, her child was born prematurely, and she died soon afterward. She became the second mother in the Bible to die in childbirth. Unlike Rachel, no loving husband was at her side as she died, and unlike Rachel also, no tomb marks the spot where she was buried.

There is this parallel, however, in her story and Rachel's. At Rachel's side was a midwife, who comforted her with these words, "Fear not; thou shalt have this son also" (Gen. 35:17). Those who attended Ichabod's mother said, "Fear not; for thou hast born a son" (I Sam. 4:20).

But Ichabod's mother held out no hope for her son, who had been born into a land from which the symbol of God had departed. She knew all too well that the child's degenerate and greedy father had died in battle, but not as a hero of the godly people of Israel. She probably remembered, too, that this child's grandfather Eli, though a good priest, was a weak and indulgent father. And she did not have the faith or the stamina to rise above such overwhelming disappointments and shocking tragedies, or the courage to live and nurture her son Ichabod.

[94]

ICHABOD'S MOTHER

Had she possessed the faith of Sarah, or the consecration of Hannah, her son Ichabod might have been illustrious and not inglorious. And he might have retrieved for the Israelites the ark of the Covenant which his father had lost to the Philistines.

Women in the Days
of the Kings

MICHAL

I SAM. 14:49
18:20, 27, 28
19:11, 12, 13, 17
25:44
II SAM. 3:13, 14
6:16, 20, 21, 23
21:8
I CHRON. 15:29

*Estranged from her husband David be-
cause of her father's jealousy of his valor.
Is next married to Phalti. When David
becomes king, he demands his wife back.
She mocks him when he dances before
the ark. She cares for sister's five children
in her last years.*

KING SAUL'S DAUGHTER—DAVID'S FIRST WIFE

THOUGH a woman of exceptional fortitude in time of trouble,
Michal, King Saul's daughter and David's first wife, lacked a
genuine appreciation of her husband's religious zeal. It is to her
credit, however, that she aided David in his early struggles long
before he became king of Israel.

Her older sister Merab had first been promised by her father to

David after he returned victorious over Goliath, the giant champion of their enemies the Philistines. She was to be his reward for the victory. But King Saul failed to fulfill his promise. He gave his daughter Merab to Adriel, the Meholathite.

Next, we learn from the Scripture, "Michal Saul's daughter loved David" (I Sam. 18:20). She was the younger daughter. It is easy to suppose that she and David had often met when her brother Jonathan, a great admirer of David, had brought him home. And to a king's young daughter the brave and strong David became a great hero.

Michal must have had a gentle mother. Her name was Ahinoam. But her father Saul was an obstinate, jealous, and murderous man. He disliked David and began to plan how Michal might be the stumbling block to David's promising career.

As he began a plot against David, Saul sent the flattering word by servants to David that he wanted him for his son-in-law. Humble as he was at this time, young David sent word back to King Saul that it was no light thing to be a king's son-in-law.

Then it was that Saul said David could have Michal if he would go out and kill one hundred Philistines and bring back the foreskins to him. Saul was sure David would be killed himself, but David surprised him. He brought back the foreskins of two hundred Philistines. And Michal became his wife.

Saul, however, did not cease plotting against David. One day, as his unsuspecting son-in-law sat entertaining him with music, a tall spear sped like lightning from Saul's hand toward David. But it missed its aim and went harmlessly over his head. David fled and escaped.

Michal, probably distraught at her father's continued attempts to take her husband's life because she was still in love with him, began to plan how she could save him. Messengers had already come to her house telling her that they would slay David in the morning.

Warning David of his approaching danger, Michal let him down through a window, and he escaped. When her father commanded David to come to him, she sent back word that David was sick, but her father, still persistent, asked his messengers to deliver the sick David on his bed.

David was already well on his way to safety when Michal, to appease her father's wrath, took a large image resembling a recumbent figure, put it in David's bed, and then made a pillow of red goat's hair. The bed with what appeared to be a sleeping figure was taken before her father, and when he discovered the trick his daughter had played on him he asked why she had deceived him.

Clever woman that Michal was, she evaded her father's question, telling him that David had said to her, "Let me go; why should I kill thee?" (I Sam. 19:17). When Michal dared to defy a madman king like her father in order to save her husband, she must have possessed real courage.

We have no record that Michal had David's faith in God's protecting power. She no doubt believed in idols. When she placed the image in David's bed, to resemble his recumbent figure, it appears that she had other idols near at hand. Commentators, however, question the size of Michal's idol that she placed in the bed. It had to be large, in order that it might resemble a reclining figure. And teraphim, like the one Rachel had carried away from her father's house, were small enough to put in a saddlebag. There is some discrepancy in this passage of Michal's idol but enough evidence to lead us to think she was not a believer in David's God of strength and mercy.

For a long time after this David remained an outlaw in exile from his wife's father. It would be almost impossible for a marriage to survive under such conditions. After some time had passed, King Saul arranged for Michal to marry Phalti, also called Phaltiel. Michal probably went with him to live in his town of Gallim.

Evidently some years passed before David and Michal ever met again. These were polygamous times, and David married Abigail, the woman of good understanding and a stanch believer in God. He also took another wife, Ahinoam of Jezreel.

When David became Saul's successor as king, he demanded that his wife Michal be returned to him. This was done. As he marched up to Jerusalem with the ark of the Covenant accompanied by 30,000 chosen men of Israel, Michal looked from a window and saw David, girded in a linen ephod, leaping and dancing before the newly restored ark. Not understanding David's religious zeal, Michal thought her husband was acting in an undignified manner.

When David saw that the ark was set in the tabernacle prepared for it, he returned to bless his own household. Then Michal came out to meet him and mocked him scornfully, saying, "How glorious was the king of Israel today, who uncovered himself today in the eyes of the handmaids of his servants, as one of the vain fellows shamelessly uncovereth himself!" (II Sam. 6:20).

Because David obviously wore nothing but the ephod, a custom not uncommon in these times, Michal "despised him in her heart" (II Sam. 6:16). We might also infer that David's acts had reflected on his wife's queenly dignity because he had mingled so freely with the common people.

There must have been other reasons, too, for Michal's resentment of David. When he demanded her back after he became king, she did not forget that he was taking her away from a husband with whom she must have spent several years. This husband, Phalti, we learn, wept as he followed Michal to Bahurim, where she was taken from him (II Sam. 3:16). But as king, David could demand whomever he chose, even a former wife who had married again.

The final record of the Michal-David love affair comes when David curtly tells Michal that he does not care for her opinion about the ephod and that he trusts the common sense of the maids and their loyalty to understand his motive. There then follows the phrase, "Therefore Michal the daughter of Saul had no child unto the day of her death" (II Sam. 6:23).

A rather conflicting passage appears later, in II Samuel 21:8, when the five sons of Michal are mentioned. Scholars seem to be convinced that this is a scribal error, that these were not Michal's sons but the sons of her sister Merab, and that she had reared them as her own after her sister's death.

Summing up the Bible portrait of Michal, first we see a young, beautiful, loving, courageous girl. But at the end we see a disillusioned, bickering woman with an inner poverty of spirit, one oppressed with many tragedies.

Not only had she been torn from two husbands, but if she lived long enough she had seen the five sons or nephews she had reared hanged in revenge for her father's wickedness. Also she had seen her father rejected by God, troubled by an evil spirit, and then killed by falling on his own sword. And his head was sent among many villages of the Philistines.

How could there be any happiness for his daughter Michal, who, like her father, had rejected God in her life?

ABIGAIL

I SAM. 25:3, 14, 18, 23, 32, 36,
39, 40, 42
27:3
30:5
II SAM. 2:2
3:3
I CHRON. 3:1

First married to Nabal, drunkard, who is owner of large herds and lands. He angers David. She acts as mediator to appease him. Takes gifts of cooked foods to David and his 600 men. After Nabal's death she becomes one of David's wives. Bears him a son Chileab.

A WOMAN OF GOOD UNDERSTANDING

BECAUSE of her good understanding, Abigail might be called the earliest woman pacifist on record. Certainly of all the famous women in the Old Testament she was the wisest.

Though she was to become David's wife after the death of her husband, Nabal, a drunkard, it is as the wife of the latter that her fine character comes into the sharpest focus. In this first picture of Abigail we come to know why David later was to have such faith in her wise counsel. From his first meeting with her David's life seems to have taken on a higher meaning and a stronger purpose. He is no longer a fugitive and outlaw but destined to become the great king of Judah and of all Israel.

Abigail was one of David's eight wives. The others were Michal (I Sam. 18:27), Bath-sheba (II Sam. 12:24), Ahinoam, Maacah, Haggith, Abital, and Eglah (II Sam. 3:2, 3, 4, 5), but Abigail was the greatest influence for good and helped David to remember that he was God's anointed into whose keeping the kingdom of Israel had been entrusted.

When David and Abigail chanced to meet, he was a shepherd

hiding from Saul in the wilderness of Paran, an extended tract along the southern border of Canaan adjoining the Sinaitic desert. He had gathered around him about six hundred followers, who constituted a bodyguard and voluntarily protected the flocks of many a herdsman from prowling thieves.

In the sheep and goat country west of the Dead Sea, and not far from where David was, lay the town of Maon. Near by was the larger town of Carmel standing in mountainous country. One of the richest men in this area was Abigail's husband, Nabal, who had some three thousand sheep and one thousand goats. Their home probably was a pretentious place on a plateau that one came upon suddenly after leaving desolate brown limestone hills, bare valleys, and dry watercourses.

It was sheep-shearing season at the home of Abigail and Nabal. Many guests had gathered, and there was much feasting. Abigail had provided abundantly for her guests, for she was a woman who had a reputation for gracious hospitality. We can imagine that her hospitable house, run efficiently and well, was a place where the stranger liked to tarry.

On such feasting occasions let us picture Abigail in a dress of fine linen, probably a vivid blue, with a softly draped headdress of shell pink forming a flattering outline for her brown hair and her delicate features. The headdress probably fell into a sash around her slender waist.

We have the Biblical record that Abigail was of a beautiful countenance as well as a woman of good understanding (I Sam. 25:3). But in the next phrase her husband, Nabal, is described as "churlish and evil in his doings" (I Sam. 25:3). His most niggardly act was directed at David, who had sent ten of his men up to the hills to ask for a little food during feasting time. David's own provisions were running low. His request was polite and just, for ten men could not carry away much food.

David and his men had helped Nabal's shepherds to protect their master's large herds of sheep and goats. It was quite natural that David's shepherds, who had befriended Nabal's man, would be welcome at feasting time. But Nabal, drinking too heavily, cried out contemptuously when he heard of David's request, "Who is David? and who is the son of Jesse? there be many servants now a days that break away every man from his master" (I Sam. 25:10).

When word reached Abigail, through one of the workers on the place, that her husband had railed at David's messengers, she listened attentively. This worker, who evidently had confidence in his mistress' sagacity, reminded her that David and his herdsmen had been like a wall of protection to Nabal's herdsmen. And he added that they had come to the house in peace, asking for that to which they were justly entitled. We can be assured that Abigail possessed an innate dignity and had won the respect and faithfulness of the workers in her household.

Wise woman, too, that she was, she lost no time, for she knew what happened when strong-minded men like David were angered. He was not one to let such an affront go unpunished. She also knew how rashly her husband acted when he was drunk. She wasted no time in lamenting the threatened danger or in making aspersions on her husband's character. Certainly she did not pause to discuss David's anger with her drunken husband.

Instead she hastily made ready to prepare special foods for David's six hundred men. She asked no advice of anyone but went to work as judiciously and quietly as if she had had months to think over her actions and make preparations for the food. She supervised the baking and packing of two hundred loaves of bread. Also, she had five sheep dressed and five measures of grain parched, and she packed two skins of wine, one hundred clusters of raisins, and two hundred cakes of figs (I Sam. 25:18). Then she had everything loaded on asses and mounted an ass herself. Let us imagine it was a white one, and as she mounted it, she beckoned to her helpers to ride before her with the food.

Only a capable and affluent woman could have made ready so much food in such haste. Only a woman of good understanding could have left so quietly, without informing her husband of her actions. If she had, she knew he would demand that she not give away his food to strangers. She knew, too, that the safety of their entire household was at stake.

As Abigail came down under the cover of the mountain, David and his men rode toward her, and she heard David telling them of her husband's ingratitude and of how he had returned to him evil for good. She overheard David say that by morning all that Nabal possessed and all in his household would be destroyed.

Abigail, unafraid, hastened toward David and alighted from her ass. In all humility she began to intercede for her husband and apologize for his bad actions. She admitted to David that Nabal was a base fellow and a fool. She then begged David to receive the food she had brought and to forgive her trespasses. She praised David, telling him that evil would not be found in him so long as he lived.

She also predicted that he would be prince over Israel and that his soul would be "bound in the bundle of life with the Lord thy God." She confirmed that God's word was sure and that God would exalt him. Abigail's supplication to David runs through I Samuel 25:24-31. In not one word do we find her forgetting her own dignity. All of the greatness which she predicted would come to David she attributed to the only source of good, God Himself. And she helped David to know he was the object of God's love and care.

What but the unquestioning faith in God could have dictated such a humble petition? In it Abigail typifies woman in her noblest, purest character. Her actions reveal that she was a diplomat of the highest order and that she understood men and had tolerance for their bad behavior.

When she had finished her mission, she did not loiter. She quickly mounted her ass and wended her way back over the hills. We can imagine that David watched her until she was lost in the distance. He probably had been impressed with her good countenance, and he was not to forget this woman who had brought all of this excellent food to his hungry men. His admiration for her one day would take on a deeper, richer meaning.

When Abigail arrived home, she found her husband still feasting and drinking. But, wisely, she did not tell him of her journey until morning. When the sober Nabal learned from Abigail how near he had come to being slain by David and his men and what she had done to avoid such an attack, he became violently ill. Ten days later he died. He probably died of apoplexy when he realized the perilous situation in which he had placed himself.

David, later to learn of Nabal's death, would affectionately remember the woman of good understanding who had come over the mountain on the ass, bringing food to appease his hunger. He was now free to wed Abigail, and so he sent his servants, telling her that he wanted her to be his wife.

She was now the petitioned and not the petitioner. She accepted David's invitation for marriage, but it was in humility and self-abasement. To his messengers she said, "Behold, let thine handmaid be a servant to wash the feet of the servants of my lord" (I Sam. 25:41). Though Abigail brought to David a rich estate and a new social position, she felt unworthy to become the wife of one whom God had singled out for His work.

Abigail was just the wife that David needed, for he was willful and tempestuous, while she was humble and gentle. Probably she helped him to learn patience and forbearance and to put aside temptation. She also helped to inspire confidence in him.

She dwelt with David at Gath and also went with him to Hebron, and there she gave birth to their son, Chileab, also called Daniel. Though little is recorded about Abigail after her marriage to David, we can be sure she was continually exposed to danger from the enmity of Saul and his followers and to captivity from neighboring nations. When the Amalekites captured Ziklag, she was taken captive but was rescued by David after he had defeated the enemy.

In their years together, David probably said to Abigail many times, as he had said to her when she first rode up to him on the ass, "Blessed be the Lord God of Israel, which sent thee this day to meet me: And blessed be thy advice" (I Sam. 25: 32-33).

WOMAN OF ENDOR

I SAM. 28:7-25

A woman with a "familiar spirit," she lives at town of Endor. King Saul goes to her in desperation. She foretells his death. Terrified, he becomes ill, and she prepares food to try to restore him as he rests on her bed.

A CAVE WOMAN WHO TOLD FORTUNES

THE King James Version calls her "a woman that hath a familiar spirit" (I Sam. 28:7). The Revised Standard Version calls her "the woman who is a medium." Modern writers have dubbed her the "Witch of Endor." Lord Byron has called her the "Phantom Seer." Kipling gives one of the most vivid portrayals of all in these lines:

> Oh, the road to Endor is the oldest road
> And the craziest road of all.
> Straight it runs to the witch's abode
> As it did in the day of Saul
> And nothing has changed of the sorrow in store
> For such as go down the road to En-dor.

Let us picture the woman at Endor as a wise old person with gnarled hands, deep, penetrating eyes, coarse, leathery skin, and

dark hair falling over her stooped shoulders. Probably she had resorted to fortunetelling because it was her only means of livelihood.
Maybe she had made some startling true predictions. Because she
had, many had gone to her cave home, seeking counsel.

However, in her magic, she broke laws that had been set down
for the people of Israel. In Leviticus 19:31 is this strong admonition:
"Regard not them that have familiar spirits, neither seek after
wizards, to be defiled by them: I am the Lord your God." Other
passages just as firmly denouncing sorcerers and stargazers appear
in Deuteronomy, Isaiah, and Jeremiah. And in an earlier part of
his reign Saul himself had "put away those that had familiar spirits"
(I Sam. 28:3).

But now he was a terrified old king, jealous of David, not respected by his own son Jonathan, and ridiculed by the people of
his kingdom. In a desperate state of mind, he planned to go down
the road to Endor, along with other material-minded people who
had forgotten God. The road he traveled led six miles southeast of
Nazareth. On the outskirts of Endor were many ancient caves. And
let us suppose this woman with the familiar spirit lived in one of
them. Probably her cave was hung with skins of wild animals to
keep out winds from the northern slope in the winter; in the summer
its portal was dark and terrifying, the last place you would expect
the king of Israel to enter.

Earlier in his career, as he valiantly fought down all his enemies,
including the Philistines, Ammonites, Moabites, and Amalekites
Saul would have scoffed at magic. Then he was afraid of no man,
but now he was a fear-ridden, weary old man, who longed to bring
back the dead Samuel, upon whom he had once leaned so heavily in
moments of depression. It was in one of these moments that Saul
told his servants to seek out and find a woman that had a familiar
spirit.

Ashamed to let it be known publicly that he was seeking aid from
such a woman, King Saul disguised himself in other garments.

Taking two men with him, he made his way to her gloomy cave under cover of darkness. This women possessed a certain wise caution, for she said to her visitor, "Behold, thou knowest what Saul hath done, how he hath cut off those that have familiar spirits, and the wizards, out of the land: wherefore then layest thou a snare for my life, to cause me to die?" (I Sam. 28:9).

But her visitor promised her there would be no punishment. Then the woman asked him, "Whom shall I bring up unto thee?" (I Sam. 28:11). And Saul commanded her to bring up Samuel, but the woman now cried with a loud voice, "Why hast thou deceived me? for thou art Saul?" (I Sam. 28:12).

She no longer doubted that she was being visited by the king of Israel. But when she was assured by Saul that she must not be afraid, she made her predictions, telling him that she saw gods ascending out of the earth. "An old man cometh up," she spoke, "and he is covered with a mantle" (I Sam. 28:14).

Convinced that the old man might be Samuel, whom he had relied upon so firmly for faith and inspiration, Saul was temporarily comforted. And the woman, by some kind of magic, brought forth the voice of Samuel, who predicted Saul's downfall and death.

The very fear that Saul had had as he made his way to see the woman at Endor was now more real. Unable to fight his battle of depression any longer, he fell from fright and fatigue on the cold, damp earth of the woman's cave. At this point she arose to nobler stature. Laying aside her role as fortuneteller, she became a hospitable and kind hostess, eager to minister to a weary old man.

"Let me set a morsel of bread before thee; and eat, that thou mayest have strength, when thou goest on thy way" (I Sam. 28:22), pleaded the woman of Endor. She and his servants compelled him then to lie down on her bed.

While he rested, she killed a fat calf that she had, took flour, kneaded it, and made unleavened bread. This food prepared by the woman of Endor was probably the last that King Saul ate, for the next day the Philistines cut off his head and fastened his body to the wall.

Maybe this woman had sensed more than she even dared to tell King Saul. She possessed a peculiar power, but suppose she had sought to use that power to lead King Saul and others on to a knowledge of God rather than into the mysteries of wizardry. What great things might this woman have achieved!

RIZPAH

II SAM. 3:7
21:8, 10, 11

A concubine of Saul. Abner takes her after Saul's death and quarrels with Saul's son over her. Her two sons are murdered, also Saul's five grandsons. She watches over their dead bodies from barley harvest until fall rain. Later David learns of her sacrifice and has her loved ones buried in family grave.

A MOTHER WHO GUARDS SONS' DEAD BODIES

S HE suffered greater tribulation than any woman in the Old Testament. For five months, from the barley harvest until the early rains, Rizpah watched over the dead, unburied bodies of her two sons resting beside the bodies of Saul's five grandsons. Rizpah's name has come to mean intense suffering, such as only a devoted mother can endure.

Others had forsaken her loved ones, who had been hanged and accursed, but Rizpah stood by them in death as she had in life. She could not hinder the seizure and hanging of her sons and relatives,

[109]

but she could watch so that no further dishonor would be done to their bodies.

Taking sackcloth, she spread it out to shield her by day and to rest on at night. Though stifled by the heat and chilled by the cold night air, Rizpah remained near those sun-scorched, weird, blackened, dishonored bodies, watching closely to save them from further harm. Now standing, now sitting, now half dead with sleepiness, and then quivering with daring effort, she drove away the dogs and vultures that would have devoured her dead.

Alone on a weary rock, week after week, for five months she remained. Probably passers-by gazed curiously from the distance at this woman watching alone, either pitying or mocking her. Some, let us suppose, called her mad and others cheered her for her courage.

Today we can gaze with admiring wonder at Rizpah's love and patience. And what faith! She believed that sooner or later God would deliver the land from famine. She also knew in her heart that her dear ones then might at least have an honorable burial. She believed that they hung there, not for their own sins, but for the sins of others, and she would not forsake them.

Rizpah, in her suffering, typifies thousands of wives, daughters, and sisters, either sitting by the bedside of loved ones or mourning at their death. Silently and alone, too, like Rizpah, many of them bear their sorrow.

Her bitter trial came largely through Saul's sins. She had been his concubine. At Saul's death she had been appropriated by Abner, Saul's general and regent for his son Ish-bosheth, who according to the law of that time would have fallen heir to Rizpah. The two men quarreled over Rizpah. Later Abner was slain by Joab with King David's knowledge. All of this came not too long after the beheading of Saul, another tribulation Rizpah had had to endure.

By him she had had two sons, Armoni and Mephibosheth. They were put to death during the famine in David's reign. Three years' famine had made David anxious. In seeking a reason for the calamity, he concluded it was because of Saul's unavenged conduct to the Gibeonites. In order to appease Jehovah, he had the two sons of Saul and Rizpah hanged, as well as Saul's five grandsons, probably the sons of his daughter Merab.

These seven heirs of Saul were hanged at Gibeah, reminding us that the sins of the father had been visited upon the second and third generation. Though Rizpah had nothing to do with Saul's sin against the Gibeonites, she had to bear some of its most fearful consequences.

She who had worn queenly garments while a concubine in the court of King Saul now donned sackcloth for mourning and probably spread sackcloth upon the rock holding the gallows upon which her sons and her husband's grandsons had been hanged. It has been suggested in one old commentary (Cobbins) that she made a tent of sackcloth and placed it over the bodies of her sons. This sounds altogether possible because sackcloth of Old Testament times was a coarse cloth woven on a loom from the hair of goats and camels.

Some commentators interpret the spreading of the sackcloth as a sign that the land had repented because of drought and famine. When Rizpah spread it out to protect the bodies of her sons, she probably made a pledge with God that she would watch over them until He relented and the rains came.

Rizpah's long watch over her sons' dead bodies is one of literature's most tragic examples of a mother's love. We wonder if her story suggested Tennyson's "Rizpah," which transfers a resolute devotion to a different but equally tragic setting.

Celebrated artists have depicted the suffering of Rizpah on canvas. Turner painted one of the most famous of these pictures. The seven bodies are depicted lying on the rock, covered with sackcloth. Rizpah has her face covered with one hand; with the other she waves a lighted torch to frighten off wild animals. A lion crouches near, and a bird of prey circles in the air.

Rizpah's suffering finally reached David's ears. He remembered that the uncared-for bones of Saul and Jonathan still lay at Jabesh-gilead. These were recovered and apparently mingled with the bones of Rizpah's sons and Saul's grandsons. Together they were buried in the family grave at Zelah.

Probably Rizpah watched the interment of the bones of Saul and their sons and wondered if any woman had ever known greater tragedy. Certainly no woman had ever shown greater endurance or stoicism amid such tragedy.

BATH-SHEBA

II SAM. 11:3
      12:24
I KINGS 1:11, 15, 16, 28, 31
      2:13, 18, 19
I CHRON. 3:5

Wife of Uriah, one of David's faithful generals. David, desiring her for his own, orders that she be brought to him. Child is born of this adulterous union; dies after Bath-sheba's husband is ordered into front of battle by David and killed. David then takes Bath-sheba for his wife. Four sons, including Solomon, are born to them. She intercedes for her son's succession to throne.

MOTHER OF SOLOMON

COMMENTATORS differ in their opinions about Bath-sheba. Some, like Frank S. Mead in his *Who's Who in the Bible*, describe her character as a "dirty, apologetic gray." Others, especially the older commentators, depict her as a woman more "sinned against than sinning."

Regardless of these conflicting opinions, several much quoted verses in the Bible center around her life. It was after the death of the child of their adulterous union that David spoke the often quoted funeral text, "I shall go to him, but he shall not return to me" (II Sam. 12:23). Nathan, the prophet, immediately denounced David in a parable, pressing home his accusation with the words "Thou art the man" (II Sam. 12:1-7). The historical note introducing the 51st Psalm calls this David's prayer for remission of sins after Nathan had denounced him for his sin with Bath-sheba. Clearly we hear his words ring out: "Wash me thoroughly from mine iniquity, and cleanse me from my sin. For I acknowledge my transgressions: and my sin is ever before me" (Ps. 51:2-3).

Jewish tradition has it that Bath-sheba recited the 31st Proverb on chastity, temperance, and the qualities of a good wife, to her son Solomon at his first marriage. Some sources, especially the Jewish again, point out that this might have been written by Solomon in memory of his mother. Other sources take the view that the Book of Proverbs probably comes from the post-Exilic period about five centuries later than the Solomonic era of 960-922 B.C.

With all of this material to assist us in addition to that which presents itself in the opening of her Bible biography (II Sam. 11:2), we can search deeply into the character of Bath-sheba. Her husband Uriah, one of King David's most trusted generals, was fighting the Ammonitish war. It is probable that Bath-sheba was a bride. We know she was "very beautiful to look upon" (II Sam. 11:2). We also know she came from a God-fearing family, for her father's name was Eliam (Ammiel), which in Hebrew means "God is gracious."

The setting of the opening scene of her story, the roof-top of Bath-sheba's home, and the time, eventide, suggest a romantic novel. Bath-sheba was bathing, as was the custom in this era of about ten centuries before Christ, on the roof of her Jerusalem home. David's new palace on the eastern ridge commanded a view of her house. He had gone out on his roof-top for a walk in the cool night air, always more refreshing on a Jerusalem evening than the air inside closed walls.

As King David promenaded on his palace roof, he saw the woman washing herself. Artists have pictured Bath-sheba as having luxuriant golden tresses that fell over shapely shoulders, also as having exquisite features and skin. Probably King David had become accustomed to indulging his fancy freely in the matter of attractive women and he was immediately attracted to Bath-sheba.

Following this opening scene, we have the frank statement of fact, "David sent messengers, and took her; and she came in unto him, and he lay with her; for she was purified from her uncleanness: and she returned unto her house" (II Sam. 11:4). According to the laws, Bath-sheba could not have resisted had she desired, for a woman in these ancient times was completely subject to a king's will. If he desired her, he could have her. Consequently her part in the story is neither praiseworthy nor blameworthy. Even Sarah, some centuries before, because of her beauty had been taken into the harems of two kings, Abimelech and Pharaoh.

The Bible narrators give us no indication of Bath-sheba's thoughts or feelings in the matter. "I am with child" (II Sam. 11:5) was the message she sent to David; and she left him to deal with the situation.

In order to avoid a court scandal, he acted quickly and treacherously toward Bath-sheba's husband Uriah, a man valiant and strong. First King David called Uriah to Jerusalem and insisted that he go down to his wife, but Uriah slept in his barracks with his men. Still the conscience-stricken David, eager to throw the burden on Bath-sheba's husband, tried a second time to prevail upon Uriah to go to his wife. But the conscientious, deeply consecrated soldier told David that the ark and Israel and Judah abided in tents and that his commander-in-chief, Joab, and David's servants were encamped in the open field. Probably Bath-sheba's husband had respect for the law which forbade intercourse to warriors who had been consecrated for battle (I Sam. 21:4). Another time David sought a way out of his predicament by making Uriah drunk, but still he would not go down to his wife. Finally, David ordered what practically amounted to Uriah's murder. He treacherously wrote out the order that Bath-sheba's husband be placed in the forefront of the hottest battle. And Uriah, listed as one of the "mighty men," died in battle at David's order.

The crime was David's, but what about the penalty for the crime? Was that not Bath-sheba's? "She mourned for her husband" (II Sam. 11:26), we are told. Her grief may have been routine. Again, her grief may have been more poignant because of her own transgressions, for she was already with child, David's child.

Though we have no other expression of her feelings, we do have a vivid record of how David felt after he had gone in to Bath-sheba. We can almost hear him cry out, as he prays for the remission of his sins, "Hide thy face from my sins, and blot out all mine iniquities. Create in me a clean heart, O God; and renew a right spirit within me" (Ps. 51:9-10). When their child, born out of wedlock, died, David spoke his famous lament mentioned above: "I shall go to him, but he shall not return to me."

II Samuel 11:27 tells how, when the mourning was passed, David brought Bath-sheba to his palace and made her his wife. She bore him a son, Solomon, whose name means "the peaceful," an indication that he was probably born after David's wars had ended. In addition to Solomon, Bath-sheba had three other sons by David, Shimea, Shobab, and Nathan, but it is as the mother of Solomon that she takes her honored place among the famous women of the Bible. In the genealogy of Jesus (Matt. 1:6), she is mentioned as the former wife of Uriah and mother of Solomon by David.

Once introduced into the palace, Bath-sheba quickly gained a commanding influence at court. During the years of Solomon's youth there is no record of her. But when King David was old and dying, she carried out the most important mission of her life. She intervened to have her son Solomon succeed his father as king of Israel. The Abingdon Bible Commentary refers to this visit as "guileful intervention" on Bath-sheba's part. On the other hand, the same commentary grants that she must have been a "remarkable" woman. "She was David's favorite wife," continues this account, "who kept her ascendancy over him long after her youthful charms had vanished."

Evidently Bath-sheba became a strong force in the court party that wanted to make her son, Solomon, king at the time when Adonijah, David's son by Haggith, was plotting to become king. Absalom, David's third son by Maacah, had been killed by General Joab who shot three darts at him while his hair entangled him in a tree. The fact that the prophet Nathan, who had once denounced David, now conspired with Bath-sheba to have Solomon made king seems to be evidence enough that she had won great respect.

Bath-sheba's plea before the aged King David for their son Solomon, running through I Kings 1:17-21, shows wisdom, finesse, courtesy, and vision. Touched by Bath-sheba's entreaty for their son, King David said to her, "As the Lord liveth, that hath redeemed my soul out of all distress, . . . assuredly Solomon thy son shall reign after me, and he shall sit upon my throne in my stead" (I Kings 1:29, 30). Soon their son was on his way, riding on David's own mule to Gihon Spring in the valley below Jerusalem to be anointed king over Israel by Zadok the priest and Nathan the prophet.

Only an intelligent, respected woman, in whom the aged king had great confidence, could have won so great a victory. Only a righteous woman, it would seem, could have been sought out by the prophet Nathan. And only a much loved mother could have been so warmly greeted as was Bath-sheba when she went to her son after he became king. When she came before him, he accorded her the place of honor as queen mother on his right side, a place of power and authority.

Because of her influence with her son, Adonijah later appealed to her for Abishag, King David's young concubine. Bath-sheba went to the king with Adonijah's request. Not knowing what his mother's request would be, King Solomon said, "Ask on, my mother: for I will not say thee nay" (I Kings 2:20). He did say nay, however, and even ordered Adonijah's death, for he was wiser than his mother and knew that it was an ancient Semitic custom that the man who inherited the women of the dead king was his successor. Though Bath-sheba failed in her petition, she demonstrated that she was a kind woman, one to whom her son, now holding the scepter, turned with pleasure and with honor.

We know that the stormy scenes of her young womanhood had all passed. Though she had lost the child born of adultery, it had been her pleasure to educate for the kingdom another son, to see him anointed king, and then to sit by him when he began to rule.

Not only is Bath-sheba mentioned in I Chronicles 3:5 under the name of Bath-shua, the mother of four of David's sons, but she is accorded in Matthew 1:6 a special place in the genealogy of Jesus. Though there is a question about whether the Book of Proverbs was written by her son, it bears a striking relationship to her life, opening as it does with many dark pictures of a woman as man's seductress, but closing happily with the picture of the ideal woman who is a trusted companion and devoted mother.

Bath-sheba lives on, even today some twenty-nine centuries later, as the honored and serene mother of Israel's wisest king, as a wife possessing a noble calmness and gentle dignity, and as a woman of queenly carriage as well as one who was "very beautiful to look upon."

TWO MOTHERS
of SOLOMON'S TIME

I KINGS 3:16-28

A child is born to each of two harlots dwelling in same house. One child dies in night when mother overlays it; she claims living child. They appeal to Solomon, who shows great wisdom in settling the argument.

"GIVE HER THE LIVING CHILD"

AFTER King Solomon had stood before the Ark of the Covenant at Jerusalem and had had a great feast for all his servants, there came before him two strange women. They were harlots, who dwelt in the same house. King Solomon, who presided over Israel with pomp and power, received these women as would a judge presiding over a court of justice.

Each had given birth to a son. One child had been born three days before the other. Like most infants of such a tender age, they looked much alike. The mothers probably appeared before Solomon dressed in the simple apparel of women of the servant class.

Quite in keeping with maternal love the real mother rushed excitedly before King Solomon and spoke in this manner: "And it came to pass the third day after that I was delivered, that this woman was delivered also: and we were together; there was no stranger with us in the house, save we two in the house" (I Kings 3:18).

Lowering her voice, she said poignantly, "And this woman's child died in the night; because she overlaid it" (I Kings 3:19). Excitement returning, she hastened to add, "And she arose at midnight,

[118]

and took my son from beside me, while thine handmaid slept, and laid it in her bosom, and laid her dead child in my bosom" (I Kings 3:20).

We can almost hear the anxious voice of this mother speaking and we can easily visualize the eager expression that came across her face as she continued her story: "And when I rose in the morning to give my child suck, behold, it was dead: but when I had considered it in the morning, behold, it was not my son, which I did bear" (I Kings 3:21).

These touching words bespoke a real mother's love. Her instinct told her that the dead child was not her own. But now the other harlot interrupted the conversation to tell King Solomon her version of the story. "Nay; but the living is my son," she shouted, "and the dead is thy son" (I Kings 3:22).

King Solomon stood looking on, probably recalling that only a short time before he had asked God to give him an understanding heart to discern between good and bad (I Kings 3:9). And he did not forget that God had promised such spiritual discernment. Now with two harlots claiming the living baby, he needed it.

What fright must have come into the heart of the real mother. What boldness was yet there in the heart of the mother whose child was dead because she had overlaid it in the night.

A less wise person might have dismissed the case for want of real evidence, but Solomon, in his wisdom, devised a clever trick. He commanded an attendant to bring him a sword, and he held the sword in his hand. Surely there must have come across the face of the real mother an expression of fear and anxiety. Though she knew not what Solomon intended to do, as she watched him brandish the sword she must have thought of her child with even greater tenderness. Then she heard these fatal words from King Solomon's lips: "Divide the living child in two, and give half to the one, and half to the other" (I Kings 3:25). The real mother hastened to say, "O my lord, give her the living child, and in no wise slay it." But the other said, "Let it be neither mine nor thine, but divide it" (I Kings 3:26).

King Solomon now knew which was the real mother. The two mothers, by their very words, had revealed their identity.

We can imagine how grateful the real mother was as she reached for her child and held it again in her arms. We can see her tears turning to smiles, and know that the heaviness that had enveloped her heart was now replaced by joy.

The fame of King Solomon's wisdom, because of the verdict he had rendered in the case of the two mothers, now spread over Israel. Though the story is short, requiring only fourteen Bible verses for the narration, it has become the most frequently quoted example of Solomon's judicious judgment, and one of the Bible's most stirring examples of mother love put to a trying test.

THE QUEEN OF SHEBA

I KINGS 10:1, 4, 10, 13
II CHRON. 9:1, 3, 9, 12
MATT. 12:42
LUKE 11:31

Comes from Saba to prove Solomon's wisdom and wealth. Brings with her a large retinue, also lavish gifts for Solomon. Art, music, and literature memorialize her. Jesus mentions her.

SHE CAME TO PROVE

THE first reigning queen on record who pitted her wits and wealth against those of a king was the Queen of Sheba. She came to Jerusalem from her kingdom of Saba in southwestern Arabia to investigate all that she had heard about Solomon, Israel's wisest and wealthiest king. The real purpose of her visit was probably the trade zone demarcation and alliance she worked out with Solomon. Solomon's commercial expansion followed after her visit.

Rather startling it is to know that in this period of more than nine centuries before Christ Sabean women occupied as high a place as did the Queen of Sheba. The *International Standard Bible Encyclopedia* states that "in almost all respects women appeared to have been considered the equal of men and to have discharged the same civil, religious and even military functions."

Great drama centers around the approximately 1,200-mile journey that the Queen of Sheba made by camel caravan from Arabia to Jerusalem. The journey probably took more time than is at present required to circle the world in a slow boat. That long, winding caravan, the queen riding on a camel with gold trappings studded with precious jewels, made its slow way probably through the Arabian Desert, across the land of Moab and into Jerusalem. This may have been one of the most imposing caravans ever to enter Jerusalem, for it is described as a "very great train, with camels that bare spices, and very much gold, and precious stones" (I Kings 10:2).

Let us suppose the Queen of Sheba brought with her also frankincense and myrrh, such as later were brought to the infant Jesus. Some interpreters point out that these may have come to Jesus from devout merchant princes from the Arabian spice and incense trade routes, for they, too, came out of the "east" to Bethlehem.

For many centuries the Queen of Sheba's visit has been a popular subject for the old masters. Rubens depicts her as an elegant, dignified woman, wearing apparel that was neither too costly nor gaudy. In Raphael's fresco in the Vatican she is depicted as having a girlish figure, entering Solomon's court in great haste and running up the steps of the dais to meet the king. Other artists, such as Sir E. J. Poynter, who painted her in 1891 and whose work is in the Gallery at Sydney, New South Wales, portray the Queen of Sheba as a woman splendidly attired and loaded with gorgeous jewels, typical ɔf the wealth and magnificence of the land of southern Arabia from which she came.

Ancient Himyaritic inscriptions depict the fame of Saba. Pliny and Strabo, too, write of its culture and political power. The Old Testament mentions it in a number of passages, among which are Psalms 72:10, Isaiah 60:6, and Jeremiah 6:20.

The riches of this Sabean queen's kingdom are evident from the Bible text centering around her, for she brought to Solomon 120 talents of gold (I Kings 10:10). That, according to Bible scholars, would be equivalent today to about $3,600,000 in United States of America gold coin. Solomon's annual income at this time has been estimated at more than $20,000,000, so what she brought was not out of keeping with what he had and what he in turn generously bestowed upon her. Their exchange of gifts is one of the first examples of good public relations for business purposes on record.

King Solomon derived a large part of his revenue from the traffic of spice merchants, tolls, dues, and iron and copper mines. He is said to have exceeded all monarchs of his time in wealth. The Queen of Sheba probably was a very wise woman herself and saw in her visit an opportunity for trade between her country and Israel. She was right; a new century of commercial expansion followed.

She was one of many rulers from far and wide who sought to learn about Solomon's wisdom. Others sent ambassadors, but she was the only one to go herself. She was a courageous, resourceful woman, who took an active part in increasing the prosperity of her own people. In this she was successful.

When she reached Jerusalem King Solomon's wisdom and the magnificence of his palace and other public buildings surpassed her expectations. After viewing all his splendor and receiving lavish gifts herself, she made the famous comment, "I believed not the words, until I came, and mine eyes had seen it: and, behold, the half was not told me" (I Kings 10:7).

She was impressed not only with Solomon's wisdom and ability to answer hard questions but, womanlike, with the magnificence of his buildings, the richness of the apparel worn by those in his court, and the elegance of his royal table. All drinking vessels, she noted, were of gold, and all the vessels of the house were of pure gold. Also, she admired greatly the well-ordered dignity of his court, the fine costumes of even his servants, and the splendor of the arched viaduct that led from his palace to the Temple.

"Blessed be the Lord thy God" (I Kings 10:9), the Queen of Sheba said to King Solomon. It is probable, as Jewish writers believe, that she was converted to the worship of the true God, but there is no record of her making a gift or offering in the Temple. Probably, coming as she did from an idolatrous country, whose chief god was Attar, she had only three things in mind—trade, culture, and worldly wisdom.

Many legends surround the Queen of Sheba's visit. There is one that she and Solomon had a love affair. Their son was said to have been named Menelek and it was thought that he migrated with his followers to Abyssinia. The present royal house of Abyssinia (Ethiopia) claims descent from Solomon and the Queen of Sheba, but there is no record of this in the Bible. The Book of Kings is frank about Solomon and his many wives. It says that he "loved many strange women, together with the daughter of Pharaoh, women of the Moabites, Ammonites, Edomites, Zidonians, and Hittites" (I Kings 11:1), but the Queen of Sheba is not mentioned.

Other fantastic legends which gathered around her journey to the court of Solomon may be read in Sura 27 of the Koran. Mohammed himself, it is probable, derived his information from Jewish sources. Her visit, one of the most romantic in history, has also been dramatized in Karl Goldmark's well-known opera *The Queen of Sheba*, which makes frequent use of Biblical material. No reference to her has yet been found in the Sabean inscriptions so far unearthed. But her visit was so well known to the people of Israel that the story of it was handed down even to Jesus' time, and his reference to her is recorded in Matthew 12:42 and Luke 11:31.

The Queen of Sheba, who came to prove, lives on now, nearly thirty centuries since her visit, as a woman whose spirit of adventure and whose resourcefulness, courage, and curiosity have not been surpassed by any queen in history. And certainly her sense of good public and international relations is unparalleled among women of the Bible.

CHAPTER 4

Women in an Era
of Political Decline

JEZEBEL

I KINGS 16:31
    18:4, 13, 19
    19:1, 2
    21:5, 7, 11, 14, 15, 23, 25
II KINGS 9:7, 10, 22, 30, 36, 37

Daughter of Zidonia and worshiper of Baal, she becomes wife of King Ahab of northern Israel. Attempts to force her lewd cult on his godly people. Persecutes prophets of God, including Elijah. He flees twice to wilderness. Her children rule wickedly after her husband is killed. She dies a horrible death.

HER NAME IS A SYNONYM FOR WICKEDNESS

JEZEBEL's degrading and idolatrous cult of Baal that she brought with her to Samaria, northern kingdom of Israel, from her native Zidonia about 869 B.C. ate like a cancer into the vital structure of the Hebrew religion during her more than three decades of power. Though the daughter of a king, the wife of a king, and the mother and grandmother of kings, she was neither a good wife and mother nor a just ruler. Her own father, Ethbaal, priest-king of Tyre, murdered his brother to become king. It is possible that Dido, founder of Carthage, was related to Jezebel, for Dido is thought to have been a princess of Tyre who at about this time led a group of colonists to north Africa.

Jezebel brought with her into Israel customs that were not only fearfully cruel but sensual and revolting. At her table no less than 450 priests of the great nature-god Baal were fed. Baal was believed to control the weather and to give or withhold fertility, while one of his consorts, Asherah, goddess of love, presided over temples which became centers of legalized vice. Jezebel introduced many of these temples into Israel.

According to the Deuteronomists, the great crime of Ahab of Israel was that he married this Phoenician princess Jezebel. Her elaborate, sensuous entourage introduced into Israel the lewd Baal worship which tended to destroy manhood and drag womanhood into shame.

When she tried to impose the materialistic and sensuous cult of her native Tyre upon Israel, she denied the ultimate value of spiritual victory and became the enemy of the one God, a God of purity, righteousness, law, and order.

In her evil power over her husband, Jezebel might be compared to Shakespeare's Lady Macbeth. In her fanaticism, she might be likened to Mary, Queen of Scots. Her death, though far more bitter and bloody, suggests the death on the guillotine of another alien queen, Marie Antoinette. And like Catherine de' Medici, Jezebel is remembered as an outstanding example of what a woman ought not to be.

The young bride Jezebel entered Israel with every opportunity to do good, had she turned her forces in that direction. Dr. Edward B. Pollard, in *Oriental Women*, Volume IV of "Woman in All Ages and Countries," has suggested that the 45th Psalm was a Hebrew epithalamium, written in honor of Jezebel's marriage to Ahab. None of its ideals concerning the new-made queen was ever realized in

Israel, for her marriage, instituting an alliance between her many gods and Ahab's one God, could bring nothing but corruption, dissension, and death.

Jezebel was such a domineering person that she soon became the master of her husband and in turn the despot of the nation. One of her first acts was to order the extermination of the prophets of the Lord (I Kings 18:4, 13). These were the prophets who were attached to various shrines (II Kings 2:3, 5) or who roamed the countryside (I Sam. 10:5-13). Her strongest enemy was the great prophet Elijah, who defied her to the end. By divine command he fled to the wilderness, only to return stronger in his knowledge of God and more determined to fight the evil cult of Baal.

During one of the periodic famines that cursed the land he pronounced that it was one of the direct cosmic consequences of Israel's sin. Jezebel, of course, was the sinister figure in that sin.

Becoming alarmed at the increasing dependence of the people in northern Israel upon idols, Elijah demanded a contest on Mount Carmel between the powers of Israel's God and the powers of Jezebel's god, Baal. One of the most dramatic struggles in history followed. The test was whether the priests of Baal could bring rain after the long drought; they failed. Elijah, who prayed to the omnipotent God, was victorious. Out of the heavens came an abundance of rain. Jezebel was so infuriated when her priests were defeated that she threatened Elijah's life. He fled from her wrath to the wilderness a second time.

She continued to dominate Israel from her ivory-decorated palace, built by her father-in-law Omri on a 400-foot hill of Jezreel. From its lofty tower she could command a view of prolific olive orchards that stretched in the valleys eastward to the Jordan. On beyond she could see the mountains of Gilead. Westward she could see the wide plain that ended at the foot of Mount Carmel. In this great panorama spreading before her was the vineyard of a man named Naboth.

King Ahab looked on this vineyard with envious eyes, because it adjoined his palace and he desired it for an herb garden. He tried to purchase the land from Naboth, but Naboth knew his rights under the law and firmly refused to sell it. Jezebel was incensed that her husband, a king, could not force his subject, a common man, to sell. "Dost thou now govern the kingdom of Israel?" (I Kings 21:7), she exclaimed in contemptuous impatience. And when she saw how weak her husband was in asserting himself, she declared, "I will give thee the vineyard of Naboth the Jezreelite" (I Kings 21:7).

Then Jezebel took the matter into her own hands. She wrote letters to the officials in her husband's name and sealed them with his seal. In these letters Jezebel arranged to have Naboth falsely accused of blasphemy against God and treason against the king. The bold, heartless Jezebel knew that the penalty for these crimes was stoning to death. Her letters were sent with the knowledge that her commands must be obeyed, and that Naboth would be taken out and stoned to death. This was done.

Confronting her husband, the king, Jezebel triumphantly declared, "Arise, take possession of the vineyard of Naboth the Jezreelite, which he refused to give thee for money: for Naboth is not alive, but dead" (I Kings 21:15). Naboth's sons also were stoned to death. Now that there were no heirs, possession of the vineyard reverted to the king.

Jezebel had plotted treacherously to gain her way; but her high-handed action aroused the religious zeal and democratic fervor of Israel's common man, of whom the prophet Elijah became the aggressive leader. He took grave exception to what Jezebel had done and told King Ahab that he had sold himself to do evil in the sight of the Lord. He predicted that dogs would lick Ahab's blood in the very field which had been acquired from Naboth, and that Jezebel would be eaten by dogs (I Kings 21:23). Elijah also foretold that every member of the house of Ahab and Jezebel would be dishonored in death.

JEZEBEL

One would imagine that Jezebel would have been stricken with fear, but she had too much confidence in her own might and the power of her gods of evil. Some three years later, however, her husband was brought back from battle mortally wounded, and the dogs of Samaria did lick up his blood from his chariot.

Jezebel survived her husband for about ten years. As queen-mother she continued to exert a malign influence over Israel, first through her eldest son Ahaziah, who was also a worshiper of Baal according to his mother's cult. But as Elijah had warned, Ahaziah was fatally injured by a fall from a window, after he had been king less than two years.

Jezebel's second son Jehoram came to power next and ruled seven years. During his rule Jehu, an army leader who had been commissioned by Elijah to overthrow the Ahab dynasty, came to Jehoram and announced there could be no peace in Israel "so long as the whoredoms of thy mother Jezebel and her witchcrafts are so many" (II Kings 9:22). This son also was murdered by Jehu, who cast his body into the vineyard which had belonged to Naboth.

Jezebel faced the most gruesome death of all. From the tower of her palace one day she looked out and saw Jehu, the destroyer of her family, approaching. She knew her death was certain, so she adorned herself like the queen that she was. She "tired" her head with regal trappings. She took a paint made of a black lead-ore powder mixed with oil and applied this to her eyelids to make them appear lustrous. A queen to the last, she hoped that she might overawe Jehu.

As he entered the gate, she shouted down to him from her window the bitterest, most insulting taunt she could think of: "Had Zimri peace, who slew his master?" (II Kings 9:31). Zimri had been another chariot captain who revolted against his king and set fire to the palace at Tirzah but died in the wreckage.

When Jehu raised his eyes to the palace window and saw the defiant queen sitting there like a tragedienne playing a part, he yelled to her eunuchs, "Who is on my side? who?" (II Kings 9:32). Probably hating their mistress as much as Jehu and his army hated her, they gladly complied with Jehu's order, "Throw her down" (II Kings 9:33). The painted queen, in her regal trappings, was tossed down to Jehu; her blood spattered the walls of her ivory-colored palace and the horses standing below, and Jehu's horse trod her under foot. Her thirty years of tyranny over Israel had ended.

Jehu went in and ate and drank and ordered that the cursed woman be buried, for after all she was a king's daughter. But when the attendants went out to bury her, they found no more of her than the skull and feet and the palms of her hands. As Elijah had declared, the dogs had eaten the flesh of this woman who typified government without God.

The final words spoken over this heathen queen's body were, "And the carcase of Jezebel shall be as dung upon the face of the field in the portion of Jezreel; so that they shall not say, this is Jezebel" (II Kings 9:37). The terror that had been visited upon her and her family was testimony to the Israelites that God's forces are always supreme.

Jezebel's evil lived after her. Her daughter, Athaliah, carried the fatal influence she had inherited from her mother into Judah, southern kingdom of Israel, when she became the wife of another Jehoram. After his death Athaliah's son, another Ahaziah, came to the throne; and when Jehu also killed him, Athaliah seized the government. She ruled only six years before she was supplanted by Joash and killed. When the horses trampled over her body, which lay just inside her palace gates, her fate was not unlike that of her mother, Jezebel.

That Jezebel's name made a deep impression upon the Hebrew mind may be traced in the Book of Revelation. A heretical and idolatrous influence is referred to as "That woman Jezebel, which calleth herself a prophetess, to teach and to seduce my servants to commit fornication, and to eat things sacrificed unto idols" (Rev. 2:20).

Jezebel's name even appears in the dictionary as a term of reproach. It came into use in England during the sixteenth century when painting the face was accepted as prima-facie evidence that a woman had loose morals. Certainly no woman's name in history has become so commonly accepted as a synonym for wickedness.

WIDOW OF ZAREPHATH

I KINGS 17:8-24
LUKE 4:25, 26

Elijah asks impoverished widow for cake. She willingly makes it for him from her last meal and oil, but her provisions do not fail through the year of drought that Elijah remains with her. He not only teaches her law of abundance but raises her son from the dead.

"SEE, THY SON LIVETH"

IN CONTRAST to the cruel and unscrupulous Jezebel, who had threatened to have the prophet Elijah slain, stood one obscure woman who opened her humble home to him. She was a nameless widow, identified only by the name of the town in which she lived in Phoenicia at Zarephath, eight miles south of Zidon on the road to Tyre.

The land had had two and a half years of drought, and the widow was hungry. So was her son. All she had left to eat was a handful of meal in a barrel and a little oil in a cruse. No doubt she was so low in spirit that the radiance had gone from her face and the quickness from her step; and she was so undernourished that her clothes must have hung loosely about her emaciated body.

While she was gathering sticks at the city gate, there came across her path Elijah, roughly clad in a garment of coarse camel's hair, girt with a leather girdle. He also wore the mantle of his prophetic office, and this probably attracted the immediate attention of this impoverished widow.

By divine direction Elijah had come to this woman from the brook of Cherith, where he had fled from Jezebel's wrath. He could have starved at Cherith, but God had supplied his every need, even in the midst of drought. He had drunk at the brook, and the ravens had brought him bread and flesh twice a day. But when the brook had dried up God had directed him to Zarephath, saying, "Behold, I have commanded a widow woman there to sustain thee" (I Kings 17:9). Because Elijah's own faith had been tested and because he had learned to believe so firmly in God's sustaining power, he was able to approach the widow of Zarephath with the positive assurance that God could supply all her needs, even in the midst of famine.

"Fetch me, I pray thee, a little water in a vessel, that I may drink" (I Kings 17:10), he called to her. And as she started forth in search of water in this dry land, he afterwards called to her, "Bring me, I pray thee, a morsel of bread in thine hand" (I Kings 17:11).

Then it was that the widow unburdened her heart to the prophet, saying she had only a handful of meal in a barrel and a little oil in a cruse. "Behold, I am gathering two sticks," she said, "that I may go in and dress it for me and my son, that we may eat it, and die" (I Kings 17:12).

Though she was greatly discouraged, Elijah came to her with a message of faith and hope. "Fear not," he spoke firmly; "go and do as thou hast said: but make me thereof a little cake first, and bring it unto me, and after make for thee and for thy son" (I Kings 17:13). What a test of self-denial for a hungry mother, who probably was even more conscious of her son's hunger. What a test also of her faith!

Proving equal to such a great test, she yielded to Elijah's command that he himself should be fed first from her scanty store. She made a cake as he had requested, probably a hoecake or corn cake, using the meal in the barrel, mixing it with the oil in the cruse and with hot water, and then frying it in oil. In return for her obedience to the prophet's command, she was to know the fulfillment of the prophet's promise uttered in the name of God, that neither the barrel of meal nor the cruse of oil would be exhausted before the drought ended, but there would be a plentiful supply for a full year for herself and son and the prophet.

Even in the midst of drought, the widow of Zarephath was to experience the continual miracle of nature in all its abundance. And she would be the center of this miracle, first because she had been willing to give all she had and next because she was willing to believe there would be more.

The wonder of it all was that this widow, though humble and impoverished, had been willing to accept from the prophet a knowledge of God, which Jezebel, a proud and merciless queen, had fought so bitterly. A queen would go down to her death fighting God, while a widow, a Phoenician too, would come back to health and plenty because she had faith to believe in God.

After the widow had demonstrated her faith in God's providence, she was to be tested again. This time her son was taken mortally ill and "there was no breath left in him" (I Kings 17:17). Probably he died of a disease caused by the malnutrition he suffered before Elijah came. The widow's faith, not yet strong enough to stand up against such a test, wavered. Bitterly upbraiding Elijah, she said, "What have I to do with thee, O thou man of God? art thou come unto me to call my sin to remembrance, and to slay my son?" (I Kings 17:18). Then it was that this prophet of God, who later would hand down his knowledge of healing to another great prophet, Elisha, proved God's healing power.

"Give me thy son" (I Kings 17:19), he first demanded. And he took the boy from his mother and went alone with him into an upper room and prayed fervently to God. Elijah, stretching himself on the child three times, cried, "O Lord my God, I pray thee, let this child's soul come into him again" (I Kings 17:21).

Afterward Elijah brought the child to his mother, saying, "See, thy son liveth" (I Kings 17:23). Another miracle had taken place in the home of the widow of Zarephath. The prophet who had demonstrated to her the law of abundance had also miraculously demonstrated God's power to heal. In both miracles the Phoenician woman had been brought to a clearer knowledge of God's goodness. She could now assert with firmer faith, "Now by this I know that thou art a man of God, and that the word of the Lord in thy mouth is truth" (I Kings 17:24).

With Elijah as her teacher, she had learned how to conquer negation, how to rise out of limiting beliefs, how to walk free, strong, and unafraid. He had helped her to understand that God is known only as He reveals Himself, and that faith is the key to His revelation.

Jesus, preaching at Nazareth nine centuries later, would refer to the story of Elijah's healing of the son of the widow of Zarephath (Luke 4:25, 26). And a short time after this message, Jesus himself would raise from the dead the only son of another widow, who lived at Nain (Luke 7:11-15).

The widow of Zarephath, however, was the first woman on record to know the meaning of those glorious words, "See, thy son liveth." Only a woman who comes to know that God sustains, controls, guides, and is omnipotent can be the center of a miracle of healing and of abundance.

THE SHUNAMMITE

✳

II KINGS 4:8-37
8:1-6

Offers hospitality of her home to prophet Elisha. Turns over upper room to him. He tells her she shall have a son in due time. Child, at about age twelve, is stricken while in field with father and dies in mother's arms. Without telling anyone she hastens to Elisha for help. He returns and raises child from dead. During a famine Elisha urges her to take her child and go to Phoenicia. She remains away seven years. Home restored to her by king after being seized during her absence.

THE GREAT WOMAN

IN THE King James Version of the Bible the Shunammite woman is called great (II Kings 4:8). This undoubtedly means that she was a wealthy and influential woman, but her story shows that she was great in other ways also—in her faith, her wisdom, and her silence. Living as she did at Shunem, a village on the edge of the rich grain fields of Esdraelon, she has come to be known as the Shunammite.

History had been made on the site of her home. Here on the ground she walked daily King Saul and his son Jonathan had been killed in battle. Here also the soldiers of Israel had won mighty victories against the Philistines. Elijah, the prophet of the "still small voice," often was seen to pass by on the road in front of her house, a road that led from Nazareth across the Plain of Esdraelon to Jerusalem. Probably she had heard of Elisha, upon whom Elijah's mantle had fallen. She knew that this man of God, as he had come to be known by the people, had increased the oil in the jars and vessels of the widow of one of the prophets, who had then been able to pay her debts. This and other miracles, no doubt, had brought wonder to the mind of the Shunammite, who was particularly receptive to God's word.

It is quite evident that she was a woman of property, a leader in her community, one who reached out hands to bestow kindness upon rich and poor alike. Little is said of her husband. We do know that he was old (II Kings 4:14), probably much older than she was. From the story, however, we later can see that he had confidence in his wife's judgment and bestowed upon her all the good things of life.

Because their home was one of the most inviting places on the outskirts of Shunem, we can imagine that the traveler, like Elisha, would like to pause there and refresh himself. One day the Shunammite shared bread with Elisha, and after that he stopped often at her home when he came that way. Finally she said to her husband, "I perceive that this is an holy man of God, which passeth by us continually. Let us make a little chamber, I pray thee, on the wall; and let us set for him there a bed, and a table, and a stool, and a candlestick: and it shall be, when he cometh to us, that he shall turn in thither" (II Kings 4:9-10).

The upper room that the Shunammite prepared for Elisha was reached by an outer stairway from the garden. Cool, quiet, and private, it became a favorite retreat for the prophet when he visited neighboring towns. Let us imagine that sweet-smelling balm perfumed it, bright-colored coverings were on the bed; and on the table was kept, let us suppose, wine, oil, honey, and dates. Often the Shunammite, we can be sure, would serve Elisha fish, bread made of meal, oil, and water, and milk from her own goats.

A man who breathed a spirit of soothing, healing beneficence wherever he walked, Elisha often came to Shunem. He was a man who enjoyed the comforts of a home and who liked people. This family, in turn, was blessed to have as their guest the prophet, who was known for his work all over the northern kingdom.

One day Elisha asked his hospitable hostess what could be done to repay her. But she made it clear that she was not seeking honor or recognition or favors from him. Then Elisha discussed the matter with Gehazi, his servant. Gehazi reminded Elisha that the woman had no son, the sacred desire of every God-loving woman in Israel. Elisha said, "Call her" (II Kings 4:15). Then Gehazi called the Shunammite and she stood in the doorway of the guest chamber. Elisha told her that when spring came around again she would embrace a son. Probably she had been barren so long that she could scarcely comprehend what she had been told; but she did conceive and bore a son the next spring.

Can we not imagine the mother's strong affection for the son who came through the blessing of the great prophet? And would it not be natural to suppose that such an unexpected blessing increased her adoration for God?

Several years passed, maybe ten or twelve. The Bible gives us no record other than that one day the boy went out among the reapers with his father. It was the harvest season, and the whole valley around the village glowed like a furnace in the intense heat. Not a breath of air was stirring, and not a leaf moved in the trees. Even the sand was parched and stung like hot ashes to the bare feet.

The child had not been long in the heat of the sun before he complained to his father, "My head, my head" (II Kings 4:19). The father, turning to his servant, said, "Carry him to his mother" (II Kings 4:19).

Until noon she held him on her lap, but he grew worse and died, probably of a sunstroke. Though confronted with the death of her only son, this mother's trust in God became supreme. Acting quickly, she carried her son up the outside staircase, entered the prophet's chamber, and placed the lifeless body upon the bed. No murmur of complaint, no loud wailing escaped her lips. She did not even call loudly to her husband, but kept silent until she could go to the prophet.

In all likelihood she recalled the story of how Elijah had raised from the dead the son of the widow of Zarephath. The Shunammite believed her lifeless son could in like manner be the center of a miracle. So firmly did she trust in the healing power of God, and in Elisha's ability to bring it forth, that not once did she say, "My son is dead."

Elisha, she knew, was not subject to doubt and fear but could bring life back into her son's body. So she hurried up the steep slope of Mount Carmel. To her servant she said nothing, except, "Drive, and go forward" (II Kings 4:24). That literally was what she was doing, driving forward in faith, never for one moment faltering or doubting.

As Elisha saw the Shunammite approaching from the distance, he said to Gehazi, "Behold, yonder is that Shunammite: Run now, I pray thee, to meet her, and say unto her, Is it well with thee? is it well with thy husband? is it well with the child?" (II Kings 4:25-26).

The remarkable faith of this mother in God's power to heal found expression in her calm answer, "It is well." And she rushed to kneel and touch Elisha's feet. As Gehazi, evidently wanting to protect his master, tried to push her away, Elisha sensed that the woman needed him. And he spoke: "Let her alone; for her soul is vexed within her: and the Lord hath hid it from me, and hath not told me" (II Kings 4:27). Still not confirming the death of her son, she answered Elisha, saying, "Did I desire a son of my lord? did I not say, Do not deceive me?" (II Kings 4:28).

Hurriedly ordering Gehazi to take his staff and go to the child, Elisha understood the seriousness of the situation, especially when the Shunammite further implored, "As the Lord liveth, and as thy soul liveth, I will not leave thee" (II Kings 4:30). Elisha arose and followed her.

Gehazi hastened ahead with Elisha's staff and placed it upon the face of the child, but there was no sound or sign of life. When

Elisha, traveling more slowly, finally came to the child, he went into the room alone, shut the door, and prayed solemnly to God. Like Elijah, who had stretched himself upon the child of the widow of Zarephath, Elisha, too, stretched himself upon the child until his flesh was warm. When the child had sneezed and opened his eyes, the prophet summoned Gehazi and said, "Call this Shunammite" (II Kings 4:36).

Seeing that her child breathed, smiled, and stretched out his arms to her once more, the Shunammite fell at Elisha's feet powerless, voiceless, and conscious only that her child lived again. The prophet, who had lived in a spirit of victory, had given her a wonderful demonstration of a spiritual victory.

Later, when famine was spreading in the direction of the rich grain country of Shunem, Elisha warned the Shunammite to leave her home and to go to the land of the Philistines with her son, so as to escape the great desolation of drought. The prophet had come from Samaria only a short time before, and so great was the famine there that some of the people had turned to cannibalism.

Elisha, knowing that food was so scarce that an ass's head had sold for fourscore pieces of silver, stopped by the house of the Shunammite to warn her and her son of the approaching famine. (There is no record of the father. Probably he had died by this time.) The Shunammite quickly did as Elisha had directed and did not look back upon the comforts she left behind, but pressed on with her son to the land of the Philistines.

Her move is but briefly told in the first two verses of II Kings 8. In the very next verse we learn that the Shunammite returned to her home seven years later, only to find that her house and land had been confiscated. Again she kept her silence until she could appear in person before King Jehoram.

At the moment that Gehazi was telling the king how Elisha had restored a dead body to life, the Shunammite walked in. This, explained Gehazi, is the woman whose son was raised from the dead. "Restore all that was hers, and all the fruits of the field since the day that she left the land, even until now" (II Kings 8:6), the king ordered.

From the beginning to this dramatic conclusion, the Shunammite's life is an example of victorious living. Her peculiar charm is her serenity in moments of trial, her firmness in affliction, her calm yet energetic prosecution of her son's rights before the king, and her unselfish endurance, amid anxiety and anguish. She won every claim to greatness, because at the sudden death of her only son she could go forward and seek the man of God, who she knew could heal her son. And when he asked how it was with the child, she could answer, "It is well."

In the gallery of Bible women there is no better example of positive faith. The Shunammite did not allow negative ideas to enter her mind because she had such sublime confidence in the power of God.

ATHALIAH

II KINGS 8:26 11:1, 2, 3, 13, 14, 20 II CHRON. 22:2, 10, 11, 12 23:12, 13, 21 24:7	*Daughter of Jezebel and wife of Jehoram, king of Judah. Her son succeeds father to throne. When son is murdered she usurps throne, first destroying all but one of royal of House of Judah. She reigns six years. Is murdered and trampled upon by horses.*

ONLY WOMAN EVER TO RULE OVER JUDAH

WOMEN are ever extreme; they are better or they are worse than men," history has often testified. Athaliah, the only woman ever to sit on the throne of David and rule, was the extreme in wickedness.

ATHALIAH

Evil ran in her veins. She was the granddaughter of Omri, who waded through slaughter to a throne he never inherited. She was the daughter of Ahab, the legitimate successor of his unscrupulous father, and of Jezebel, whose name is synonymous with wickedness. Reared in the northern kingdom of Israel, at Samaria, where the palace of her parents was surrounded by groves and idols of Baal worship, Athaliah grew up in an atmosphere that completely denied the one God. Because of the lewd cult worship of Baal, introduced by her mother, the kingdom was swept by immorality and godlessness.

Athaliah, probably for political expediency, was married to Jehoram, eldest son of the pious Jehoshaphat, king of Judah. She went with him to Jerusalem, capital of the southern kingdom. When he was thirty-two years old, he came to the throne, and Athaliah sat beside him. Just as her mother had done when she came to Samaria from Tyre, Athaliah promoted her Baal worship among the people. Because her husband's brothers were loyal to the faith of their nation, King Jehoram had them murdered. Athaliah, much more determined in character than her husband was, probably instigated these murders.

Jehoram reigned eight years and died unmourned of an incurable disease foretold by Elijah. The Philistines had captured all his secondary wives and sons, except Ahaziah, Athaliah's own son, who now came to the throne. As queen-mother, Athaliah was more powerful than ever. Her son was young and she had had the experience of dictating through her husband. We have the record that Ahaziah "walked in the ways of the house of Ahab: for his mother was his counsellor to do wickedly" (II Chron. 22:3).

Within a year Athaliah's son was wounded in his chariot by Jehu, commissioned by Elijah to overthrow the dynasty of Athaliah's father. Her son escaped to Megiddo, where he died. Athaliah seized the throne and resolved to destroy "all the seed royal," her own blood relations, among whom were her own grandchildren. Had one of these young princes become king, her place as queen-mother would have been usurped. She also knew that if she had the power of chief ruler she could further promote her Baal worship.

Judah had six years of unrighteous government under Athaliah. From II Chronicles 24:7 we can assume that she even had a portion of the Temple of Jehovah pulled down. And she used the material in the building of a temple of Baal.

Fortunately for the kingdom of Judah, Jehosheba, her step-daughter, had rescued Joash, one of the royal infants, from her bloody massacre at the time she came to the throne. Jehosheba had hidden the child for six years, and at the proper time her husband, the high priest Jehoiada, brought forth the lad, now seven years of age. With the aid of mighty men, he proclaimed him king.

When Queen Athaliah heard the people celebrating the young king's accession in the temple, she went there and screamed, "Treason, Treason" (II Chron. 23:13). The high priest ordered that she be slain, not in the house of the Lord, but after she had left it. She was therefore slain as she was entering the horses' gate by the palace, close by the Temple.

The horses trampled over her body where she lay dead at the gates. In her miserable end, Athaliah bore a singular resemblance to her mother Jezebel, who was abandoned to the dogs. Athaliah was left in a horse-path, to be trampled upon. Like her mother she died a queen, but without a hand to help her or an eye to pity her.

The final Biblical record alludes to Athaliah as "that wicked woman" (II Chron. 24:7). Jean Baptiste Racine's tragedy *Athalie,* written at the instigation of Madame de Maintenon and first performed at Versailles in 1690, is based on the life of this wicked queen, who lived the latter part of the eighth century before Christ.

HULDAH

II KINGS 22:14
II CHRON. 34:22

A Hebrew prophetess to whom King Josiah sent his high priest Hilkiah to ask concerning the book found in the Temple. She tells him that, because of idolatry, Jerusalem will be destroyed. She prophesies that King Josiah will be spared.

"THUS SAITH THE LORD"

THOUGH many of the Hebrews were given to idolatry and were ignorant of God, still the lamp of divine truth was kept burning in the heart of a woman. That woman was Huldah.

To a high degree, Huldah possessed two great qualities, righteousness and prophetic insight, and because she possessed the former she was able to use the latter wisely. This prophetic power, never trusted to the undeserving, was given to her because she loved God with all her heart.

Evidently Huldah was known in the kingdom of Judah far and wide or she would never have been sought out by King Josiah, who sent five of his own personal messengers to her with the Book of the Law, which had been recently discovered during repairs in the Temple at Jerusalem. He had faith in Huldah's spiritual powers and he wanted her to tell him whether the book was genuine or not. Here is a clue to Huldah's intellectual and spiritual perception.

The Scriptures give us no graphic description of this early Hebrew prophetess, except to say that she was the wife of Shallum, whose family had been singled out as keepers of the wardrobe, meaning

[143]

either the priest's or the king's wardrobe, probably the latter. At least this would place her close to life inside the palace and Temple.

The King James Version says that Huldah "dwelt in Jerusalem in the college," but the Revised Standard Version says "she dwelt in the Second Quarter" (II Kings 22:14), indicating the area of Jerusalem in which she lived. On some maps the Second Quarter is shown to be the section in front of the Temple. Jewish tradition has it that Huldah taught publicly in a school. Other tradition has it that she taught and preached to women.

We can justly infer that she was a woman of distinction. Among the messengers that King Josiah sent to her were his high priest, Hilkiah, who had found hidden away this amazing roll of manuscript, the lost Book of the Law, the brilliant work of a group of prophets and priests who had recorded the Yahwistic spiritual ideals. Another messenger was Shaphan, the scribe in the temple, to whom Hilkiah had first taken the lost book. Parts of this book are still found in Deuteronomy. It is now thought to be the first book of the Bible that was canonized.

Only a deeply devout woman, one of real intellectual attainments, would have been sought out by a king and a priest to give her opinion as to whether or not this scroll was indeed the word of the Lord. It turned out to be one of the most important scrolls in the history of Israel.

Huldah not only confirmed its authenticity but also prophesied concerning the future, saying that the Lord would bring evil upon Judah, because the people had forsaken Him and had turned instead to images. As a reward for Josiah's humility and tender heart, Huldah prophesied that he would be gathered unto his fathers before this terrible doom came upon Israel.

Commentators have questioned why King Josiah sent his personal messengers to consult a woman. Why were they not sent to a man? Josiah, who had come to rule at age eight, doubtless had learned to rely a great deal on his mother Jedidah as queen-mother.

HULDAH

We know little about her, but we do know that Josiah's father Amon was murdered in his own palace by his servants because of his idolatry. But King Josiah centralized religion at Jerusalem, exalted the Levites, threw out the shrines of the false gods, and led his people to new spiritual heights. We naturally assume that the godly Josiah had a godly mother. Because of her, he would have a sympathetic appreciation of a woman as righteous and as spiritually discerning as Huldah?

Noteworthy it is that in the short account of Huldah's prophecy the scribe repeated four times her phrase, "Thus saith the Lord," making us know that Huldah did not think of herself as an oracle, but only as a channel through which God's word came.

Huldah's prophecy gave King Josiah greater courage to put into action the laws written in the Book of the Law, which had been sent to her for verification. After this, Josiah had the scroll read in the house of the Lord and made a covenant to walk after the Lord and to keep his commandments. And because of it, he fought evil in Judah more zealously.

High regard he had for Huldah's prophecy when he acted so promptly, and when he also sought to make himself more worthy of the promised forbearance of God, though he knew the threatened evil to his country and his people could not be averted.

Only a woman who studied immutable spiritual laws and who prayed unceasingly could have been given insight into the mystery of the future. But Huldah was a woman who could throw back the veil of Israel's future because she had lived so close to God.

ESTHER

Name appears 55 times in ten chapters of Old Testament book bearing her name.

From throngs of virgins, Esther is chosen to be wife of King Ahasuerus of Persia. She succeeds Queen Vashti, who has been deposed. She averts a general massacre of her race planned by the wicked Haman, prime minister. Her service to her people gives rise to Feast of Purim.

"FOR SUCH A TIME AS THIS"

THE Book of Esther, one of only two books in the Old Testament bearing the name of the woman around whom the narrative centers, opens in all the oriental splendor of an Arabian Nights tale. Some scholars call it a historical novel; others term it a festal legend.

The setting is Persia, and Esther becomes the first notable woman in the Bible who lived outside Palestine, though she was of a noble Jewish family carried into captivity when Nebuchadnezzar reduced Jerusalem to what Isaiah has called a wilderness of thorns and briars.

Esther is the central figure in what is one of the most controversial books in the Old Testament, because not once does the name of God appear in it. But its significance and importance to Jewish history stems from the fact that it has become a patriotic symbol to a persecuted people of the ultimate triumph of truth and justice. And the courage of Esther becomes the dominating factor in the salvation of her people.

Many authorities agree that the governing purpose of the Book of Esther is to explain and justify the celebration of the Feast of

Purim, observed in March by the Jews. Though the author of the Book of Esther is not known, historians confirm the fact that he showed an amazingly accurate knowledge of Persian palaces and customs, and critics place his work among the masterpieces of literature. None of the characters is more skillfully presented than is Esther herself.

Like many great characters in history, Esther makes her first appearance as one of the humblest of figures, an orphan Jewess. But four years later she rises to the position of a queen of amazing power, a power which she manages to use wisely.

The setting where she is placed is the sumptuous palace of the Persion Empire in the time of Artaxerxes I (404-358 B.C.). The curtains were fastened with cords of fine linen and purple to silver rings and pillars of marble. The beds were of gold and silver, upon a pavement of red, blue, white, and black marble. The wine was served in vessels of gold and flowed in abundance. All of this is vividly described in Esther 1:6, 7.

The ancient writer's estimate of Esther's importance to the story becomes apparent, for in this short Bible book her name appears fifty-five times. The name of no other woman in the Bible is recorded so often. Only Sarah, whose name appears as Sarah thirty-five times and as Sarai sixteen times, comes near to approaching this record.

The queen who preceded Esther was Vashti, respected as a woman of nobility and honor and one who had the courage to refuse an unjust command from her husband. After much feasting and drinking, he had commanded seven eunuchs to bring Queen Vashti before him so that he might show the princes her beauty. That was during a palace feast. Vashti refused. The king became so incensed that he issued an order that her royal position be given to another.

Vashti's refusal opened the way for the coming of Esther, who had been reared by her cousin Mordecai, a Benjamite official at the palace gate. He had seen the king's royal notice that beautiful young virgins would be assembled for the king's harem in Shushan, and that the maiden who pleased the king would take the place of Vashti. So it was that Mordecai sent forth his lovely cousin Esther.

Of all the maidens gathered in Shushan, Hadassah—that was Esther's Hebrew name—was perhaps the only one who worshiped the true God, though this fact is never mentioned. Educated as a daughter in the house of Mordecai, a wise and devout Israelite, she had probably learned from him the glorious truths about God treasured by her people. In that throng of virgins, she may have been the only one who had not worshiped idols or some of the many heathen gods. From her infancy, devout Jewess that she was, she probably had bowed her knee to Jehovah, and in this rich Persian kingdom she was in touch with a power not counted in terms of marble or gold or silver.

When she was presented to the king, he loved her above all the women who had been brought before him, and he set the royal crown upon her head. After she became queen, her name was changed from Hadassah, meaning "myrtle," to Esther, meaning "star." And she soon played a stellar role in the lives of her people, who were threatened with destruction. Early she dedicated herself, not to the pleasure, comforts, and luxuries of a palace, but to the dreams, hopes, and ambitions of her people.

When Esther became queen, King Ahasuerus had no idea that she was a Jewess. He had been attracted to her because of her surpassing loveliness, and he celebrated her entrance into the court with a great feast, which introduced her as queen of one of the most powerful empires in the world.

Let us picture her, if we may, as she moved about this magnificent palace with grace and dignity, wearing robes of gold and purple and handsome jewels which set off to advantage her garlanded black hair, olive skin, and eyes radiant because of all the wonder that now stretched before her. We can imagine she soon felt that she had been placed upon this high pedestal, not because of an accident, but for a great purpose.

Queen Esther soon gained favor with the people when she showed that she had sound judgment, fine self-control, and the ability to think of others first. It was not long before she learned that Haman, her husband's favorite, hated her people and demanded that they bow down to him. This Haman has been described by modern Jewish writers as a typical Hitler, manifesting so intense a hatred that it became an evil intent on destroying a God-fearing people. Opposed to such powers of evil as Haman possessed stood the courageous Esther, ready to defend her people even with her own life.

When her maids and eunuchs brought her word of a serious feud between her cousin Mordecai and Haman, she was deeply distressed. She knew she must act promptly and wisely. Soon she received a message from her cousin placing upon her this great responsibility: "Who knoweth whether thou art come to the kingdom for such a time as this?" (Esther 4:14). Challenging words these were for a young, inexperienced queen.

Her triumphant place in the hearts of her people became assured because she accepted her own divine destiny. Quietly she issued orders that all Jews in Shushan hold a fast in her behalf, and she joined them in this fast, which in itself suggested Esther's strong belief in prayer.

Following the fast, she prepared to go before her husband and intercede for her people. If the king, a capricious man, was in a good mood, she might gain her point; if not, she could lose her cause and also her own life.

As Esther made ready to appear before the king, one of the most courageous assertions made by a woman in the Bible is credited to her. "So I will go in unto the king, which is not according to the law: and if I perish, I perish" (Esther 4:16), she said. Here is a woman who had not only high courage but sincere faith and a devotion to the cause of her people.

Also she had exhibited real loyalty in her co-operation with her cousin Mordecai, who had reared her and was largely responsible for the fact that she now sat on the throne of Persia. The king's affection she seemed also to have won wholeheartedly. As she appeared before him in her most royal apparel, his first tender words to her were, "What wilt thou, queen Esther? and what is thy request? it shall be even given thee to the half of the kingdom" (Esther 5:3).

Prudent as well as fearless, Queen Esther knew that, though she had won her husband's love and confidence, she was dealing with powerful and sinister forces. It was best to move slowly with the king.

She answered him saying that she had one request, and that was that he join Haman with her for dinner. The king ordered that Haman be brought quickly. The latter was elated because he was sure he was now in the good graces of the queen as well as the king. It would be easy to do away with his enemy Mordecai. Haman rushed home and bragged to his wife Zeresh and friends about his invitation from the queen. They told him that now was the time for him to protest against Mordecai. "Why not," they asked, "prepare a gallows on which to hang Mordecai?"

Still proud of himself, Haman proceeded with a merry heart to Queen Esther's banquet. Providence was on the queen's side. After the banquet the king could not sleep. He called for the book of memorable deeds. There he found written the story that Mordecai had saved his life earlier from two palace eunuchs who had plotted to destroy him and that Mordecai had never been rewarded for the deed.

The next morning Haman was waiting in the court for an audience with the king, and his mission was to request the king to hang Mordecai. Haman had a surprise awaiting him. He learned that the king desired to pay honor to Mordecai.

At a second banquet to which Haman had been invited by Queen Esther, again she was asked by her husband what he could do for her. And she fell at his feet with tears in her eyes, telling him, "We are sold, I and my people, to be destroyed, to be slain, and to perish" (Esther 7:4). Then turning she said, "The adversary and enemy is this wicked Haman" (Esther 7:6). And at that moment he sat in the banquet room as their guest, but he now humbled himself before Esther, begging for his life. It was too late. The king was indignant. He ordered that Haman be hanged on the gallows that had been prepared for Esther's cousin, Mordecai.

After that Esther won even greater confidence from the king. He turned over to her the House of Haman and held out to her the golden scepter. Again exhibiting solicitude for the permanent protection of her people, she was instrumental in having it written into the law that the Jews not only could defend themselves but could slay their enemies.

Esther has often been criticized for this, but it must be remembered that she was dealing with an implacable enemy. Moreover, she was seeking security for her people and not for herself.

The Jews, then in Persia, celebrated their deliverance from the wholesale massacre that had been planned by Haman. And they called the celebration a Purim Festival, because Haman had cast *pur* (a lot) to ascertain a favorable day for carrying out his plot to destroy the Jews.

To this day the Purim Festival is celebrated on the fourteenth and fifteenth of March when the Roll of Esther is read in Jewish synagogues all over the world. Queen Esther's last decree was that this feast be held annually, "and it was written in the book" (Esther 9:32). It became a law that stands even today.

Esther herself lives on in the hearts of her people and is still commemorated at the Purim Festival as the woman who rose up as a savior of those Jews who were refugees in Persia about twenty-four centuries ago. She has become one of their greatest heroines because she served with fearlessness, intelligence, deep insight, and prudence.

Her name has been immortalized in art by Gottlieb Bierman, Julius Schrader, Tintoretto, and others; in literature by Jean Baptiste Racine, who wrote a play based upon her life, and in music by Handel, who composed an oratorio with the English words from Racine's

Esther. In Windsor Castle also are fine Gobelin tapestries depicting Esther's dramatic story.

THE VIRTUOUS WOMAN

PROV. 31:10-31

The glories of a good woman are skillfully portrayed in these twenty-two verses. Preceding chapters admonish against a woman who is not virtuous.

HER PRICE IS FAR ABOVE RUBIES

NOTHING can add to the sheer beauty of the Bible portrait of the virtuous woman, though an entire sermon could be preached on each single phrase about her. Summarizing as it does the most noble attributes of the wife and mother, this is literature's most perfect picture of the ideal woman.

Her chastity, her charity, her diligence, her efficiency, her earnestness, her love for her husband and children, even her business foresight, are brilliantly illuminated in words that rise up majestically from the page. But the light in all its effulgence shines upon her godliness. This quality, the Bible seems to say, is what gives meaning, purpose, and direction to her life.

Many of the verses in the Book of Proverbs, of which this is the conclusion, are written in the style of the parent talking to a son just reaching manhood. It is as though a mother and a father instruct their son in practical piety. Like the refrain in a song, "my son, my son" appears eighteen times, and you can almost hear the mother's ejaculatory prayer as she counsels with her son. Such admonitions as "My son, attend unto my wisdom" or "My son, give me thine heart, fear thou the Lord, be wise, and make my heart glad" appear over and over again.

The son is warned, for example, against the "strange woman," who is likened to a "narrow pit" and who has lips that are "as an honeycomb" and a mouth that is "smoother than oil." He is warned also against the "fair woman which is without discretion," described as a "jewel of gold in a swine's snout."

Strong warnings also are given against the "foolish woman," depicted as "clamorous, simple, and knowing nothing," against the "contentious and angry woman," also the "adulterous woman," the "brawling woman" and the "whorish woman." "It is better to dwell in a corner of the housetop, than with a brawling woman in a wide house," says one Proverb. "It is better to dwell in the wilderness, than with a contentious and an angry woman," says another. In one bold stroke, we are told that the "adulterous woman" "will hunt for [his] life."

Then finally, coming to a brilliant climax, like the overpowering finale in a symphony, this mother admonishes her son to be wise and to listen to the praise of a good wife. So inspiring is the passage in the King James Version that we shall not try to add to or take from it.

"Who can find a virtuous woman? for her price is far above rubies," it begins. And then it continues:

The heart of her husband doth safely trust in her, so that he shall have no need of spoil.

She will do him good and not evil all the days of her life.

She seeketh wool, and flax, and worketh willingly with her hands.

She is like the merchants' ships; she bringeth her food from afar.

She riseth also while it is yet night, and giveth meat to her household, and a portion to her maidens.

She considereth a field, and buyeth it: with the fruit of her hands she planteth a vineyard.

She girdeth her loins with strength, and strengtheneth her arms.

She perceiveth that her merchandise is good: her candle goeth not out by night.

She layeth her hands to the spindle, and her hands hold the distaff.

She stretcheth out her hand to the poor; yea, she reacheth forth her hands to the needy.

She is not afraid of the snow for her household: for all her household are clothed with scarlet.

She maketh herself coverings of tapestry; her clothing is silk and purple.

Her husband is known in the gates, when he sitteth among the elders of the land.

She maketh fine linen, and selleth it; and delivereth girdles unto the merchant.

Strength and honour are her clothing; and she shall rejoice in time to come.

She openeth her mouth with wisdom; and in her tongue is the law of kindness.

She looketh well to the ways of her household, and eateth not the bread of idleness.

Her children arise up, and call her blessed; her husband also, and he praiseth her.

Many daughters have done virtuously, but thou excellest them all.

Favour is deceitful, and beauty is vain: but a woman that feareth the Lord, she shall be praised.

Give her of the fruit of her hands; and let her own works praise her in the gates.

Here we see a woman who uses her time wisely, who richly provides for the growing needs of her family, and who continually seeks to build her spiritual resources so as to be prepared for any emergency. We see, too, a woman who shows skill in all her household tasks, who aids the needy, who guards her tongue, and who has dignity of character. Because of all these qualities, her husband "is known in the gates," and her children call her blessed.

Verbs in the passage are especially meaningful. The virtuous woman, for example, "seeketh," "riseth," "girdeth," "maketh," "openeth," and "looketh."

Thirteen out of the twenty-two verses begin with the pronoun "She," thus placing emphasis on the woman herself. Matthew Henry, the famous English Biblical commentator (1662-1714), likened this portrait of the virtuous woman to a mirror in which all women can examine themselves, though few will find their likeness. But the woman who looks in the mirror there will catch something of the beauty of spirit and the serenity of the virtuous woman.

She has been a source of inspiration to women for more than two thousand years, and her ideals are as faithfully applicable to this generation as they were to the generations of long ago.

A singular thing about these twenty-two verses on the virtuous woman is that in the Hebrew they form an acrostic. That is, each verse begins with a letter of the Hebrew alphabet in order, beginning with aleph, beth, gimel, daleth, and so on. Because of its alphabetical acrostic form these twenty-two verses have been called "the ABC of the Perfect Wife."

Since this passage is found at the end of a chapter whose title mentions King Lemuel and his mother, the questions often have been asked, Who was this King Lemuel? Who was his mother? Neither has ever been satisfactorily identified.

Tradition attributes the writing of Proverbs to Solomon. If this were so, this chapter might draw its inspiration from the wise counsel of Solomon's own mother Bath-sheba. But modern scholars do not accept this theory. They look upon Proverbs as embodying not only the wisdom of Solomon but that of many old Hebrew sages.

The story of the virtuous woman fittingly ends the study of the great women of the Old Testament. Though this good wife was not a real woman but an ideal one, she does typify almost all the admirable qualities of the actual women of Hebrew history.

Centuries later, at the beginning of the New Testament, comes Mary, Mother of Jesus, who more than any woman in the Bible embodies all the best qualities of womanhood. We see clearly that the virtuous woman of Proverbs was a motivating force in the refined and enlightened society of her day. As woman goes so the world goes. In the new Christian community that was to come, Mary, the Mother of Jesus, would be a radiant center.

CHAPTER 5

Women in Christ's Time

MARY, MOTHER OF JESUS

MATT. 1:16, 18, 20
　　　　2:11
　　　　13:55
MARK 6:3
LUKE 1:27, 30, 34, 38, 39, 41, 46,
　　　　56
　　　　2:5, 16, 19, 34
ACTS 1:14

Angel Gabriel appears to Mary at Naza-reth and announces she is to have a son. She hastens to Judaea to be with her cousin Elisabeth, also with child. After three months Mary returns to Joseph. They travel to Bethlehem where Jesus is born and Wise Men come. After her purification she and Joseph take Jesus to Temple and offer Him to Lord. Mary is with Jesus at Marriage at Cana; she also stands with other women at Crucifixion. Later she helps establish His church.

"BLESSED AMONG WOMEN"

As the mother of Jesus Christ, Mary stands apart from all women in history. In art, music, and literature she has become the embodiment of all that is fine and noble in womanhood. Even to unbelievers she is the subject of adoration. No woman in the entire history of the world has been so honored and revered.

[156]

MARY, MOTHER OF JESUS

The world's most majestic poems, novels, and plays have had Mary and her son as their central figures. In the most magnificent cathedrals she is depicted on canvas, in stained-glass windows, in bronze, marble, and stone. Through the centuries the most triumphant hymns and the best-loved carols, lullabies, and folk songs have told of her pre-eminence among women.

Adoration of her is ageless, classless, raceless, and timeless. Each nation where the Christian message lives thinks of both the Madonna and the Child as their own. Her face may carry the features of the southern European in one great painting, the Ethiopian in another, and the oriental in another. We find great representations of the Madonna up and down Europe, Asia, Africa, North America, South America—in fact everywhere that the New Testament has shed its light.

Many names of praise, such as "Mother of Mercy," "Mother Most Blessed," "Queen of Heaven," "Mother Most Pure," "Virgin Most Powerful," and "Spiritual Vessel," have been bestowed upon her. The angel Gabriel and her cousin Elisabeth said of her: "Blessed art thou among women" (Luke 1:28, 42).

Yet her greatness had a humble beginning. She was an obscure peasant girl living in Nazareth twenty centuries ago. But her story has spread to the ends of the earth. Though her life came to its tragic yet glorious climax at the foot of the cross, it continues to inspire and uplift millions. Though she reared her son in obscurity and had neither wealth nor acclaim, the world has worshiped at her feet all down the centuries.

Though Mary herself never wore fine clothes, the Madonnas through the ages have been draped in the most costly of garments, and people have left at her feet the world's most precious jewels. Though she never exalted herself, literature has raised her to the highest pinnacle of any woman in history. Though she never entered a palace, her picture has graced the most magnificent palaces. Though she never traveled any farther than from Palestine to Egypt, and then by donkey, her story still travels to the farthest corners of the earth. And though she suffered as much as any woman in the world's history, her suffering changed to joy at her son's resurrection.

Today, as in the time of Jesus' birth, Mary is the embodiment of one of the greatest and still unexplained miracles of the Bible, the Virgin Birth. Because of this, she is unique in the history of women, as is her son, who brought salvation to mankind.

She is great, not only in being the most perfect woman recorded in history but because of her part in the miracle of the Virgin Birth. This has been no better explained in almost 2,000 years than has the origin of the sun, the moon, and the stars.

We can imagine that as a young girl in Nazareth, Mary was more serious and pious than other girls of her age and more given to believing in the wonders of God. Yet she was too humble to think that she would be the center of mankind's greatest miracle, the birth of the Christ Child. Even in her early years we can see that she had completely surrendered her whole being to the higher, holier will.

The story of the Virgin Birth appears in the Bible in two separate places, thus strengthening the account. The First Gospel (Matt. 1: 18-21) tells the story from the point of view of Joseph. The angel appearing before Joseph tells him, "Fear not to take unto thee Mary thy wife: for that which is conceived in her is of the Holy Ghost. And she shall bring forth a son, and thou shalt call his name Jesus: for he shall save his people from their sins."

The Third Gospel (Luke 1:27-35) tells the story from the point of view of Mary. It seems quite likely that Luke acquired this information from his association with Mary herself, or from one who knew Mary well, for the narrative in the first portion could only have come from Mary herself. One commentator has been so bold as to speculate that Mary might have written some parts of the first two chapters of Luke, because it is so completely from her viewpoint.

In Luke the angel appears to Mary saying, "Fear not, Mary: for thou hast found favour with God. And, behold, thou shalt conceive in thy womb, and bring forth a son, and shalt call his name Jesus."

Mary's first recorded words, "How shall this be, seeing I know not a man?" (Luke 1:34), are in themselves remarkable, because they bespeak her purity and her humility.

The angel then told her that "The Holy Ghost shall come upon thee, and the power of the Highest shall overshadow thee: therefore also that holy thing which shall be born of thee shall be called the Son of God" (Luke 1:35). She accepted this annunciation with faith and resignation. When she answered, "Behold the handmaid of the Lord; be it unto me according to thy word" (Luke 1:38), she showed that her thoughts and longings were ever directed to God alone. She was willing to obey and surrender herself to divine love, and her reverence for the body as the inviolate temple of God became all the more secure.

The accounts of the conception of Jesus in Matthew and Luke are so similar that one confirms the other. These Gospel writers only use different words. Matthew says that Mary's son will be conceived through the "Holy Ghost," while Luke says He will be conceived through the "Holy Spirit, the power of the Most High."

Even Jesus later confirmed His supernatural birth when He declared, "Ye are from beneath; I am from above: ye are of this world; I am not of this world" (John 8:23).

Scholars interpret the story of the Virgin Birth differently. Some see all birth as a miracle, and warn that by overestimating the sanctity of virginity one may depreciate the sanctity of marriage. Others see the Virgin Birth as of less importance than the supreme miracle, which was the actual appearance in the world of One who in His mind and spirit completely expressed and embodied the reality of God.

The story of Mary and the birth of the Christ Child is the most holy story in Scripture. In a setting of majestic poetry and imagery and in the presence of angels, the most divine idea ever conceived has its inception with the angel's first words, "Hail, thou that art highly favoured, the Lord is with thee: blessed art thou among women" (Luke 1:28). This "Hail Mary" inspired the words of the famous

Ave Maria or angelical salutation. The first words of the song are taken right out of this.

With even the most liberal scholars the miracle of Christ's birth is but the framework. The appearance of Christ himself is the picture. All of the liberal scholars, no matter what their interpretation of the Virgin Birth, approach this story with the deepest reverence. They regard Mary's part as having divine significance.

Probably in her early twenties or younger at the time of the conception, Mary went quietly and prudently to her older and more experienced cousin Elisabeth to tell of the angel's visit. In these times such a journey, requiring three days, presented many problems, but Mary surmounted all of them, thinking not of the difficulties but only of the urgency of her visit.

Before this, Mary had already been introduced as a "virgin espoused to a man whose name was Joseph, of the house of David" (Luke 1:27). The betrothal in these times usually preceded the wedding by about a year. Mary's majestic quality of faith shines through this period. As she hastened to Elisabeth, we see that she had surrendered her whole being to the higher, holier will. Elisabeth, a pious older woman, already six months pregnant—and her child would be John the Baptist—greeted Mary with the same salutation as that of the angel: "Blessed art thou among women." And she added, "Blessed is the fruit of thy womb" (Luke 1:42). Finally she addressed Mary as the "mother of my Lord" (Luke 1:43).

More humble even than before, Mary set forth to magnify the Lord in those stirring lines (Luke 1:46-55) which have come down to us as the immortal magnificat. It is Mary's hymn of praise to God for His wonderful works. This jubilant song pours from her heart and in its richness and sweep sets forth the wide range of her spiritual experience. In it we can see that Mary knew the age-old Psalms of her people and also the Song of Hannah. Out of them she made a new, sublimer prayer to God. It suggests parts of Psalms 21 and 109, and also has lines from other Psalms. It sings of God's power, of His name and mercy and of how He exalts the humble. There is such spiritual fullness in this Magnificat that mothers of the world always can turn to it for new faith and new belief in the Almighty.

We can visualize the joyous three months that Mary and Elisabeth had together. And yet we wonder, too, if ever a shadow crossed their paths and if they had a premonition of what was to come to their sons. Elisabeth's son, John the Baptist, would be beheaded by Herod to please his stepdaughter and his wife Herodias, and Jesus would be nailed to the cross. But both of these prospective mothers were women of such triumphant faith that they were willing to accept God's plan in their lives and their sons' lives.

After Mary had spent some three months with Elisabeth in Judaea, she returned to Joseph in Nazareth. Though faced with serious problems of her coming marriage and the social implications of her pregnancy, nowhere is there a reference to her unwillingness to place her whole womanhood at the disposal of her Creator.

One great branch of the Christian faith believes that Joseph was many years older than Mary and had been married before, and that his children by this former marriage are the brothers and sisters mentioned in Mark 6:3: "Is not this the carpenter, the son of Mary, the brother of James, and Joses, and of Juda, and Simon? and are not his sisters here with us?" Other commentators conjecture that Mary and Joseph, after the birth of Jesus, had several children, born the normal way. Still others suggest that the "brothers" and "sisters" could have been Jesus' cousins by his mother's sister (John 19:25).

The belief that Joseph was Jesus' legal father only, and that Jesus had no actual brothers and sisters, suggests the perpetual virginity of Mary. In any case, Joseph, humble and industrious laborer that he was, played a vital role as the protector of Mary, the legal guardian and one who provided for the child Jesus. We can picture Joseph, kindly and good, at work in his shop in Nazareth, planing cedars from Lebanon, sawing hard woods from the hills, and making ox yokes and well buckets. And he passed on his skill to his son.

Joseph's love for Mary makes us certain of the devotion she attracted to herself. Never did she need him more than in those days when a decree had gone out from Caesar Augustus that a census of the Roman world must be taken. And Joseph went up from Nazareth to Bethlehem, "to be taxed with Mary his espoused wife, being great with child" (Luke 2:5). Mary, too, it is thought, was of the house of David, and according to ancient tradition her parents were two holy persons, Joachim and Anna. Some Christian faiths, in the dogma of the Immaculate Conception, hold that Mary, from the moment of her conception, was preserved from all stain of original sin.

For Mary this journey from Nazareth to Bethlehem, some ninety miles by donkey up and down hill, was to be long and arduous. We can imagine that she baked the bread that would be required, dried the meat, filled a sack with lentils, and poured water from the well into a goatskin. She also packed the swaddling clothes that she would need before the return.

Let us imagine further that Joseph saddled their old and patient donkey and packed upon its back goat's-hair blankets for them to lie down upon and to use as a cover also, for the December nights in the Judaean hills often were cold and rainy. Several nights no doubt they slept under a large tree, if they could not find a hut for shelter.

Each morning as they set forth, Joseph would help Mary gently upon the donkey and then walk at her side, watching carefully so that the donkey would not make a misstep. The sun warmed them in the day and the stars shone over them at night as they descended the Jordan and followed the eastern bank of the river as far as the city of Jericho. This was a warmer though a longer route than that leading across the plain of Esdraelon; and it was a less arduous route for Mary, though difficult at best.

When Mary and Joseph reached Bethlehem there was no place

at the inn, for the town was teeming with people who had come to be enrolled. The innkeepers, like some of us today, did not know when the great possibilities of God had come right to their doors. So it was that many turned Mary and Joseph away; and finally when Mary could wait no longer because her child was about to be born, she and Joseph found rest inside a stable of the inn. There Mary delivered her son and wrapped Him in the swaddling clothes that she had brought from Nazareth, and laid Him in the straw of the oxen's crib.

Every woman who has brought forth a child can imagine that Mary, as her child was born, was uplifted by her sustaining faith in God, and that her exultation was great as she beheld Him for the first time. Beautiful mother that she was, she had brought forth a child beautiful of form, and with an indescribable radiance in His face.

When the shepherds, who had seen the "glory of the Lord" and had heard the angels' words as they tended their flocks, came and told Mary of the angel's message, she accepted quietly the positive affirmation of the heavenly message: "For unto you is born this day in the city of David a Saviour, which is Christ the Lord" (Luke 2:11). She might have gone forth among the people and exclaimed, "Look, I am the mother of the Saviour." Others wondered at what the angel had said to the shepherds, "But Mary kept all these things, and pondered them in her heart" (Luke 2:19). Wonderful mother —she was to hold in her heart all the intimations of a divine significance for her child which had come to her in angelic words!

Mary's divine mission of being the mother of the only begotten Son of God never faltered from the manger to the cross on Calvary. She displayed great wisdom, as well as spiritual discernment, in the circumcision of her son, in His presentation at the Temple, and in her own appearance at the Temple for her purification forty days after His birth. These were all according to the old Mosaic law.

Luke, one of the greatest poets of the New Testament, tells that

Mary and Joseph took the babe into the Temple and placed Him in the arms of Simeon, a righteous and devout man, who saw that this child had the light of God on His face. Again Mary must have marveled at what Simeon said to her about her child: "Behold, this child is set for the fall and rising again of many in Israel; and for a sign which shall be spoken against" (Luke 2:34). And she must have questioned his prophetic words, though she expressed no fear when he said, "(Yea, a sword shall pierce through thy own soul also) that the thoughts of many hearts may be revealed."

Mary's destiny was further manifested when the aged Anna, standing in the Temple with Simeon, "spake of Him to all them that looked for redemption in Jerusalem" (Luke 2:38).

Quietly Mary left the Temple and became a mother who gave her best to her child so that it could be said of Him that He "increased in wisdom and stature, and in favour with God and man" (Luke 2:52).

The evil of man's might crossed Mary's path very soon, however. Matthew tells that, after the visit of the Wise Men bearing princely gifts, Joseph was warned in a dream to take Jesus and Mary and flee to Egypt. From Bethlehem, which lies about 2,000 feet above sea level, the way descended to the lowlands. There was no road, only a steep path which for centuries had been trodden by man and beast. Their first morning, as the sun burst forth, they looked down upon the land of the Philistines, and on the second day they may have reached Gaza, the last of the larger towns. And then the measureless desert stretched out before them, the yellow sand dunes glowing against the low horizon and softly fading one into the other. As they journeyed, Mary gently watched over Him whom God had promised of old to her fathers. And as she reached the banks of the Nile, her own people's history came alive to her.

Mary and Joseph remained in Egypt until the death of Herod and then they traveled eastward back over the desert. On and on they plodded, finally reaching Galilee and their own beloved town of Nazareth.

Mary watched over her son as He grew, with loving care, feeding Him, clothing Him, and leading Him gently by the hand. Guided by her, He gained in knowledge of the spirit until He came to love God's house above all others. With His mother and father He made annual trips from Nazareth to Jerusalem for the Feast of the Passover.

When He was twelve years old, it is recorded that after they had left the Temple and had started on the homeward journey, they missed Him. First thinking that He was journeying with another group of pilgrims on the dusty road behind, they were not concerned that their son was not at their side. The road was thronged with people, some on foot, some on donkeys, and some on fine riding camels. But at nightfall Mary and Joseph became anxious and turned back to find Him. After a three-day search they discovered Him in the Temple, sitting among the doctors of law.

Turning to her son, Mary said to him, "Son, why hast thou thus dealt with us? behold, thy father and I have sought thee sorrowing" (Luke 2:48).

Jesus indicated His divine Sonship when He answered, "How is it that ye sought me? wist ye not that I must be about my Father's business?" (Luke 2:49). Again we hear, like a refrain in a song, "his mother kept all these sayings in her heart" (Luke 2:51). Strange new emotions, however, must have entered her being. The gulf of His divine parentage that had begun to separate her from her son now made her know that He felt God to be in a special sense His father.

Joseph disappears from the narrative after this incident, and Mary is depicted alone. It is probable that Joseph died about this time, though no record of this fact is given.

Mary reappears in the story in John 2 at the Marriage at Cana in Galilee. This was her son's farewell to His private life and the beginning of His public ministry. Probably Mary was approaching her fiftieth year. Her cousin Elisabeth's son, John the Baptist, who had already gathered about him a group of disciples, had predicted that Jesus was the Messiah.

When Mary saw that the wine was giving out at the feast, she said to her son, "They have no wine" (John 2:3). For the first time He answered her not as her son but as the Messiah, calling her "Woman" and saying, "What have I to do with thee? mine hour is not yet come" (John 2:4). Though He expressed His complete subordination to the will of God, this must have been a trying test of Mary's faith, but she kept submissive, patient, trustful. She would remain so, even when her son was crucified and laid in the tomb. Thinking not of herself but of Him, she now experienced a new sense of exultation when she saw that wine filled the empty jars. What a great thing for a mother to witness, the first of her son's miracles!

From now on Mary remained in the background. We get our next brief glimpse of her when she and His brethren visit Him as the multitude sat about Him (Mark 3:31-35; Matt. 12:46-50; Luke 19:19-21). Again He dismissed His personal relationship to His mother, saying, "Who is my mother, or my brethren?" further explaining, "For whosoever shall do the will of God, the same is my brother, and my sister, and my mother" (Mark 3:35). She no doubt was beginning to know that for those who live the life of the spirit the human family bond is transcended by a wider love. Her love, too, was enlarged, and consequently, she could bear more bravely what was to come, the crucifixion of her son.

In this she would have much to bear, but her knowledge of God and His promise would sustain her. And because she bore nobly such loneliness and such heartache at the foot of the cross, countless people down the centuries, in moments of anguish and pain, have found comfort. Mary's silent endurance of what she could not change is her great lesson at the cross to the world.

As she saw her son accept death as the price of salvation, she knew that she still had to assist in the furtherance of His mission by her service to His grief-stricken disciples.

The last human tie with her son was breaking, but she had the fortitude and faith to remain with Him to the end. As He was lifted high on the cross, He showed His tender solicitude for her in his last words. He saw His mother and the disciple He loved standing to·gether and He said, "Woman, behold thy son!" and to the disciple, "Behold thy mother!" It came about as Jesus planned that "from that hour that disciple took her unto his own home" (John 19:26, 27). In this hour of greatest agony, Jesus forgot not to entrust His beloved mother to the care of John, the Beloved Disciple.

Mary appears again after the Resurrection. No record is given of what she felt at this triumphant time when it was found that her son had arisen. The witness to the Resurrection came through Mary Magdalene, who had gone to the tomb with other women.

Mary the mother was to experience new confidence in her own mission after she learned that her son had arisen from the dead. She now was not so conscious of her own motherhood as she was of the divine Sonship of Jesus.

The last mention of Mary is when she was gathered with the infant Church after the Ascension. She was praying with the apostles in the Upper Room in Jerusalem (Acts 1:14). We can know that great now was her faith in the Eternal. In her service to the early Church, Mary typifies "the noblest qualities in womanhood."

It is no wonder that the adoration of the Madonna has prevailed throughout the Christian and civilized world for nearly 2,000 years, and that human genius, inspired by faith, has been dedicated to the portrayal of Mary as the mother of Christ.

There is no record of the time or manner of her death. This is unimportant, for in reality she lives on as the world's most beautiful example of motherhood. The world seems to know today why she was hailed, "Blessed art thou among women."

ELISABETH

LUKE 1:5, 7, 13, 24, 36, 40, 41, 57

Mother of John the Baptist and wife of Zacharias, also a cousin of Mary, mother of Jesus. First to greet Mary as mother of the Messiah, when Mary comes to spend three months with her before Jesus is born.

MOTHER OF JOHN THE BAPTIST

ELISABETH holds two distinctions that lend immortality to her name. She was the mother of John the Baptist, forerunner of the Messiah, and she was first to greet her cousin Mary as mother of the Messiah. Elisabeth also occasioned two of the greatest poems in the New Testament, Mary's Magnificat (Luke 1:46-55) and Zacharias' Benedictus (Luke 1:68-79), both of which are parts of the ritual in the Christian Church today.

Like her husband Zacharias, Elisabeth was a godly person. She was not only the wife of a priest but the daughter of a family of priests of the house of Aaron. She also bore the name of Aaron's wife Elisheba (Exod. 6:23), the Hebrew for Elisabeth.

The town where Elisabeth lived was in the hill country of Judaea, in a desert tract west of the Dead Sea, possibly near Ain Karem, four miles north of Jerusalem. Her house, let us suppose, was within walking distance of Jerusalem's great Temple, where her husband officiated at stated times. As the wife of a priest, Elisabeth gave loving attention to her husband's priestly vestments and to her home, where godly people came to talk over Temple matters. We have Biblical record that both Elisabeth and her husband were "righteous before God, walking in all the commandments and ordinances of the Lord blameless" (Luke 1:6).

Elisabeth is introduced by Luke as a woman well stricken in years and barren, just as had been Isaac's mother Sarah. To Elisabeth it was foretold that her son would "be great in the sight of the Lord, . . . and he shall be filled with the Holy Ghost, even from his mother's womb" (Luke 1:15).

This message from Gabriel had come first to Zacharias when he went into the Holy Place of the Temple of the Lord to burn incense and to pray. A multitude was praying in the court outside. Probably Elisabeth was with them, or she could have been praying in the quiet of her home. It is easy to imagine the joy and wonder that filled her heart when she learned of the good tidings that had come to her husband. We can be sure that she received the message in a spirit of humility and reverent responsibility.

Elisabeth, who believed strongly in miracles, must have walked more prayerfully now about her house, though her husband was so overwhelmed that he had lost his ability to speak. The angel Gabriel had told Elisabeth's husband that he would not speak again until these things, which had been foretold, had come to pass, because he had not the faith to believe in such a miracle.

Though Elisabeth was old in years, let us imagine she was still vigorous and walked with a vibrant step. She was a woman, too, who thanked God for the wonders in the lives of His people. Even the stars that shone above her little home represented God's goodness to men. If He could make the stars shine, He could bring forth to her a son, who would glorify Him. How could she doubt? The human body itself was a miracle so wondrous that only God could create it and bring into being both human life and infinite mind. A child was the fruit of the womb and only God could bestow it as His gift to man and woman.

In the sixth month that Elisabeth was with child, her cousin Mary, the Virgin, now in Nazareth, received word that she would bear a son and that His name would be called Jesus. Mary had greater faith when the angel explained to her, "And, behold, thy cousin Elisabeth, she hath also conceived a son in her old age: and this is the sixth month with her, who was called barren" (Luke 1:36). The women now had a common bond. They knew that with God nothing was impossible.

With new rejoicing in her heart, Mary arose and went with haste into the hill country where Elisabeth lived. When she arrived at Elisabeth's home, the latter received her visitor with the stirring words, "Blessed art thou among women, and blessed is the fruit of thy womb" (Luke 1:42). Then Elisabeth asked in a modest spirit and with a new sense of wonder, "And whence is this to me, that the mother of my Lord should come to me?" (Luke 1:43). On Mary's arrival she had received a special inspiration of the Holy Spirit. This had enabled her to recognize in her kinswoman a fulfillment of the promise of God Himself, to know Mary as the mother of the coming Messiah. Elisabeth unconsciously illustrated the meaning of her own name, which in its Hebrew form signifies "God is an oath." To her, God's word was all powerful.

For three months Elisabeth entertained in her house the mother of the child who one day would be acclaimed the Christ. Though with child herself, and filled with great dreams for him, Elisabeth, humble, unselfish woman that she was, could accede that Mary would bear a child greater than her own.

During these three months that Mary visited Elisabeth, we can imagine that they unburdened their hearts to each other and that Elisabeth had many words of wisdom for Mary, who was young enough to be Elisabeth's daughter. Yet in their common experience of approaching motherhood the age difference became insignificant as they joyfully planned for the birth of their sons, who were to be so near the same age.

Happy were they then in that they could not look across the years to the end of their sons' lives. Mary's son would be crucified on the cross by an angry mob. Elisabeth's son, John the Baptist, would be beheaded by Herod, ruler of Galilee. As Elisabeth and Mary visited together, we wonder if they had any premonition of what was to come. Certainly they found much joy in each other, because they loved and understood each other and had the same strong belief in God.

They have been depicted together in Christian art all over the world, from the early Christian paintings on the walls of the cata-combs in Rome to such splendid examples of the Renaissance as Raphael's "Visitation" in the Gallery in Madrid, Spain.

Shortly after Mary's return to her home, Elisabeth gave birth to her son. We know she watched over him with a feeling of tenderness, veneration, and awe. On the eighth day, as is still the custom in Jewish families, a great gathering of neighbors and kinsmen came for the circumcizing and naming of Elisabeth's child. Some of those present called him Zacharias, after his father, but Elisabeth, remem-bering what the angel had said, declared positively, "Not so; but he shall be called John" (Luke 1:60).

Though still without his speech, Zacharias showed how he relied on his wife in the naming of his child when he wrote, "His name is John" (Luke 1:63). After that affirmation Zacharias' mouth opened and his tongue was loosed. Another miracle had come to pass in the home of Elisabeth. Her husband was healed of his speechlessness and spoke his famous Benedictus glorifying God as the divine deliverer.

What a joyful moment for Elisabeth. Her husband could speak again and at her side was a promising son. The hand of the Lord was with her. Like his father, John the Baptist became just and holy and ministered unto the people.

Elisabeth's story ends as her son's story begins to unfold. We can only hope that she lived to rejoice in his early ministry, while his good tidings were reaching forth and turning many to repentance. The tribute of John the Baptist to Jesus as one mightier than himself and his beautiful spirit of renunciation when he said, "He must in-crease, but I must decrease" (John 3:30) are a reminder of the spirit of his noble mother.

Elisabeth's most lasting memorial as the great mother of John the Baptist is found in the words of Christ when he said, "Verily I say unto you, Among them that are born of women, there hath not risen a greater than John the Baptist" (Matt. 11:11).

ANNA

LUKE 2:36-38

An aged widow, she lives in the Temple at Jerusalem. Serves God with fastings and prayers night and day. Speaks first words of messianic hope to those looking for redemption in Jerusalem.

FIRST TO ACCLAIM THE CHRIST

HUMBLE, staid, serious, unearthly in spirit, a woman of a strangely expectant faith—that was Anna the prophetess, the first person to proclaim Jesus as the Christ. In the little band of men and women who looked for the Redeemer, she was the one figure that stood out in bold strokes.

This was a period when Rome dominated the entire Mediterranean world, ruling an empire larger than the Greeks, the Persians, or the Egyptians had known. The Empire was strong and powerful. Its science, philosophy, theology, wealth, ecclesiastical and social power reigned supreme and were in opposition to any such idea as the coming of a Messiah. But there were a few, like Anna, who knew that the prophecies long foretold would be fulfilled.

ANNA

Why was the first one in Judaea to proclaim the Christ this gentle, elderly woman? Luke depicts Anna as dwelling in an ivory tower of the spirit, aloof from worldly preoccupations. She lived on a plane apart from material things and "served God with fastings and prayers night and day." He calls her a prophetess and in that she joins other eminent figures—Miriam, Deborah, and Huldah. Anna stands foremost among prophetesses in the New Testament.

In Luke's brief description of Anna we learn that she was a woman of great age, who "had lived with an husband seven years from her virginity; and she was a widow of about fourscore and four years." From that passage commentators determine her age differently. Some say that she was eighty-four years old. Others interpret the text to mean that she had been a widow eighty-four years. If she had been married seven years, she was now probably well over a hundred years old. But her exact age is of no great consequence.

More important is Anna's spirituality. The mention of her is so brief that little of her character can be given. But there is enough to liken her to a bright star that sweeps above the horizon and then suddenly dips down out of sight.

Denied the triumphs of motherhood, she had scarcely absented herself from the Temple since her early widowhood. Probably she held the place in the Temple of a deaconess or Sister of Charity.

It is easy to visualize Anna as a woman erect for her years, walking about the pillared Temple of Jerusalem in a flowing black dress with a shoulder shawl of a brighter hue, probably purple, and paler drapery about her white hair.

Onlookers, however, would not observe too closely Anna's attire, but her face, a face that showed neither hate nor cynicism nor malice, but a gentle sweetness and a serene spirituality. She seemed to say, "I am one of those who never ceases to believe in the great wonders of God." Her faith was the kind that gives meaning to the words of Joel quoted later by Peter in his great speech at Pentecost: "I will shew wonders in heaven above, and signs in the earth beneath" (Acts 2:19).

Anna belonged to the godly remnant. Perhaps she, like the Wise Men, had searched the skies the night Christ was born and had seen the "star in the east." She was one of those who had time to enjoy all of God's beauties, such as the stars that lighted the sky at night, the dawn that broke in all its effulgent color over the Temple, and the setting sun as it dipped behind the tall spires shadowing the Temple's rugged stone walls.

Though an old woman of the ancient tribe of Asher, a daughter of Phanuel, Anna was young in hope. She not only confessed the Christ but spoke of Him to all who were looking for the redemption of Israel. Is not this the real clue to Anna's creative, active, significant self?

Among these others looking for redemption and the coming of the messianic age were people of a simple faith, people who like Anna were more engrossed in spiritual things around the Temple than in material things, people who read the Scrolls of the Law and the Prophets daily and believed fully what Isaiah had spoken when he said, "Behold, a king shall reign in righteousness" (Isa. 32:1). "And there shall come forth a rod out of the stem of Jesse" (Isa. 11:1). She believed, too, in what the prophet Micah had said, "But thou, Beth-lehem Ephratah, though thou be little among the thousands of Judah, yet out of thee shall he come forth unto me that is to be ruler in Israel" (Mic. 5:2). She believed, too, in what Isaiah had said in Isaiah 2:2-4, and what Micah had said in almost the same words in Micah 4:1-4.

We know that Anna was a woman who listened to the reading of the scrolls of the sacred scriptures (the Bible of her time) and believed fully in the prophecies they contained. Not only did she believe, but she watched unceasingly for the coming of the Messiah.

The time for her to see Him with her own eyes finally came. It was at His presentation in the Temple as an infant according to the customs of the chosen people, and at the ceremonial service of His mother's purification, forty days after His birth. The favored mother,

Mary, with Joseph, had now come up to the holy city on Mount Zion from Bethlehem, to present the most mysterious offering that had ever been laid before that altar.

Probably Anna watched Mary cross the large open space within the Temple walls, called the Court of the Gentiles, and ascend the beautiful steps of the uncovered gateway leading into the Court of the Women, a higher area which lay like a terrace above the outer court.

Just as the venerable Simeon uttered his famous *Nunc Dimittis,* saying, "Lord, now lettest thou thy servant depart in peace, according to thy word: For mine eyes have seen thy salvation" (Luke 2:29-30), Anna stood watching the wondering priest. No sooner had she seen the enraptured Simeon lift the child Jesus in his arms than she caught the heavenly inspiration that animated the priest and the baby's parents.

Turning to the bystanders who had waited so long for the redemption of the Lord, Anna declared that this was the promised Messiah, the Hope of Israel, the Redeemer of the world. What greater prophecy could there be than this concerning an unconscious, helpless babe?

This aged woman had seen God more than events, and God in events. She had seen because she was intimate with grace, providence, and redemption.

As Joseph and Mary quietly wended their way out of the Temple with the child Jesus, we can see Anna unobtrusively returning to her thanksgiving and prayer in the Temple. In all probability she did not live to witness the public manifestation of the Christ, much less to hear His divine teachings and promises. But she had been there to behold Him and to thank God for Him and to speak of Him to all those men and women of prayer and devotion who had looked for the redemption He was to bring.

MARTHA and MARY

MARTHA
LUKE 10:38, 40, 41
JOHN 11:1, 5, 19, 20, 21, 24, 30,
    39
    12:2

MARY
LUKE 10:39, 42
JOHN 11:1, 2, 19, 20, 28, 31,
    32, 45
    12:3
MARK 14:3-9

Sisters of Bethany open their home to Jesus. Martha bustles about; Mary is more pensive. To Martha Jesus announces the victory over death. Mary anoints his feet with oil. Both are at last feast in Bethany.

"THE MASTER IS COME"

BOTH Martha and Mary belong in the gallery of famous Bible women. It was to Martha that Jesus first declared, "I am the resurrection, and the life: he that believeth in me, though he were dead, yet shall he live: And whosoever liveth and believeth in me shall never die. Believest thou this?" (John 11:25-26). Countless millions down the centuries have been comforted by these words first received by Martha. To her sister Mary goes the distinction of having anointed Jesus before He trudged to the cross. Through this loving attention to the Christ, Mary showed every evidence of knowing more of His secret power and wisdom than His disciples did. Because of this, she rises up as one of the most spiritually sensitive women in the New Testament.

Bethany, where these two sisters lived, was a quiet little village on the southeast of the Mount of Olives, beside the Jericho Road. It was a short and pleasant walk from here over the Mount of Olives to the Temple at Jerusalem.

[176]

We can picture the house where Martha and Mary lived as one of the most comfortable in Bethany, for we have every evidence that they were women of means, and gave of their means as well as themselves. Mary, for example, used her own costly ointment on Jesus.

Their house was probably a two-story place with a broad outer stairway leading to an upper room. The staircase, let us suppose, led up from a well-shaded court; and it was here that Jesus often paused to refresh Himself. Both house and garden were inviting, for Martha excelled as a homemaker.

She and Mary were as unlike in disposition as Esau and Jacob had been. While Martha was practical and unemotional, Mary was impassioned and imaginative. Martha probably was the older and mothered Mary; and she took the lead as homemaker. Probably Martha was a widow and Mary had never married. Despite their differences, Martha and Mary exhibited a close bond of sympathy for each other.

Like most attentive, eager-hearted, and affectionate hostesses, Martha strove for perfection around her house, especially when a guest the family loved as much as they did Jesus came for a visit. Mary was the more pensive and the quieter of the two. As Martha bustled about her home duties, she did not have Mary's calmness or her holy trustfulness.

Craving a fellowship of the spirit attuned to His, Jesus stopped one day at the home of the Bethany sisters on His way to the Feast of Dedication at Jerusalem. Martha seemed busier than usual, while Mary sat in deep humility at Jesus' feet, drinking in His every word. Martha, like most busy homemakers, became concerned that Mary sat idly by while there was work to be done. We can be sure that Mary was not selfish in her withdrawal from homemaking, but she knew that Martha had the ability to carry on without her. And probably it was Martha's house, not Mary's, in which they lived.

Instead of gently entreating Mary to help her during a rush period, Martha turned and said, "Lord, dost thou not care that my sister hath left me to serve alone? bid her therefore that she help me" (Luke 10:40). And Jesus answered and said to her, "Martha, Martha, thou art careful and troubled about many things: But one thing is needful: and Mary hath chosen that good part, which shall not be taken away from her" (Luke 10:41-42).

In these few words we have a careful delineation of the character of the two sisters. Probably Martha had prepared too lavish a meal, when a simple one would have sufficed. And Jesus was more interested in food for the soul than in food for the body. Yet Martha was tender in her service to her Lord.

The second scene in the New Testament in which Martha and Mary figure prominently is narrated in John 11:1-46. This is their most triumphant scene, for it deals with the raising of their brother Lazarus from the tomb. And it was here that Jesus declared to Martha, "Whosoever liveth and believeth in me shall never die" (John 11:26). Martha, a woman of great discernment, responded with one of the most magnificent confessions of faith in the New Testament, "Lord, I believe that thou art the Christ, the Son of God, which should come into the world" (John 11:27).

Lazarus had been in his tomb four days when Martha learned that Jesus was approaching on the road to Bethany. She went outside the village to meet Him, while Mary remained behind sitting in the house. But both she and Martha finally spoke to Him exactly the same words, "Lord, if thou hadst been here, my brother had not died" (John 11:21, 32). Of the weeping Mary Jesus asked, "Where have ye laid him?" And they said unto Him, "Lord, come and see" (John 11:34).

"Jesus wept" (John 11:35), and the two sisters became the first named women recorded in the New Testament to witness Jesus' expression of grief for a friend. They knew their brother had been Jesus' well-loved friend. They also realized that Jesus was grieved not only at their brother's death but also at the indignation and unbelief of some of the people who stood there. Their loving attitude toward Jesus in a moment of trial drew a striking contrast to the hate and jealousy of some of the others standing by.

The sympathy of the two sisters must have been comforting to Jesus. Though their temperaments were poles apart, now they were one in spirit, and Jesus understood and loved both of them. As they stood there looking at the recessed tomb of their brother Lazarus, a tomb carved horizontally in the rock with a slab to close the entrance, they remembered the promise that they would "see the glory of God" (John 11:40). And they did.

Lazarus walked from the tomb, heavily bound in his grave clothes, and Martha and Mary heard the Master say, "Loose him, and let him go" (John 11:44). They were witnessing the forerunner of a similar miracle, when Jesus Himself would rise from the tomb.

In the scene where Lazarus came forth from the tomb, Martha and Mary stood by more loyal than ever, while the jealous-hearted already were plotting against Jesus. The loyalty of the two sisters meant much to this lonely man and to other believers in Bethany, who looked to Martha and Mary for leadership because of their close friendship with Jesus.

The third and final scene in which Martha and Mary figured prominently was at the last feast in Bethany, six days before the Passover. Both Matthew and Mark intimate that this feast was in the home of the deceased Simon the leper. John makes no mention of this. Because Martha was a notable housewife, the banquet most probably was entrusted to her. In this last feast at Bethany, Martha and Mary were the central figures with Jesus and Lazarus. Many had come out of curiosity to see Lazarus, but Martha and Mary were there to express gratitude because Jesus had raised their brother from the tomb.

Mary, impelled to express her adoration, took a pound of ointment of spikenard, very costly (John 12:3), and came softly behind Jesus and poured the precious perfume on His feet, wiping them with her hair. The same service is mentioned in John 11:2. We learn in Mark 14:5 that the ointment might have sold for more than 300 pence, or about sixty dollars at that time, but with a purchasing power now about four times what it was in the first century.

Mary was following the custom of this time, that of refreshing guests at banquets by pouring cool and fragrant ointments on their heads and sometimes their feet. She knew how Jesus' enemies despised Him and were drawing Him into their net. Yet she did not try to dissuade Him from going up to Jerusalem. He who had brought back her brother Lazarus from the grave would not willfully try to grasp at mortal life Himself.

Mary, who knew that some things were worth dying for, in this act of pouring ointment on Jesus was endeavoring to show Him that in her eyes whatever course He chose would be right and good.

Poised, pure, we see her standing meekly and reverently by after she had poured the costly ointment on Jesus' feet. We also see Martha, understanding sister that she was, with a look of love in her eyes as she saw her sister administer the ointment.

Then these two sisters heard Jesus say what has been called the loneliest sentence in literature, "Let her alone: against the day of my burying hath she kept this" (John 12:7). The implication here is that some of the ointment was left to be used in the preparation of the body of Jesus for burial.

Though others, including Judas, criticized because Mary had been so extravagant and had not given this wealth to the poor, Jesus praised her for her gift to Him who, unlike the poor, would not always be with them. In His appreciation of her gift, Jesus invited others to enjoy God's many blessings, not only the lovely things of the earth and the sky and sea but also such a creation as fragrant ointment.

Mary herself had not inscribed her memorial on a gravestone. She had poured out her precious ointment in wholehearted devotion to the living Jesus and her broken alabaster vase would fill the world with its fragrance down the ages.

Paradoxical as it may seem, in a little while Judas would accept thirty pieces of silver, the equivalent of about twenty dollars and a sum one-third less than the cost of the perfume. In accepting twenty dollars from the chief priests, Judas set in motion the Crucifixion. Yet Mary, who was called extravagant in the giving of a gift that cost sixty dollars, showed she understood the wiser use of money. She was willing to expend a large sum to provide beauty and comfort for a loved one.

We can be certain that Martha, too, sanctioned her sister's lavish gift to their Master, who so soon would trudge to the cross alone.

THREE SICK WOMEN

WOMAN WITH FEVER
MATT. 8:14, 15
MARK 1:30, 31
LUKE 4:38, 39

WOMAN WITH ISSUE OF
BLOOD
MATT. 9:20-22
MARK 5:25-34
LUKE 8:43-48

WOMAN CROOKED FOR 18
YEARS
LUKE 13:11-13

Three diseased women come to Jesus. All three go their way whole again, for he heals them.

AND JESUS HEALED ALL OF THEM

ONE had a high fever from which she could not arise. One had had a hemorrhage for twelve years. Another had been bent in body for eighteen years. And Jesus healed all three of them.

The woman who had lain ill with a high fever was the mother-in-law of Simon, to whom Jesus later gave the name of Peter. We can imagine that she assisted much in the ministry of her disciple son-in-law, but now she had what Luke, the physician, calls a "great fever," and was so sick that she could not arise. Probably it was malaria, very common then in this region.

We can imagine that she was a woman with gray hair and a worn countenance, and that her son-in-law had a genuine affection for her. Jesus had just come to the home of Simon Peter, probably at Capernaum or Bethsaida. Only a short time before, according to Matthew, He had healed a leper and a centurion's servant who had palsy. Now it was probably early afternoon, when the fever had risen to its highest point, and the woman's family sat anxiously watching her.

Jesus came to her bedside and merely touched her hand, and the fever left her.

The remarkable thing about Simon's wife's mother is that after she was healed "she ministered unto them." All three Gospel writers, Matthew, Mark, and Luke, report this fact. Because she owed her health and life to Christ, she could express her gratitude only in service in His ministry.

Then there was the woman who is the prototype of those who see their powers wasting away in an incurable disease. This woman had had an issue of blood for twelve long years. She was weak and weary and disheartened, for she "had suffered many things of many physicians and had spent all that she had, and was nothing bettered, but rather grew worse" (Mark 5:26). Even Luke, the physician, admitted she could not be healed by a physician (Luke 8:43).

This woman, according to the law of the time, was regarded as unclean and was restricted in her contact with others. Dared she expect even a light touch from Jesus? But she believed that if she could touch merely His garment she would be made whole again.

So it was she gently touched the broad edging of His long tunic. It was like the turning on of a great light in a dark room. She felt

His healing energy go through her body immediately, and He too sensed that power had gone from Him, for He turned and said, "Who touched me?" (Mark 5:31).

The woman, fearful of what He might say and trembling with joy at what had happened to her, came and poured out to Him the story of her long suffering. All this occurred on a crowded street, probably in Capernaum, when Jesus was on His way to the bedside of Jairus' daughter.

Matthew and Luke report that Jesus said to this woman, "Daughter, be of good comfort: thy faith hath made thee whole" (Luke 8:48). Mark gives a more stirring portrayal when he reports the phrase, "Daughter, thy faith hath made thee whole; go in peace, and be whole of thy plague" (Mark 5:34). What triumphant words for a woman who had suffered for twelve years!

Many, like this woman, have gone to physicians and have not been cured, but she had been healed instantaneously by the greatest physician of them all. And she went forth in peace again.

Later legend gives this woman the name of Berenice of Veronica. Eusebius of Caesarea (A.D. 264-340) in his *Ecclesiastical History,* tells of a bronze statue that was erected to her at Caesarea Philippi. But inanimate things like statues could never tell her story. Only Jesus' triumphant words, "Thy faith hath made thee whole; go in peace" (Luke 8:48), ring forth the certainty and the wonder of her healing.

Finally there was the woman who had had a spirit of infirmity for eighteen years. Her body was crooked. Probably she had suffered from a serious accident or from some crippling disease like arthritis.

Imagine what it would be like not to walk straight for eighteen years. Think of how broken one would be in spirit. This woman probably had lost all hope, because her body had been bent for so long.

Then, on the Sabbath, she came before Jesus in her crippled condition. So serious was her ailment that she could not raise herself up and look into His face.

Turning to her and laying His hands upon her, He said, "Woman, thou art loosed from thine infirmity" (Luke 13:12). What a positive declaration! The woman could once more walk forth well and whole again.

The most amazing thing about this woman, Luke tells us, is that she glorified God. She did not take her healing for granted, but offered a prayer of adoration to the Giver of all good.

The healing of this woman and the other two, one with fever, the other with an issue of blood for twelve years, makes more insistent the question, "Why are ye so fearful? how is it that ye have no faith?" (Mark 4:40).

HERODIAS

MATT. 14:3, 6
MARK 6:17, 19, 22
LUKE 3:19

As the second wife of Herod Antipas, she demands through her daughter the head of John the Baptist, because he had denounced her marriage. She receives this ghastly gift on a platter.

SHE OCCASIONED THE BEHEADING OF JOHN THE BAPTIST

THE most striking example in the New Testament of how far reaching can be the evil influence of a heartless, determined woman in a high position is the story of Herodias. Not only did she occasion the beheading of John the Baptist, but it may even be that she helped to hasten the crucifixion of Christ. It was to her husband, Herod Antipas, that Jesus was sent by Pilate, and Herod

[184]

might have delayed the verdict. This was the same Herod whom Jesus earlier had compared to a "fox" because of his cunning (Luke 13:32).

Herodias herself, like her husband, was descended from a line of wicked people. Though the story in the Bible relates only one scene in her life, the beheading of John the Baptist, let us view her entire life from the pages of history in order better to understand what kind of woman she was.

Her first marriage had been to her half-uncle Herod Philip. She entered into a second incestuous and illicit union when she divorced him to marry his half-brother Herod Antipas, who was the stepbrother of her father Aristobulus. This Herod Antipas was tetrarch of Galilee and Peraea during Jesus' time and he is mentioned more frequently in the New Testament than any other Herod.

To Herodias' first union had been born her dancing daughter, to whom Josephus gives the name of Salome, though in the New Testament she is never identified in any way except as Herodias' daughter. The daughter was born of the Herod family on both her father's and mother's side and must have been brought up in the evil atmosphere of the family. We are told she excelled in sensuous dancing.

History shows us that evil ran all through Herodias' life. She was a granddaughter of Herod the Great, who carved out his empire with a sword and sought to destroy the child Jesus (Matt. 2:13). The family line of Herod has become so entangled as to make it a veritable puzzle to historians. They record that he had ten wives and killed his first wife Mariamne, the only human being he ever seems to have loved. Herodias' father, Aristobulus, was the son of Herod the Great by this Mariamne.

After Herodias' first marriage to Herod Philip, history records, she lived in Rome, where her husband had been exiled and disinherited because his mother had taken part in a plot against his father, Herod the Great. There Herodias and her husband, Herod Philip, entertained as their guest her husband's half-brother, Herod Antipas. He had come to Rome to receive his investiture as tetrarch and at this time was married to the daughter of King Aretas of Arabia.

Herod Antipas, while a guest in his half-brother's home, indulged in a guilty relationship with the brother's wife, Herodias. Desiring to be closer to the throne than she could ever be with her present husband, a more retiring man, Herodias was willing to pay any price for a regal position, regardless of principles or people involved.

She persuaded Herod Antipas to divorce his wife, and she in turn divorced her husband and left Rome for Tiberias, the capital city of the province of Galilee, where Herod Antipas was now tetrarch. With her went her daughter, who probably was just entering her teens.

Great artists have depicted Herodias as a beautiful woman, who wore a crown from which a thin veil fell in long, graceful folds. Beneath it was her dark hair, adorned with pearls. Her dress was of a flowing, rich, regal fabric. Richard Strauss has made more real her wickedness in his opera *Salome,* with its setting in Galilee, where her second husband, Herod Antipas, had great power.

The only one who had the courage to speak against this incestuous union of a man of such power was John the Baptist, who said to Herod, "It is not lawful for thee to have her" (Matt. 14:4). She was his brother's wife. Herod would have put John to death at once, but he feared the multitude (Matt.14:5), which looked upon John the Baptist as a prophet. In Mark 6:19 we learn that it was Herodias who felt especially bitter about John and desired his death but was held back by Herod.

Herodias, however, was not a woman who could easily forget John the Baptist's stinging rebuke of her marriage. Vindictive as well as cruel, she determined that she would get rid of this man; and so she entered upon her foul scheme.

Her daughter danced for Herod in the palace on his birthday, as Herodias sat looking on. The daughter pleased Herod so much that he said to her, "Ask of me whatsoever thou wilt, and I will give it thee" (Mark 6:22). The Scriptures tell us further that the daughter went forth and said to her mother, "What shall I ask?" And the mother made her ghastly request for "the head of John the Baptist."

The daughter became her mother's puppet as she danced to please Herod. Though he "was exceeding sorry" (Mark 6:26), Herodias had her way. She was the evil influence for both her daughter and her husband and the sole instigator of one of the most horrible crimes ever committed against a just and holy man.

According to the portrayal given us in Strauss's opera *Salome*, the daughter danced with many veils and then flung them off one by one, as Herod looked on with lustful eyes. Then when she had concluded her dance, he sent and had John the Baptist beheaded and ordered that the head be brought on a platter and presented to Salome, who in turn gave it to her mother.

Though her husband and daughter committed this horrible crime against John the Baptist, they were merely the tools of Herodias. She was actually more responsible than either of them for the outrage because she had planned it. As Jezebel had made a tool of Ahab to slay the prophets of Jehovah, so Herodias had made a tool of Herod Antipas to behead John the Baptist. Though the Bible follows through to the very end of Jezebel's life, when she was eaten by dogs, the Bible story of Herodias ends with the delivering to her of the head of John the Baptist.

However, ancient history relates that after this she became so jealous of the power of her brother, Agrippa, who had been made a king, that she induced her husband to demand of the Roman emperor Caligula the title of king for himself. But Agrippa sent word to Caligula that Herod had been plotting with the emperor's enemies. When Caligula questioned Herod and Herodias in Rome, he was not satisfied with the answers of the guilty pair.

Instead of making Herod Antipas king, Caligula took from him even the title of tetrarch and added the tetrarchy of Galilee to the kingdom of Agrippa. The emperor banished Herod to Gaul. This is all related by Josephus.

Because of his friendship for her brother, Caligula offered Herodias her freedom, but she chose exile and disgrace with her husband. Strangely enough, this is the only time that we have any historical record of a praiseworthy action on her part.

Legend has it that Herodias and Herod died in Spain. Did she have time to live with her guilty conscience and to realize that the beheading of the holy and just John the Baptist was a crime for which she must suffer to the end of her days? Did she come to see that one word which she might have spoken could have saved Christ? At the time of Jesus' trial Pilate, fearing to render an unpopular verdict, had sent Jesus to Herod, for Jesus was from the town of Nazareth in Herod's tetrarchy of Galilee. But Herod had "mocked" and sent Jesus back to Pilate (Luke 23:11).

Did Herodias ever realize that, had she stood on the side of God and righteousness, the history of this period might have had a different ending? She had been warned by John the Baptist of her evil choice in the matter of her marriage, but she had hardened her heart to this message of God. With but one exception, her life had followed an evil pattern to the end.

SYRO-PHOENICIAN WOMAN
(Also Called The Canaanite Woman)

MATT. 15:21-28
MARK 7:24-30

Lives on border of Holy Land and is not of Jewish faith, but when Jesus comes into her country, she entreats Him to heal her afflicted daughter. In His test of her faith she shows patience, and He heals the daughter without even seeing her.

"O WOMAN, GREAT IS THY FAITH"

SHE was a mother who had suffered unbearable tribulation because of the affliction of her daughter, who was "grievously vexed with a devil" (Matt. 15:22). Matthew calls her "a woman of Canaan," meaning of course the ancient land of Canaan, signifying she was of Semitic stock but was not Jewish. Mark accurately calls her a Syro-Phoenician after her country of Phoenicia, which belonged to Syria and was on the northern frontier of Palestine, about three days' journey by foot from Jerusalem.

By culture and language this woman was Greek, by religion a pagan, by position in her community a nobody. Yet with Christ these differences meant nothing. Wearied in every nerve and fiber of her being by the constant care her daughter needed, she made an importunate demand upon Him on His arrival in Syro-Phoenicia from Galilee. She had watched her child's paroxysms so long and was so grieved by them that she probably could scarcely hold back a woman's tears as she came toward Him. But she did hold back her tears.

[189]

She walked toward Him with new courage and faith. Her faith was based on wondrous stories she had heard of how He had healed the deaf, the dumb, and the blind, and those with evil spirits of many kinds. These stories had been brought to her ears by her own people from Tyre and Sidon. They, with the multitudes from Judaea and Jerusalem, had a short time before heard Jesus when He preached the Sermon on the Mount.

No doubt she had heard, too, His story of the widow of Zarephath, who had fed the prophet Elijah, of another race and country, out of her scanty store. Though this Syro-Phoenician woman knew that she was not of Jesus' own people, she had the courage to believe that the family of God included Jew and Gentile alike, that Phoenicia, like Palestine, needed His missionary service.

And so the Syro-Phoenician woman came before Him crying, "Have mercy on me, O Lord, thou Son of David; my daughter is grievously vexed with a devil" (Matt. 15:22). How unutterably earnest that prayer! This mother was not complaining about her own burden but was lamenting the spiritual and physical distress of her daughter.

Nowhere in the Gospels do we find Jesus turning away from need as He did from this woman's. He did not even answer her entreaty. His disciples, evidently disturbed that she should interrupt Him, said, "Send her away" (Matt. 15:23). Finally Jesus said to her, "I am not sent but unto the lost sheep of the house of Israel" (Matt. 15:24).

Various attempts have been made to explain Jesus' seeming aloofness toward the woman. In no other single sentence does He express such apparent coldness. Did He desire to test the feelings of His disciples, who in their narrow Judaic exclusiveness might be unprepared for Him to bestow His blessing upon this woman of another race? Or did He also desire to test further the woman's faith? Or did He wish to teach that we must persevere, even when it might seem that His ear is turned away?

The Syro-Phoenician woman did persevere. She came and knelt

before Him, saying, "Lord, help me" (Matt. 15:25). The very terseness of this entreaty expresses all the more strongly its urgency.

Jesus' answer was a further test of her faith; He said, "It is not meet to take the children's bread, and to cast it to dogs" (Matt. 15:26). The reference to dogs sounds offensive but was not meant to be. It is only an evidence of the picturesque speech of the peoples of this time, who understood that a metaphor should not be taken literally.

At any rate the woman understood. She was not offended. She took up the figure with wit and spirit and presence of mind, answering Jesus, "Truth, Lord: yet the dogs eat of the crumbs which fall from their masters' table" (Matt. 15:27). She let Jesus know that she was aware of the infinite plenty being lavished upon the people of Israel, and that all she asked for was a crumb which might fall to the floor for a poor, unworthy creature like herself. She also had made Him know that a child is a child, and, when afflicted like her own, helpless, no matter what its race.

Her obstinate faith had brought its reward. Jesus, always loving and merciful, turned to her saying, "O woman, great is thy faith" (Matt. 15:28). And from that hour her daughter was made whole again.

The healing of this Syro-Phoenician woman's demoniac daughter was a demonstration of the instantaneous power of God. No waiting had been necessary. It also was a demonstration of how the presence of Jesus could be felt at a distance. He did not go in person to the girl, but healed her without ever seeing her.

The woman had learned that prayer is simply asking and receiving. "Your father knoweth what things ye have need of, before ye ask him" (Matt. 6:8). She who had been content to ask only a crumb had received from Christ the key to God's vast storehouse.

No doubt she went forth and spread her faith among others and paved the way for the Christian community at Tyre. Thirty years later Paul tarried there a week, and his companion wrote: "And when we had accomplished those days, we departed and went our way; and they all brought us on our way, with wives and children, till we were out of the city: and we kneeled down on the shore, and prayed" (Acts. 21:5).

SALOME, MOTHER OF JAMES AND JOHN

*

MATT. 20:20
27:56
MARK 16:1-8

Is called mother of Zebedee's children as well as Salome, but with her sons, her portrait is most clearly drawn. Of Jesus she makes a special request for them. Afterwards she is with Jesus at the Crucifixion and also at the tomb at the time of the Resurrection.

"YE KNOW NOT WHAT YE ASK"

NEXT to His own mother, the most notable mother to cross Jesus' path during His ministry was the mother of the disciples James and John.

In two places in the Gospel of Matthew she is identified merely as the mother of Zebedee's children. In Mark she is called Salome at the Crucifixion (Mark 15:40) and at the Resurrection (Mark 16:1). But immortality comes to her not as Salome or as the wife of Zebedee but as the mother of James and John.

Her two sons belonged to the inner circle of disciples. Some scholars infer from John 19:25 that she was a sister of Mary, the mother of Jesus. Other scholars dispute the inference. Whether she was or not, we know that she and her sons were very close to Jesus.

She became so humanly ambitious for her sons to enjoy extra prestige during Jesus' ministry that she made a special public request of Him. Toward the end of His ministry she and her sons knelt before Him, and she said to Him, "Grant that these my two sons may sit, the one on thy right hand, and the other on the left, in thy kingdom" (Matt. 20:21).

In His wisdom, Jesus answered this zealous mother thus: "To sit on my right hand, and on my left, is not mine to give, but it shall be given to them for whom it is prepared of my Father" (Matt. 20:23).

Quite natural it is to suppose that the other ten disciples were ambitious for these places, too, and must have felt that this mother had made a very selfish request. Probably she needed Jesus' tender rebuke in order to learn that true spiritual greatness was not a thing to be given but to be earned, and that it could be earned only through sacrifice.

Then Jesus followed His rebuke of the mother of James and John with His marvelous definition of true greatness: "Whosoever will be great among you, let him be your minister" (Matt. 20:26).

This mother had been presumptuous enough to put her own human ambition for her sons James and John above their spiritual preparation. But in her zealousness she typifies many mothers. However, she provides a striking contrast to Mary, Mother of Jesus, who never at any time expressed any human ambition for her son. Even when great things were spoken to her about Him, she "pondered these things in her heart."

But the mother of James and John publicly expressed her dreams and hopes, probably before the multitude. We cannot be too severe on her, for she remained one of the most faithful followers of Jesus to the end, making us know that she never faltered in her service to His mission.

And evidently she handed down a rich spiritual legacy to her sons.

Her son John was the disciple who most perfectly apprehended the spirit of Jesus and to whom Jesus entrusted His own mother at the end. He may have written the Fourth Gospel, though some scholars question this.

John had attended the preaching of John the Baptist at the Jordan and doubtless came back with Jesus to Galilee and was with Him at the wedding in Cana. He also was with Him at the raising of Jairus' daughter and at the Transfiguration. Finally, at the last supper he occupied the place next to Jesus at the table (John 13:23). Because of his deep spiritual insight and loving disposition, John had merited his mother's request.

The other son, James, probably the older of the two, was a faithful disciple also. After the Crucifixion we find James with other disciples in Galilee and in Jerusalem. His life ended by the sword at the hands of Herod Agrippa, and James thus became the first of the twelve apostles to seal his testimony with his blood. There is no record that he sat next to Jesus, but he became one of His most trusted apostles.

Both sons of this ambitious mother succeeded nobly, and she could hold her head proudly to the end. Because of her unusual request, Matthew has given her a special place in his Gospel. However, Mark says that it was the sons, and not the mother, who made the request to sit on the left and the right of Jesus (Mark 10:35-40).

There is every evidence that this mother and her sons and their father Zebedee gave of their substance as well as of themselves all during Jesus' ministry. The mother was one of that faithful band of women whose special sympathetic service helped His mission.

It is natural to suppose that she occupied a rather prominent place in her own community, for her husband Zebedee was a fisherman whose boats were probably moored near the banks of a small stream that empties into the Sea of Galilee. And he had servants who are mentioned as attending to duties with his fishing boats, an indication that he was a man of some means. Their home was on the shores of the Sea of Galilee at Capernaum or at Bethsaida.

In the days of Jesus' ministry this ambitious mother of James and John had probably confused worldly position and spiritual greatness. But like others, she learned many noble lessons from Christ. And as one of the faithful who ministered to Him until the end she probably became an example herself of Christ's definition of true greatness, as did her two sons, who became His unrivaled servants.

WOMAN OF SAMARIA

JOHN 4:7-42

Meets Jesus at well at Sychar. He recalls her sinful ways but does not censure her. She opens her mind and heart to His message and carries it back to others in Samaria, where field is ripe for many other conversions.

"GOD IS A SPIRIT"

ALONE, this nameless woman trudged from the village of Sychar to the ancient well dug in a field that had once belonged to Jacob. The high noon sun beat down upon her, and as she glanced toward Mount Gerizim in one direction and Mount Ebal in another, she saw but a few wandering shadows cross the Plain of Shechem. Even the well-watered vineyards looked lifeless to her in the glare of the midsummer Judaean sun.

She had felt famished in body and soul as she had set forth with a water jug on her shoulder. It was strange that this woman who had lived for carnal pleasures should feel this way, for she had not thought too much about her soul.

Her sandals, we can imagine, pounded heavily upon the ancient cobblestones that were burning like hot coals from the heat of the midday sun. They fitted loosely and were dirty and worn. Her cotton dress, probably of faded blue crash, was carelessly draped about her, and her loose, flowing headdress, of another drab color, outlined a face once pretty and gay, but now sad and hard. Her figure, once voluptuous, now showed age and weariness.

This woman had chosen the noontime to go to the well, probably to avoid the gossipy women who usually gathered there in the early morning, while it was cool, and at twilight, when the shadows from the mountains folded in over the plains.

Today her feet pounded more heavily than usual. Her loose way of life had brought disillusionments and heartaches. She longed to find a new way to live, but it was too late, she probably thought to herself.

As she neared the well, she remembered how often she had come there for water; but today, for the first time, she sensed a new weariness of spirit. It was unlike anything she had experienced before. Her heavy footsteps broke the silence and intruded upon the solitude of a gentle-faced man, who sat by the well refreshing Himself.

This man, Jesus, had come down only a little while before from the brown hills of Ephraim into the hot valley of Shechem. He was on His way to Galilee from Judaea and most probably was weary, for He had trudged over hot sands and rough stones for several hours. The sound of approaching footsteps had aroused Him from His quiet meditation.

Having deliberately chosen the Samaritan Road, an unpopular road for a Jew like himself to travel, He probably now sat pondering the hatred that existed between the Jews and Samaritans and wondering why all men could not love one another. This hate, He remembered, dated back to the Assyrian conquest when some of the Israelites, left behind when the ten tribes were deported, had intermarried with Assyrian invaders and colonists of other nationalities. The racially mixed population of Samaria had set up on Mount

Gerizim a rival temple to the one in Jerusalem, and this had antagonized the Jews. At a time when the old hate still smoldered, this wretched, worldly woman of Samaria came upon this godly man of the Jews.

As he sat quietly on a hard stone step beside the well, He saw the woman drawing water, and He spoke somewhat quickly to her, saying, "Give me to drink." The request came as a surprise to the woman. With an incredulous smile she answered, "How is it that thou, being a Jew, askest drink of me, which am a woman of Samaria? for the Jews have no dealings with the Samaritans."

Jesus answered her, "If thou knewest the gift of God, and who it is that saith to thee, Give me to drink, thou wouldest have asked of him, and he would have given thee living water." The woman of Samaria was puzzled. Turning, she said to Jesus, "Sir, thou hast nothing to draw with, and the well is deep: from whence then hast thou that living water?" Then she questioned Him further, "Art thou greater than our father Jacob, which gave us the well?"

The only living water this woman knew was the water which flowed freely from the springs. Like a miracle, as she stood in the presence of this man of God, a change came over her. She began to drink into her inner being His words: "Whosoever drinketh of the water that I shall give him shall never thirst; but the water that I shall give him shall be in him a well of water springing up into everlasting life."

So uplifting were Jesus' words that the woman of Samaria was suddenly transported to a new level of life. For the first time she received a glimpse of what the living water this great man talked about so confidently could mean.

With a great longing in her heart to know more about it, she said to Jesus, "Sir, give me this water, that I thirst not, neither come hither to draw." The prophetic insight of Jesus was revealed when He spoke: "Go, call thy husband, and come hither."

If their conversation was to continue, Jesus realized that it was best for the woman's husband to be present, because it was not customary for a rabbi to hold a long conversation with a strange woman. He had desired to awaken the sleeping conscience of this woman, and He had. She was forced to answer that she had no husband, and Jesus said to her, "Thou hast well said, I have no husband: For thou hast had five husbands; and he whom thou now hast is not thy husband: in that saidst thou truly."

No one had ever reprimanded this woman in such an honest manner before. She, who evidently had been the subject of so much gossip, was bewildered. Here sat a man she had never seen before, but He was revealing her past. Had He sensed her innermost heartaches? She did not know, but she was certain His presence inspired her reverence.

She must have known that great things often come at unexpected moments. But she was stunned when she realized how much this moment would change her own life. The spell of Jesus' spirit had made her forget entirely how parched had been her lips and how tired her feet. As she stood contemplating the significance of this meeting, these words flowed freely from Him, as freely as the water had flowed from the well into her jug:

"God is a Spirit," He said to her, "and they that worship him must worship him in spirit and in truth." To her He had spoken that tremendous truth, the foundation of our knowledge of God. Now she could glimpse the spirituality of all true worship, for gently the Master had raised her up. He had asked for water, which was temporal, but He had in turn given her the eternal gift of spiritual fountains for the soul.

So revived was she that she said to Him, "I know that Messias cometh, which is called Christ: when he is come, he will tell us all things." Then it was He revealed to her that long-awaited message: "I that speak unto thee am he." And because she received this message, she has an immortal place in the Bible.

After this revelation, Jesus' disciples, who had come to meet Him, interrupted the conversation and bade their Master eat, but He told them that He had partaken of the food of the spirit.

The remarkable conclusion to the story of the woman of Samaria, as told by John, is that she left her waterpot and on winged feet went forth to say to others in Samaria, "Come, see a man, which told me all things that ever I did: is not this the Christ?"

In the face of this repentant, careworn woman the Samaritans must have seen a new, piercing light. She could make even the un-believers know that she had drunk from spiritual fountains of water. The people, longing to receive the same gift, now streamed out toward Jesus, and He and His disciples stayed with them for two days. Many of the Samaritans believed in Him, but they said it was not because of what the woman had heard but because of what they also had seen and heard. For the first time they called him Christ, the Saviour of the world.

Many conversions followed. The disciples who were with Jesus now understood what He had meant when He said, "Lift up your eyes, and look on the fields; for they are white already to harvest."

The story of the conversion of the woman of Samaria has a universal meaning. She is the prototype of women everywhere who live for carnal pleasures. Comforting it is to know that today, as in the time of Jesus, there is a fountain to refresh eternally all these who are parched by sin and suffering.

That fountain is God Himself, who must be worshiped in spirit and truth, by saint and sinner alike. In fact the sinner, like the woman of Samaria, may draw closer to Him and more quickly than the self-satisfied, righteous person who has a tendency to look down on those he considers less righteous than himself.

This woman's story confirms the belief that God is no respecter of persons and that Christ came to show the inner meaning of worship. His profound teaching had quickened, enlightened, and illumined the spirit of this worldly woman. She could now know what it meant to take of the water of life freely—not the water in the well at Sychar, near which she had stood, but the spiritual refreshment which had come into her own soul after her encounter with Jesus.

Paradoxical it is that this woman of very common clay in the sight of the world had been chosen to receive Christ's teaching that "God is a spirit."

MARY MAGDALENE

*

MATT. 27:56, 61
    28:1
MARK 15:40, 47
    16:1, 9
LUKE 8:2
    24:10
JOHN 19:25
    20:1, 11, 16, 18

Jesus casts seven demons out of the woman of Magdala. She becomes one of His most faithful followers, going with Him all the way to cross. She is first to know He has arisen and to report this to His disciples Peter and John.

"SEE, HE IS RISEN"

CHRIST'S empty tomb was first seen by Mary Magdalene, and she was the first to report to the disciples the miracle of the Resurrection, the greatest event the Christian world has ever known.

One of the most stirring narratives in literature is John's description of Mary Magdalene's visit to the sepulcher. He depicts her as being alone. Other Gospel writers say that other women were with her.

Evidently going on ahead, Mary Magdalene saw that the big circular stone had been rolled back along the groove and had left the entrance clear. Hastening to Peter and "the other disciple, whom

Jesus loved," who is thought to be John, she told them, "They have taken away the Lord out of the sepulcher, and we know not where they have laid him" (John 20:2).

These disciples followed Mary Magdalene to the sepulcher. John went in first and gazed in silent wonder at the open grave, and then Peter came and saw that the grave was empty and that the linen cerements were lying neatly folded in the empty sepulcher.

One, at least, of the disciples and possibly both of them "saw and believed" and then went back to their homes. Mary Magdalene, possessing a woman's sensitivity and able to believe even what eyes cannot behold, returned once more to the tomb and looked inside. This time she saw two angels in white sitting there, the one at the head and the other at the feet, where the body of Jesus had lain.

Strange it was that the first word spoken inside the empty tomb should be "Woman." And then there followed the angels' question: "Why weepest thou?" Mary Magdalene answered, "Because they have taken away my Lord, and I know not where they have laid him" (John 20:13). Then she turned, and Jesus stood before her. Not until He spoke her name, "Mary," did she recognize that He was Jesus.

Though she had not found Christ, He had found her and had called her by name. Then she turned to Him with her cry of recognition of her Master: "Rabboni" (John 20:16).

As Mary Magdalene stood there in the softly breaking dawn, Jesus had spoken in a voice so tender that it must have penetrated to her heart. "Touch me not; for I am not yet ascended to my Father: but go to my brethren, and say unto them, I ascend unto my Father, and your Father; and to my God, and your God" (John 20:17). Mary, awe-stricken, hastened to tell the others that she had seen the Lord and that He had spoken these things to her.

In Christ's resurrection Mary Magdalene had witnessed not a mere resuscitation but a changing to another form, a form not subject to the ordinary laws of the flesh but ready now for a new mode of existence and a new set of relationships, a form not temporal but eternal. Yet He was still alive, active, able to reach out and to speak.

Mary Magdalene went forth to prepare others for this change in their Master. Her long watch by the grave in the early morning had been an evidence of her faith. Because of her faith she became the first witness to the Resurrection.

In a little while followers would see and feel where the nail holes had been in His hands and the spear wound in His side, but they would learn that this body could not be pierced again, for it had taken on an indestructible form.

Who was this Mary Magdalene to whom Jesus appeared after His triumph over death? John gives her the leading part in his narrative. Matthew, however, writes that with her were "Mary the mother of James and Joses, and the mother of Zebedee's children" (Matt. 27:56). In 28:1 he writes, "As it began to dawn toward the first day of the week," Mary Magdalene and "the other Mary," who could have been Mary of Cleophas, came "to see the sepulcher." Mark tells that "Mary, the mother of James the less and of Joses, and Salome" accompanied Mary Magdalene (Mark 15:40). Luke gives the prominent place to Mary Magdalene and adds the names of "Joanna, and Mary the mother of James, and other women" (Luke 24:10).

All of this has confused scholars, but evidently Mary Magdalene had a more significant role at the time of the Resurrection than any other woman. Also in several places in the narrative she stands beside the mother of Jesus.

Fourteen times Mary Magdalene is mentioned by name. In eight of these passages her name heads the list. In one her name follows the name of the Mother of Jesus and the other Mary. In five it appears alone. These concern the appearance of Christ to her, as narrated by John.

Where did the name of Mary Magdalene originate? It is derived from Magdala, the Greek form of Migdol or Watchtower. The town of Magdala, from which she came, is identified today as Mejdel, at the south of the Plain of Gennesaret, where the hills reach forth to the lake of Galilee.

We can be confident she was a woman who walked erectly, even to the tomb, one who was young and pretty, well-favored and warm-hearted. The master painters depicted her with auburn hair; a woman beautiful of face and form.

From the Scriptures it is easy to infer that she was one of the influential women of the town of Magdala, who gave of her sub-stance as well as herself to Jesus' ministry, for she had profound gratitude in her heart for His healing of the seven demons with which she had been afflicted (Mark 16:9).

What were these "seven devils"? Some commentators have sug-gested that they indicate a nervous disorder that had recurred seven times. Others describe them as evil spirits from a superhuman cause.

There is a very strong body of contemporary evidence from highly trained and competent missionaries in the Orient and elsewhere show-ing that demon possession exists in the areas known to them and exhibits the same phenomenon as that described in the four Gospels. The Chinese, both educated and uneducated, have distinctive terms for the various patterns of mental disorder, but they distinguish the phenomenon of demon possession from other types of mental dis-order.

Whatever it was that afflicted Mary Magdalene, Jesus had healed her, and she had become His faithful and devoted follower. Into her living death He had come with the power of life, and had taught her victory over her so-called demons. And after His healing, she had become a fully poised woman, one who could watch at the tomb quietly and unafraid.

Since medieval times Mary Magdalene has been one of the most maligned women in the New Testament, largely because some scholars of an earlier period chose to identify her with the unnamed sinful woman of Luke 7:36-50. The first mention of her in Luke

8:2 follows closely upon this account of the sinful woman. But there is positively no way to identify her as Mary Magdalene. These unfair aspersions have become popular, but they are not at all accurate.

Frank S. Mead in his *Who's Who in the Bible* says, "We have had Mary Magdalene in the pillory for 1900 years, flinging mud: we should have been pilloried. This Mary was never a harlot; there is no evidence anywhere for that. At most she was neurotic. And Jesus healed her." The *International Standard Bible Encyclopedia* expresses the opinion that "The identification of this Mary with the sinful woman is, of course, impossible for one who follows closely the course of the narrative with an eye to the transition."

Because of the misinterpretation that Mary Magdalene has suffered at the hands of the few, the *Concise Oxford Dictionary* gives "reformed prostitute" as the meaning of "Magdalene." Painters, since medieval times, have also made the mistake of depicting Mary Magdalene on canvas as the penitent sinner. Some skeptical writers have described her as a paranoic in the habit of "seeing things" and have declared that what she saw at the tomb was not real.

But if we follow the Scriptures fully, we see a Mary Magdalene who displayed the highest qualities of fortitude in moments of anxiety, courage under trying circumstances, love that could not fail, and humility and unselfish devotion to the Saviour who had been crucified. Her faith is a monument to the healing power of Jesus. Her action in serving Him in life and ministering to Him when the mob had turned against Him and had finally left Him in the grave alone is characteristic of woman in Bible history at her best.

The last glimpse of Mary Magdalene as she hastened to the disciples to say "I have seen the Lord" has all the dramatic power of victorious faith. What a magnificent commission hers was, to be a witness to Christ's conquest over death and to be the first to go forth to tell others that she had seen the Lord! No woman ever ran to deliver a more triumphant message.

John makes us realize that Mary Magdalene did not hesitate to do as she had been commanded. She left the grave and forgot her useless spices. A great transformation had taken place in her own being, for she had witnessed a change from the material conception of life to the spiritual, a transformation whereby man was ruled not by the flesh but by the spirit. It is no wonder she could report with firm conviction His words, "I ascend unto my Father," for she knew the true meaning of His deity and divine exaltation.

PILATE'S WIFE

MATT. 27:19

After a dream, on the night of Jesus' arrest, she sends a message to her husband asking him not to condemn this just man, but Pilate is influenced by surging crowds, who cry loudly, "Crucify him."

"HAVE THOU NOTHING TO DO WITH THAT JUST MAN"

A WOMAN with a strong conviction of right and wrong, Pilate's wife has become one of the New Testament's immortals, though only thirty-eight words appear there about her. Her immortality is based upon the fact that she had the courage to testify to Jesus' righteousness and innocence at the time of His trial and approaching crucifixion.

Unfortunately, though she was the governor's wife, her voice was not strong enough to overcome the forces of evil represented by the corrupt priests and elders, who had taken counsel against Jesus to put Him to death.

Pilate's wife had had a dream the night armed men in the employ of the chief priests had arrested Jesus. The hearing before her husband, Pilate, began in the early hours of the next morning.

These thirty-eight words, appearing in Matthew, vividly portray the character of this woman: "When he was set down on the judgment seat, his wife sent unto him, saying, have thou nothing to do with that just man: for I have suffered many things this day in a dream because of him" (Matt. 27:19).

Pilate, the Roman governor of Judaea, received this message from his wife while he was sitting on the judgment seat. Archaeologists believe that the Roman judgment hall was part of the Tower of Antonia erected by Herod the Great and situated in the Upper City of Jerusalem at the northwest of the Temple Hill. It was near the Via Dolorosa or Sorrowful Way, known today as the most famous street in the world.

Though Pilate's wife spent most of her time at their palace at Caesarea Philippi by the sea, she had now come to Jerusalem with her husband for the yearly festival of the Feast of the Passover.

At this time she was probably living in the Herodian Palace at Jerusalem, a luxurious abode with an area large enough to accommodate a hundred guests and furnished and adorned with costly objects, including silver and gold vessels for serving. It had large wings built of white marble and rich, mosaic-paved porticoes with columns of many-colored marble. Through them she could see flashing fountains and luxuriant gardens in which cooed flocks of milk-white doves.

But because this palace commanded a view of the open spaces of Jerusalem, she no doubt had looked out on the streets and seen the multitudes following Jesus. And she had come to appreciate the kindly ministry of this man and to know of the many wonders He had performed.

Tradition says that she leaned toward Judaism and may have been a Jewish proselyte and a secret follower of Jesus. Later Christian tradition has given her the name Claudia Procula, meaning "follower at the gate," though the Bible makes no reference to her other than as Pilate's wife.

With little justification some authorities have identified her with the Claudia mentioned by Paul in II Timothy 4:21, which reads, "Do thy diligence to come before winter. Eubulus greeteth thee, and Pudens, and Linus, and Claudia, and all the brethren." This Claudia no doubt was a Roman Christian.

On the strength of the tradition that Pilate's wife was a follower of Jesus and that her name was Claudia, the Greek Orthodox Church has canonized her and set aside October 27 as her feast day. Ethiopian Christians also pay special honor to her.

The dream she had, which gave her the courage to send a message to her husband, suggests the dream of another Roman woman before a critical day. That was Julius Caesar's wife, Calpurnia, who, having seen her husband before her in a dream, covered with wounds and streaming with blood, entreated him not to leave his house for the Roman Senate on the Ides of March. But he did and was assassinated.

So it was that Pilate's wife also sent a message by a servant imploring her husband not to condemn Jesus. With a woman's delicate intuition she had sensed the approaching evil, and with a wife's concern she had tried to save her husband from his terrible decision to put a just man to death. But the mob had shouted stronger and louder and Pilate was afraid of the mob.

Her intervention caused Pilate to hesitate and once more to give the mob its choice between Jesus and Barabbas, an insurrectionist, murderer, and robber, but they had chosen instead to crucify Jesus.

We can visualize Pilate's wife, a woman who held the highest position in Palestine, as having the step and stature of a queen, but with a nature so tender and gentle that she tried to temper her husband's violence by entering a courageous plea for Jesus. Her decision had come as a result of her dream, where she had awakened to two convictions, that Jesus was an innocent man and that her husband would be inviting disaster if by reason of his authority he should take action against Him.

She was right. Her husband's administration ended abruptly and it has been reported that he was banished to the south of France and ultimately committed suicide.

The brief appearance in the Bible of Pilate's wife has stimulated the imagination of poets and artists alike. And her husband's final emphatic and unhesitating acquittal, "I . . . have found no fault in this man" (Luke 23:14) echoes all too grimly this wife's earnest warning, "Have thou nothing to do with that just man."

CHAPTER 6

Women in the Early Years
of the Church

MARY, MOTHER OF
JAMES AND JOSES

MATT. 27:56, 61
    28:1
MARK 15:40, 47
    16:1
LUKE 24:10
JOHN 19:25

One follows Jesus to the cross and witnesses the Resurrection. The other opens her Jerusalem home to early Christians for prayer.

MARY, MOTHER
OF JOHN MARK

ACTS 12:12

THEY LABORED WITH AND FOR JESUS

APPEARING as it does in fifty-one passages, "Mary" is used more frequently than any other woman's name in the New Testament. In the Old Testament it is not used at all, though the sister

[209]

of Moses and Aaron was named Miriam, which is the old form for Mary.

It is no wonder that the Crusaders brought the name Mary back from the Holy Land, for the New Testament Marys, all six of them, represented love and faithfulness.

There are individual "Searching Studies" on three Marys: Mary, the Mother of Jesus; Mary of Bethany, who anointed Christ; and Mary Magdalene, the first to proclaim the Resurrection. Then we have Mary of Rome, who is mentioned in the "Alphabetical Listing," making the six Bible Marys.

The two Marys which we shall consider here are first Mary the mother of James and Joses, and next Mary the mother of John Mark.

The first-named Mary has often been confused with other women. She is also named as the wife of Cleophas, apparently to be identified as Alphaeus (Matt. 10:3). The two names are variant forms of the same Aramaic original. Cleophas and this Mary were parents of the apostle James the less, who had a brother Joses, the latter being the Greek form of Joseph.

Roman Catholic scholars believe that Joses and the "brethren of the Lord," as well as those called "sisters," were cousins of Jesus and children of this Mary. This theory, however, is not accepted by most Protestant scholars. The former base their belief on the John 19:25 passage, which may be interpreted as stating that Mary the wife of Cleophas was the sister of Jesus' mother. Many Protestant scholars contend that it is unlikely that two sisters in the same family would bear the same name of Mary. They identify "his mother's sister" (John 19:25) as Salome and "Mary the wife of Cleophas" as the mother of James and Joses.

We shall not try to settle such points, which have been a subject of dispute for centuries. But we shall try to picture this Mary who "followed Jesus from Galilee, ministering unto him" (Matt. 27:55, 56), this Mary who "stood by the cross of Jesus" (John 19:25), this Mary who "bought sweet spices, that they might come and anoint him" (Mark 16:1), this Mary who "in the end of the Sabbath, as it began to dawn toward the first day of the week," came "to see the sepulchre" (Matt. 28:1), this Mary "which told these things unto the apostles" (Luke 24:10).

In the First Gospel (Matt. 27:56), she is identified as Mary the mother of James and Joses; in the Second (Mark 15:40) as "the mother of James the less and of Joses"; in the Third (Luke 24:10) as "the mother of James," who was the more distinguished of her two sons; and finally in the Fourth (John 19:25) as "Mary the wife of Cleophas."

This Mary, we are assured, served Jesus in every hour of His greatest need, until finally with those other faithful few she was there when the risen Saviour appeared. We can be sure she was a woman who was generous, faithful, loving, true, and brave.

And we can be sure that she stood for the best type of motherhood, for her sons James and Joses became worthy sons of a worthy mother. James the less, meaning the younger, was one of the apostles of Christ. He has been named as a possible author of the Epistle of James and it is said that he preached in Palestine and Egypt. His brother was Joses.

Following this Mary's certain footprints all the rugged way to the cross and then to the place of burial on the morning of the Resurrection, also the footprints of her sons, who helped to establish the new Church, we know she was a godly woman who embodied all the qualities of the good wife spoken of in Proverbs 31:10-31 and many more besides.

Another Mary with whom we shall concern ourselves here is Mary the mother of John Mark. Only one passage appears about her, but because of it she has come down to us as one of the great women of the New Testament.

Acts 12:12 reads, "And when he had considered the thing, he came to the house of Mary the mother of John, whose surname was Mark; where many were gathered together praying." What greater biography of a woman could be written in twenty-eight short words?

First let us take a look at this mother through her son John Mark, who wrote the Second Gospel and was a co-worker with Paul. Peter referred to him as "Marcus my son" (I Peter 5:13). The name "Marcus" is sometimes used for Mark. Tradition declares that Mark founded the Church in the Jewish-Greek city of Alexandria.

Now let us turn to the home of this Mary, the mother of John Mark. It was said to have been on the south end of the western hill of Mount Zion, a residential section in the time of Jesus. Here may have taken place that overwhelming event known as Pentecost (Acts 2:1).

We can picture this home as commodious, for it appears that Rhoda (Acts 12:13) was only one of the maids of Mary, mother of John Mark. This suggests a household of considerable size. We can assume, too, that Mary was generous, sharing her home with early Christians. She must also have been a woman of some means, one who had real-estate holdings in her own name. At this time she no doubt was a widow.

It was to her home that Peter came after he had escaped from prison, and found the group praying for him. Usually these prayer groups, in the time of the early Church, met in upper rooms reached by an outside stairway leading up from a walled court.

It is enough to know how beloved and consecrated was this Mary, who would shelter a prayer group in her home, a prayer group to which Peter himself would turn after his escape from prison. There is no doubt but that Mary's home was a well-known center of Christian life and worship.

Also, it is evident that this Mary was closely related to Barnabas (Col. 4:10), a prophet and teacher in the primitive church at Jerusalem. She was either the sister or the aunt of Barnabas. As the mother of one of Christ's apostles and aunt or sister of another who worked so faithfully in the early Church, she had distinction enough.

Like the other Marys of the New Testament, she has not a single blot on her character. And, like the mother of James and Joses, she was a great woman. The memorial of these two Marys is an imperishable one, when we know that they, along with the other four Marys of the New Testament, labored with or for Jesus.

SAPPHIRA

ACTS 5:1

This woman and her husband withhold money for themselves that has been dedicated to the common good. When Peter confronts her with her falsehood, she lies to him about it. She falls down dead as had her husband Ananias when he came before Peter three hours earlier.

MONEY BECAME HER GOD

THE love of money was Sapphira's downfall. She and her husband Ananias, members of the early Christian community at Jerusalem, had agreed with others in that community to share all that they had with one another and to contribute to a common treasury to meet the common needs (Acts 2:44, 45; 4:32).

Sapphira and her husband were not forced into such an agreement. They could have withdrawn from the community had they not wanted to meet the requirements of those who believed with one heart and soul. But they had agreed to it voluntarily, and this agreement had become a sacred pledge for the faithful.

Moreover, as Peter clearly stated, it was not required of them that they give up all their property and even after they had sold it the proceeds still belonged to them to share voluntarily with those in need.

But Sapphira could not stand a stern test with money. She, with her husband, desired credit for giving all to the Church without actually doing so. They coveted some of the money for themselves and resorted to dishonesty and untruthfulness to keep it.

The Revised Standard Version states that "A man named Ananias with his wife Sapphira sold a piece of property, and with his wife's knowledge he kept back some of the proceeds, and brought only a part and laid it at the apostle's feet" (Acts 5:1, 2).

What a strong indictment this is of a wife. The phrase "with his wife's knowledge" makes her as guilty as her husband. We might even make a stronger indictment of Sapphira and say that she may have been guiltier than her husband, for it could have been she who chiefly coveted the money. A wife cannot always influence her husband in what is right, but she can try. We have no record that Sapphira even tried. Her husband committed evil entirely with her knowledge, and it would also seem with her support if not at her instigation.

According to early Hebrew records, the name Sapphira means "beautiful." Does this not give us a key to what her character might have been? "A beautiful woman," says Ralph Waldo Emerson, "is a practical poet, taming her savage mate, planting tenderness, hope and eloquence in all whom she approaches." But Sapphira did not choose to live up to her name.

The early meaning of Ananias' name is "Yahweh is gracious." God had been gracious to Ananias in giving him a beautiful wife and in blessing him with land. No doubt he and his wife were among the more affluent members of this early Christian community and were therefore more strongly committed to generosity and honesty than were less conspicuous members.

Let us not forget either that this was a period when there had been a great outpouring of the Holy Spirit. Luke tells us here in Acts that the people "were all filled with the Holy Ghost, and they spake the word of God with boldness" (Acts 4:31). In Acts we find many other references to the activity of the Spirit of God. It had become all powerful in men's minds. We learn of the people receiving it, being filled with it and baptized with it.

Sapphira had had the opportunity to know what this outpouring of the Holy Spirit could mean in the life of a Christian. No doubt she was familiar with the gift of Barnabas, "a good man, and full of the Holy Ghost and of faith" (Acts 11:24). She had seen him give practical expression to his faith in Christ by selling his land and bringing the money and laying it at the apostles' feet (Acts 4:37). And she knew that because of such generous giving there was not a needy person among them (Acts 4:34).

Like Barnabas, Sapphira and Ananias were committed to the same cause. They had dedicated themselves and all they owned to the common good. Like these other Christians Sapphira probably was familiar with Christ's own words, "Ye cannot serve God and mammon" (Matt. 6:24).

She knew that this new Church, now numbering about five thousand (Acts 4:4), was undergoing a stern test in all its responsibilities. She knew that a tremendous conviction of truth had welded these first believers into a great fellowship of heart and soul and that all in this fellowship lived in daily expectation of miracles.

There is the account, for example, appearing a short time before hers of the lame man begging at the Temple gate who was healed by Peter (Acts 3:2-10). All the people knew that this man who had asked for alms had been given much more than he asked for; he also had received a well, strong body, and he had gone forth "walking, and leaping, and praising God" (Acts 3:8). And the people "were filled with wonder and amazement at that which had happened unto him" (Acts 3:10).

Peter, speaking soon after on repentance, had told the people that they must repent if their sins were to be blotted out (Acts 3:19).

He had stressed that they were the children of the covenant of God (Acts 3:25).

Yes, great grace was upon the people, and many were turning away from their iniquities. It was no time to think of how great were one's possessions. It was a time to think of how great was one's faith, how great was one's knowledge of God, and how willing one was to remain true to the covenant with God.

But amid all these noble ideals Sapphira and her husband had become more interested in what they had than in what they were.

When Ananias first handed over the money from the sale of the land to the apostles, Peter's stern question was "Why hath Satan filled thine heart to lie to the Holy Ghost, and to keep back part of the price of the land? . . . Why hast thou conceived this thing in thine heart? thou hast not lied unto men, but unto God" (Acts 5:3, 4).

Ananias had no answer, and he fell dead at Peter's feet. Not knowing what had befallen her husband, Sapphira appeared before Peter three hours later; and when he asked her if the land had been sold for the amount specified by her husband, she answered, "Yea, for so much" (Acts 5:8). In this dishonest answer she revealed herself as a wife who thought it better to conceal her own and her husband's dishonesty than to be honest with the Church and loyal to God.

"How is it that ye have agreed together to tempt the Spirit of the Lord?" (Acts 5:9) Peter now asked her. Then Sapphira fell dead, and the same young men who had carried her husband out when he dropped dead came in and carried her out and buried her beside him.

Sapphira's greatest sin as a member of this early band of Christians was not that she and her husband withheld a part of the proceeds from the sale of their land but that they lied to the Holy Spirit about it (Acts 5:3). When Sapphira had come into the church with her husband when he laid this money from the sale of the land at the apostle's feet, she was pretending to be something she was not. In the eyes of the people there she appeared generous; but in the eyes of God she was a hypocrite. Through Ananias and Sapphira hypocrisy first insinuated itself into the Christian Church.

Probably Peter seemed unreasonably stern in his indictment of Sapphira. One might think he could have given her and her husband another chance, but if the Christian Church was to survive, Peter had to weed out those who would undermine it from within.

Interesting it is to note that in these passages about Sapphira and Ananias the word "church" (Acts 5:11) appears for the first time as a name for the Christian community. Again we begin to understand what an extremely important obligation rested upon Sapphira as a leading member of this first Christian Church.

The sudden death of Sapphira and her husband made others in the Church see what could happen when a husband and a wife became partners in evil and not in truth. They saw that a sin two had arranged was worse than one done singly. Two consciences must be stifled. The people saw, too, that one cannot trifle with truth and go unpunished, that there is no halfway mark with truth, that either you are honest or you are dishonest.

Great fear now came upon the Church and believers came forward in multitudes. From the cities around Jerusalem came many sick folk and many vexed with unclean spirits, and all were healed.

Because of the evil committed by Sapphira and her husband, and also because of what happened to them, a new vow for those who gave themselves wholeheartedly to the Church soon appeared. Scholars intimate that the idea of taking a vow of poverty in the Church was inspired by the incident of the lie of Sapphira and Ananias. Others who came later would not be so tempted to try to serve God and mammon.

DORCAS

(*Also Called Tabitha*)

ACTS 9:36, 39

Sews for the needy at Joppa. When she dies suddenly those she befriended send for Peter and show him garments she made. He sends them away, prays fervently, and raises her from the dead.

A WOMAN FULL OF GOOD WORKS

BENEVOLENT, compassionate, and devout woman that she was, Dorcas gave so generously of herself to others that her name today, almost 2,000 years later, is synonymous with acts of charity.

More than any Bible woman of the early Christian period, she gave new meaning to the wise counsel of Lemuel's mother, who in speaking in praise of the worthy woman said in part, "She seeketh wool and flax, and worketh willingly with her hands." "She stretcheth out her hand to the poor; yea, she reacheth forth her hands to the needy" (Prov. 31:13, 20).

The motivating principle of Dorcas' life is given in six words, "full of good works and almsdeeds" (Acts 9:36). With her sewing needle as her tool and her home as her workshop, she established a service that has reached to the far corners of the earth. We can infer that Dorcas was a woman of affluence. She could have given of her coins only, but she chose to give of herself also.

She lived thirty-four miles northwest of Jerusalem at the port of Joppa, an important Christian center during the years when the new faith was spreading from Jerusalem across the Mediterranean. The picturesque harbor was situated halfway between Mount Carmel and Gaza at the southern end of the fertile plain of Sharon. We can easily visualize her home. In all likelihood it was a mud-brick structure on a "whaleback" ridge above the sandy beach. Let us suppose the house had a large roof guest chamber, reached by an outer stairway. From the roof outside this guest chamber Dorcas could observe Joppa's needy people as they wandered up and down the beach searching for rags swept in by the waters of the sea. To these poor people, without sufficient clothing, good rags washed up on the shore must have been like gold nuggets.

It is easy to suppose that as Dorcas looked from her upper room down upon the shore and watched these destitute people she became stirred with the desire to help them. Out of this first work of hers grew the Dorcas Sewing Societies, now world-wide.

Though the Bible does not record exact details, we can be sure that Dorcas, with her nimble fingers, stitched layettes for babies, made cloaks, robes, sandals, and other wearing apparel for poverty-stricken widows, the sick and the aged. Many of those in need were downcast because they had to wear ill-fitting rags, but once clothed in the well-fitted garments she made for them they went away renewed in spirit.

Needs of the people of Joppa must have seemed perpetual, for in this seaport were many families who depended upon the sea for their living. In wooden boats the men would set forth on the Mediterranean, then called "The Great Sea," and often their boats would be torn to bits when they hit treacherous rocks or were buffeted by the winter storms of the Mediterranean. History records that the bodies of early seamen were often swept into the churning waters and then sometimes back onto the shores at Joppa.

Dorcas had great compassion for the widows and the fatherless, and people loved her because of her magnificent qualities of mind and heart. Her life suggests Paul's message to Timothy, in which he said that women should adorn themselves in "modest apparel, with shame-facedness and sobriety; not with broided hair, or gold, or pearls, or costly array; But (which becometh women professing godliness) with good works" (I Tim. 2:9-10).

Doubtless the people she helped pondered on what would happen to them if she should die. One day, as the people had feared, Dorcas, amid her labors, was seized with illness. Death came suddenly.

Saints in the Church and widows she had befriended made their way to her house, washed her and laid her in the upper room, probably the room where she had made garments for them. After they had given the ceremonial ablutions to their benefactress, they stood about her bier, weeping and planning her burial.

In this age when Peter and other apostles were performing miracles, there were a few who had faith that Dorcas could be raised from the dead. About ten miles from Joppa in the fertile Plain of Sharon was Lydda, where Peter had gone to preach. The disciples sent two men to Peter to ask if he would come to them without delay. The salty, fighting hands of Peter had become the healing hands of a saint, and they believed that he could raise Dorcas from the dead.

He knew perhaps of the good works of this woman of the Christian faith, and he left his preaching at Lydda and hastened on foot to Joppa and to the upper room of Dorcas, where she lay dead. Like Elisha, when he had healed the child of the Shunammite woman, Peter refused to recognize that Dorcas was ready for burial, even though the people stood around her dead body weeping.

Dismissing the weepers, Peter knelt down and prayed over Dorcas. No conflicting doubts or fears disturbed him. In his own mind Peter must have seen Dorcas as well and whole again. Praying fervently, he laid his big hands on the head of the woman. In a positive tone of voice, using the Aramaic form of her name, he said to her, "Tabitha, arise" (Acts 9:40).

After Peter had spoken thus, the Bible says in dramatic but simple words, "And she opened her eyes: and when she saw Peter, she sat up" (Acts 9:40). Then he called the saints and widows and presented Dorcas to them.

We can be sure that the shouts of gratitude to God when Peter "presented her alive" were louder than had been the wails at her death. The people whom Dorcas had befriended sensed a new joy, such as only those who see the dead restored to life can experience. For the woman who had lifted up so many in body and spirit had now been lifted up herself.

Nothing is recorded of Dorcas after her healing, but in all probability her service increased. And those who had witnessed her healing now believed more strongly in God, for they believed that the same God who could lift Dorcas from the dead could also lift them from poverty and squalor.

LYDIA

ACTS 16:14, 40

A seller of purple dye, she lives at Philippi but is native of Thyatira in Asia Minor. She and all her household are baptized by Paul. Her house becomes the first meeting place of Christians in Europe.

FIRST CHRISTIAN CONVERT IN EUROPE

IN LYDIA's home was cradled the church of Philippi, whose members were later referred to by Paul as his "joy and crown" (Phil. 4:1). Lydia was a businesswoman, a "seller of purple," and probably one of the most successful and influential women of Philippi. But more than that, she was a seeker after truth and thus became Europe's first convert.

The old kingdom of Lydia, of which Croesus was the last king, was the region in Asia Minor from which Lydia had come. It had five large cities, Ephesus, Smyrna, Sardis, Philadelphia and Thyatira, all located on or near the chief rivers and connected with coastal cities by good roads. The Lydian market, as it was called, had enjoyed for generations a wide and valuable trade throughout the Graeco-Roman world. This woman evidently was so closely allied with her old environment of Lydia that her personal name was actually that of her native province.

Though in her era she no doubt represented the "new woman," that is, the businesswoman who had succeeded well, she later came to represent what was more significant, the new convert to the faith of Christ. Her conversion to Christianity probably came somewhere between 50 and 60 A.D.

Because of her unique place as the first Christian convert in Europe, Lydia remains a sacred memory, even today, almost twenty centuries since she walked about the streets of Philippi selling her purple. This may have been either purple-dyed textiles or a secretion of a species of murex or mollusk from which a purple dye can be made.

Lydia was evidently a woman of determination, foresight, and generosity and had a personal charm that drew people to her. We can imagine her as a radiant woman with brunet coloring. Perhaps she wore purple well herself and dressed in it often as she made her way through the streets of Philippi.

Though a native of Thyatira of western Asia Minor, Lydia now conducted her business at Philippi, a city of eastern Macedonia on the great east-west Egnation Highway between Rome and Asia. You can almost hear the tramp of the Roman legions, with the infantry on foot and the cavalry complement on prancing horses, as they made their way along a highway that led probably past Lydia's house and through the Pangaean mountain range.

It was to these mountains that Lydia and other women in the first little group of worshipers, described by Paul in Acts 16:13, lifted their eyes. They met, we are told, on the river bank at Philippi. That river was the Gangites (the modern Angista), and its banks offered peace and quiet away from the populous hill section of the city.

Here on the Sabbath, came Paul and his companion Silas. The latter had come with Paul from Troas after he had had a vision to go over into Macedonia. It can be assumed that this little prayer group of which Lydia was a member had asked for guidance, and Paul had been sent to them for a great purpose, because they were receptive to the truth. Though small in number, they were strong in the Spirit of God.

Paul tells us that he and Silas sat down and spoke to the women gathered there. The outstanding woman among them was this businesswoman Lydia, a Gentile, who worshiped the one God of the Jews, while all about her the Gentiles were worshiping other gods. Because of her great longing to know better the wonders and powers of the one God, Lydia was in this place of prayer on the Sabbath.

Next the writer of this part of Acts, who may have been with Paul in Philippi, tells us that Lydia "heard us." She and the other women must have been startled to see two strange men appear there by the banks of the river. But they, whose souls "thirsteth for God" (Ps. 42:2), saw in the faces of these men a new light.

They listened to Paul as he related his story of the new gospel proclaimed in Jerusalem by Jesus Christ and now spreading westward into Macedonia. As Lydia listened, we are told in Acts, the Lord opened her heart and "she attended unto the things which were spoken of Paul." What a fervency of spirit, what deep humility, what keen foresight, what indomitable courage it took on Lydia's part to accept the story of this new gospel.

Soon afterward she was baptized and then her household was baptized. She made her decision to be a true Christian without hesitation. She did not think of how it might affect her business if she accepted this new faith. Her customers of the purple cloth or dye would probably have scoffed at the gospel of Christ, but Lydia did not wait to see. She put Christ first, and business afterward, and went forward and was baptized, as were members of her household.

We are not told whether these who were baptized were members of her family or those connected with her in business. They may have included both. In any case, they respected the good judgment of Lydia and were willing to follow her lead, for they recognized in her the ability to choose the right and good course.

After the baptism Lydia humbly spoke to Paul, "If ye have judged me to be faithful to the Lord, come into my house, and abide there" (Acts 16:15). Lydia desired with all her heart to know more about the new truth of Christ, and she knew she could receive it best from Paul, who had carried the gospel from Jerusalem into Macedonia. Not only did she invite Paul and Silas to come to her house, but Paul tells us that she "constrained us," that is, she overcame their reluctance and insisted that they share her hospitality. In the quiet of Lydia's house we can picture Paul spending many hours each day teaching new converts who came to him there.

Apparently Luke, and probably Timothy also were guests of Lydia. Wonderful it is to think that a woman as successful as Lydia would take the time to be hospitable to this group of Christian missionaries. Yet she seems to have carried on successfully her business as a "seller of purple."

It is interesting to note that the purple was made from the juice of a certain shellfish and was perfectly white while still in the veins of the fish, but when exposed to the rays of the sun took on many hues, ranging all the way from purple blues to crimson.

In all probability Lydia's customers included Babylonian buyers who bought the purple for temple curtains and for costumes in which to dress their idols. Among her other customers no doubt were members of the Roman imperial family, who wore the imperial purple on state occasions.

We can be sure Lydia belonged to an important group, the Dyers' Guild. An old inscription bearing those words has been discovered in ruins at Thyatira, and probably Lydia, trained in the craft of dyeing at her old home in Thyatira, took her knowledge with her to Philippi.

The Bible does not say whether she was married or not, but it is easy to suppose she was a widow, who devoted herself whole-heartedly to her business. But after Paul had come to Philippi, she had a new objective, and that was to learn more about the things of the spirit.

After she had found the truth for which she had been searching, Lydia was beset with fears no longer. She even opened her doors to Paul and Silas after they came out of prison, where they had been sent when Paul had healed "a certain damsel possessed with a spirit of divination" (Acts 16:16). Paul had rescued this demented girl from men who had been exploiting her as a soothsayer for gain. He restored her to her right mind, and her masters were so furious over their loss of her earnings that they dragged Paul and Silas into the market place. There they lodged a complaint against these new Christians and had them stripped, beaten, and cast into prison.

But Paul and Silas, fearless Christians that they were, prayed and sang in prison, and there followed a great earthquake, which opened prison doors and loosed the hands of all who were imprisoned. The keeper of the prison was so moved at these wonders that he became a convert to the new faith inside the prison walls before Paul and Silas made their departure.

After being released, they headed straight for Lydia's house. Lights, we can imagine, never gleamed so brightly as they did that first night, when other new Christians, we can suppose, gathered to hear Paul and Silas tell that an earthquake had opened the doors of the prison.

Lydia and her group had surely prayed for Paul and Silas, just as Mary, mother of John Mark, and her group had prayed for Peter while he was in prison. Lydia and these other Christians believed that they, too, would hear Paul's knock at the door, just as Rhoda had heard Peter's. That door of Lydia's house would always be open now to Christians, no matter how great their persecutions.

Because her home was a haven for Christians and because she became a great spiritual leader who helped Paul spread the Christian gospel, it would never die on these new shores. Later Paul wrote his Epistle to the Philippians, who were the same little band Lydia had helped to organize. And he said, "I thank my God upon every remembrance of you, always in every prayer of mine for you all making request with joy, for your fellowship in the gospel from the first day until now" (Phil. 1:3-5).

We can hear Lydia's little group rejoicing as they read Paul's exhortation to them to think on whatsoever things are honest, just, pure, lovely, and of good report (Phil. 4:8). We can see them gaining new strength as they read Paul's words, "I can do all things through Christ which strengtheneth me" (Phil. 4:13). These early converts at Philippi would never fear tomorrow so long as they could carry in their hearts another of Paul's messages to them: "God shall supply all your need according to his riches in glory by Christ Jesus" (Phil. 4:19).

We have no doubt that Lydia, the first to be converted, the first to be baptized, the first to open her house at Philippi, was among the most receptive to Paul's Epistle to the Philippians.

She will ever stand among the immortal women of the Bible, for she picked up that first torch from Paul at Philippi and carried it steadfastly. She was one of many to spread the gospel of Jesus Christ through Europe and then farther and farther westward, and it became brighter as the centuries unfolded.

PRISCILLA

(*Also Called Prisca*)

ACTS 18:2, 18, 26
ROM. 16:3
I COR. 16:19
II TIM. 4:19

She and her husband, Aquila, are tent-makers and teachers. Paul stays with them at Corinth. She teaches Apollos and becomes a great leader both at Corinth and Ephesus and later at Rome. In latter two places she has a church in her home.

A LEADER IN THE NEW TESTAMENT CHURCH

ONE of the most influential women in the New Testament Church was Priscilla, a Jewess who had come out of Italy with her husband Aquila, to live first at Corinth and about eighteen months later at Ephesus. They had left Rome at the time when Claudius, in his cruel and unjust edict, had expelled all Jews.

Her prominence is evidenced by many facts. She became the teacher of the eloquent and learned Apollos. The church assembled in her home, both at Ephesus and at Rome, and she was known throughout Christendom in her day. Though she and her husband "labored together," in three out of five places her name appears first, evidence enough that she played the more important part in the early Christian Church.

No doubt she was a woman of studious and religious endowments, also one of practical ability. It is recorded that she and her husband were tent-makers, and their home, in the weaving sections of Corinth and Ephesus, became a rendezvous for those wanting to know more about the new faith.

Because Paul also was a tent-maker, we can picture them weaving the goats'-hair cloth and talking over the new Christian gospel as they worked. And we know that both Priscilla and Aquila were responsive to this wonderful new message. When Paul departed from Corinth and embarked for Syria, they were with him. They came to Ephesus, and he left them there. (Acts 18:18, 19). After Paul had entered into the synagogue and reasoned with the Jews, and had again set sail for Syria, he committed the work in Ephesus to Priscilla and Aquila. When Paul returned a year or more later, he found they had established a well-organized congregation in Ephesus. There Priscilla and Aquila ranked next to Paul and Timothy in the work of the congregation.

Later Paul wrote his first letter to the Corinthians from Ephesus and sent greetings from Aquila and Prisca, "with the church that is in their house" (I Cor. 16:19). Is this not evidence enough that Priscilla presided over a devout, peaceful home, to which Christians came and were uplifted?

In his solemn charge to Timothy, a second time Paul, before his approaching martyrdom, sends salutations to Priscilla and Aquila (II Tim. 4:19). Later, after the death of Claudius, we find that Aquila and Priscilla returned to Rome. In writing Priscilla's name here, this last time, Paul used the diminutive Prisca, signifying his intimate friendship for her. The affection she and her husband had for him is manifested in those lines in which he said they had for his life "laid down their own necks" (Rom. 16:4), and unto them he gladly rendered thanks.

An amazing aspect of Priscilla's life was that, though she had to manage her household and weave tent cloth, she found time to be a thorough student of the gospel of Jesus Christ. One of her first services was not only to teach but to "expound" to the eloquent Apollos, a man well versed in the Old Testament Scriptures. Introduced to the Christian religion first by John the Baptist, Apollos had come to Ephesus to speak.

PRISCILLA

Priscilla and Aquila probably were the first to recognize that Apollos had only a superficial knowledge of the new Christian faith, and so they "expounded unto him the way of God more perfectly" (Acts 18:26).

Priscilla was doubtless wise enough to realize that Apollos' limited knowledge could hurt the Christian cause. No superficial convert herself, she was determined that this eminent man should be a well-informed, inspiring exponent of the gospel. What a great privilege was hers, to expound "the way of God more perfectly." Noted for her hospitality, she may have invited Apollos to stay in her home, for we have the phrase Priscilla and Aquila took Apollos "unto them."

We can be sure that Priscilla was not only a woman of scholarly attainments but one willing to make many sacrifices in the spreading of the gospel, for she lived at a time when a Christian faced great persecution. But Priscilla was not afraid. Many honors have been heaped upon her by early Christian writers. It was suggested that Priscilla was the author of Hebrews, but this suggestion is not supported by proof.

Historical facts, not recorded in the Bible, attest to Priscilla's fame. Tertullias records, "By the holy Prisca, the gospel is preached." One of the oldest catacombs of Rome—the Coemeterium Priscilla, was named in her honor. And a church, "Titulus St. Prisca," was erected on the Aventine in Rome. It bore the inscription "Titulus Aquila et Prisca." Prisca's name appears often on monuments of Rome. And "Acts of St. Prisca" was a legendary writing popular in the tenth century.

All of this helps us to know why writers in the New Testament broke all conventionalities and three times out of five placed Priscilla's name before that of her husband. Christians honor her because she served God "acceptably with reverence and godly fear" (Heb. 12:28), and because she was not "forgetful to entertain strangers: for thereby some have entertained angels unawares" (Heb. 13:2). Priscilla, let us not forget either, had entertained the stranger

Paul and from him had learned to strive to be "perfect in every good work. . . , working in you that which is wellpleasing in his sight, through Christ Jesus" (Heb. 13:21).

PHEBE

ROM. 16:1-2

Described by Paul as "our sister, . . . a servant of the church" and "a succourer of many, and of myself also."

A DEACONESS AT CENCHREA

PAUL introduces Phebe presumably as the bearer of his epistle to the Romans. At that time the imperial post of Rome was not available for private correspondence, and such an epistle as Paul's would have to be sent by a trusted friend or a private messenger.

How Phebe traveled from her home in Cenchrea, port of Corinth on the Saronic Gulf looking eastward toward Ephesus, there is no record. The fact that Paul left the port of Cenchrea for Ephesus by boat (Acts 18:18) might suggest that Phebe traveled in the same manner, but it is more probable she went overland as far as she could, for that was the preferred manner of travel in those days for a woman. Let us suppose she joined a caravan, traveled northward into Achaia and Macedonia, and then crossed narrow waters that took her into the Roman Empire and its capital.

This would give her the opportunity to stop at many places along the route where Christian churches had been established. To these congregations she would bring greetings and a message directly from Paul.

In choosing Phebe to carry his epistle, Paul conferred a great honor upon her. Up to this time he had not been in Rome, and in sending a personal representative there he had to exercise caution.

To be a Christian at Cenchrea was no easy matter, for ports at this period were extremely wicked places. Phebe is the only Christian woman's name recorded at that place. We can be sure she was a woman with a great and good influence. Probably she had some wealth and position, or she could not have traveled about as she did.

Though Paul describes Phebe in a few brief words, he succeeds in giving us a vivid picture of the kind of woman she was.

First, he calls her "our sister." This was the simple but affectionate designation used for a member of the Christian community in these times.

Second, he calls her "a servant of the church which is at Cenchrea." The word "servant" comes from the Greek *diaconos,* from which our word "deacon" is derived. Many commentators, because of this, have inferred that Phebe was a deaconess. In the early Church much was made of service, little of office, and it was more of an honor to be referred to as a servant than as a deaconess. Dr. Lee Anna Starr in *The Bible Status of Woman* has conjectured that Phebe was a minister, even as were Paul, Timothy, and others.

Third, Paul calls Phebe "a succourer of many." This polite phrase means a great deal. It seems to suggest one who has been the patroness of the unprotected and despised, one who has come to the aid of converts in need, one who has fought the battles of those who were oppressed.

Fourth, Paul adds the phrase that she was a succourer "of myself also." It has been conjectured that Paul might at one time have been ill when he stopped at Cenchrea and that Phebe had ministered to him. She might have mothered him as did the mother of Rufus.

Phebe, we can easily imagine, presided over a hospitable place, where Paul felt at home, as he did at the home of Priscilla and Aquila in Corinth, and as he did at the home of Lydia, while at Philippi. No doubt Phebe's Cenchrea home was the meeting place for early workers in the Church of Christ, as were the homes of Priscilla and Lydia. Surely, too, Phebe devoted herself unstintingly to the ministry of the Church.

When Phebe set out for Rome, she carried Paul's letter, which became a record of all he and others owed her for her great service to them. This obligation was made the basis of an appeal to the Roman Christians to receive her with confidence and respect, and to aid her to the utmost of their power.

An added note of Paul's is that they receive her "as becometh saints" (Rom. 16:2). This suggests the thought of co-operation in the same religious service. It is difficult to decide whether Phebe is to be received as becometh a saint, as she herself would deserve, or in such a manner as would be a matter of course with the Roman Christians if they were what they professed to be. At any rate, Phebe is regarded by Paul as a woman worthy of being in the company of saints.

Whether Phebe laid down her life in Rome, as did Paul and so many of the Christians of her time, we do not know. Whether she turned back to Cenchrea, we do not know either. But we can be sure that her goodness and sympathy, her loyalty and kindness, and her industry and trustworthiness marked her as a woman whose ministry inspired all who came into her presence.

DRUSILLA and BERNICE

ACTS 24:24   ACTS 25:13, 23
                                                            26:30

Both hear Paul when he appears in the judgment hall at Caesarea. But they have lived in such wickedness that they cannot accept Paul's words of righteousness. Drusilla is an adultress and Bernice has consorted with her brother Agrippa.

TWO EVIL SISTERS WHO HELPED CONDEMN PAUL

WHEN Paul was brought a prisoner into the judgment hall at Caesarea and accused unjustly of sedition and profanation of the Temple, important auditors were two shameless sisters, first Drusilla and then Bernice. They stand sharply etched in the Bible, not only because they heard Paul speak but because their worldly lives draw such a sharp contrast to that of the consecrated Paul.

The Bible does not tell us too much about these sisters. Their main record is found in Josephus, and the information that he gives helps us to delineate the role they play in Acts. We learn first that they were daughters of Herod Agrippa I, who has gone down in history as the first royal prosecutor of the Church. They were the great-granddaughters of Herod the Great, who at the time of His birth had sought to destroy the child Jesus. Because of Herod's decree to massacre all the innocents, Mary and Joseph had fled with their child into Egypt. Bernice and Drusilla were nieces of Herod Antipas, who had had John the Baptist beheaded at the request of his wife Herodias and her daughter by another marriage.

History further relates that great hate existed between these two sisters. Drusilla, the younger, was beautiful and was persecuted by

Bernice, who must have been a fascinating woman but a much plainer one.

Acts introduces us first to Drusilla, who at this time was about seventeen years old but mature for her years. At fourteen she had been married to King Aziz of Emesa, but her present husband Felix, procurator of Judaea, had employed a Cypriote magician Atomus to seduce Drusilla from her husband. In defiance of Jewish law, Drusilla, a Jewess, had left her husband to marry Felix, a Gentile, and had come to Caesarea to live with him.

No doubt she already had heard much about Paul, the greatest Christian of this time, who was in bonds in Caesarea. We can easily assume that Drusilla was curious to see Paul; and evidently to please his beautiful young wife, Felix had sent for Paul to come before them in the judgment hall. It was Paul's second appearance before Felix. The first time Paul had explicitly denied the accusations made against him and had demanded that witnesses be produced.

When he came before Felix the second time, Drusilla was with her husband and heard Paul's memorable message "concerning the faith in Christ" (Acts 24:24). What greater privilege could have come to a woman in those times? Yet Drusilla no doubt scoffed at such a message.

After Paul had spoken of faith, he then turned to reason with Drusilla and Felix on righteousness, temperance, and the judgment to come (Acts 24:25). Could he have been speaking of these things because of the corrupt administration of Felix and of his irregular and unlawful marriage with Drusilla?

As he spoke of righteousness, could he have been referring to Drusilla's treatment of her first husband and her willingness to enter into an illegitimate relationship with Felix? When he spoke of temperance could he have been referring to Drusilla's passionate desire for pomp, power, and position? When he spoke of the judgment to come, could he have been warning Drusilla that she would finally pay the price for her scandalous conduct? And she did. One tradition has it that some years later she perished with her son by Felix beneath the lava in the great eruption of Vesuvius when Pompeii was destroyed.

Felix, even less responsible than his wife Drusilla, trembled and dismissed Paul, saying, "Go thy way for this time; when I have a convenient season, I will call for thee" (Acts 24:25). And Luke tells us in the next verse that Felix "hoped also that money should have been given him of Paul, that he might loose him."

We can picture Drusilla, a lover of pomp and glory, departing from the judgment hall in her regal attire and sparkling jewels. A woman proud of her husband's position, she held her head high as she marched beside her Roman procurator husband in his royal purple.

Probably Drusilla had lightly dismissed from her mind Paul's words on faith in Jesus Christ as the foolish belief of a religious fanatic. In her heart she now hated Paul, a man of high and holy standards, for he had made her more conscious of her own sins and she had no intention of doing anything about them.

The time of power for Drusilla and Felix was short. Two years later we find that he was succeeded by a new procurator, Festus. Drusilla and her husband went the way of many who abuse their power. They lost it and are never mentioned again in Bible history.

But Paul, though a prisoner, is a greater power than ever at Caesarea and of course he is a power for good. He has come to plead his case again, this time before Drusilla's even more evil elder sister Bernice. The latter had come from Rome with her brother Agrippa II to make an official call upon the new procurator Festus.

There must have been much gossip in Caesarea about Bernice, for in Rome she had been known largely for her incestuous conduct. She had been married first to her uncle Herod of Chalcis. After his death she had gone about publicly with her brother so frequently that she probably was one of the most talked about women at the Roman court.

[235]

So it was, as the official consort of her brother, Agrippa II, that she now sat as an auditor when Paul appeared once more in the praetorium at Caesarea. Like her sister—and all the Herods for that matter—Bernice was fond of show. We can see her entering with great pomp and making her way to a gilded chair beside her brother. And of course she would be wearing her most regal brocades and her finest jewels.

Like her sister, she would perhaps be curious to see Paul, a man so different from the men she had known. No doubt she had heard that the one charge against Paul was based upon "one Jesus, which was dead, whom Paul affirmed to be alive" (Acts 25:19). Clever woman that Bernice was, she probably recalled how close the faith in that one Jesus had been linked with the destinies of her family.

Here she sat, a woman who evidently had great influence over her brother. Probably one word from her might have freed Paul from prison. But did she speak such a word? No. We can almost see her smiling derisively as Festus declared to her brother that all the multitude had cried that Paul "ought not to live any longer" (Acts 25:24). Then she heard Festus further declare that because he had no certain thing to accuse Paul of he had brought him before King Agrippa

There she was with Agrippa throughout the memorable scene when Paul declared his story. She heard his thrilling account of his conversion. She heard his declaration about Christ. She heard him speak of the Resurrection. She heard him declare further that he had been sent by Christ to turn the people "from darkness to light, and from the power of Satan unto God, that they may receive forgiveness of sins, and inheritance among them which are sanctified by faith that is in me" (Acts 26:18).

Again, what a great privilege for a woman to have heard such a memorable message from Paul's own lips. So eloquent was Paul's plea that her brother Agrippa replied, probably ironically, "Almost thou persuadest me to be a Christian" (Acts 26:28).

After this stirring scene, Agrippa the king rose up "and the governor, and Bernice, and they that sat with them" (Acts 26:30). And when they were gone they talked between themselves, saying, "This man doeth nothing worthy of death or of bonds" (Acts 26:31), yet they did nothing to release him from those bonds.

So, like her sister Drusilla, Bernice departed from the judgment hall in all the pomp and ceremony that she loved. For a moment a golden opportunity had been opened to her. She could have gazed into a spiritual realm with this steadfast Christian Paul, but her conception of what it was to be a Christian was too faint and dim.

His declaration may have brought some slumbering thoughts later of a better way of life than any she had witnessed at court, but it did not change Bernice's way of life. She went forth again, history records, continuing the same scandalous relationship with her brother. To hush up this scandal she later married King Ptolemy of Sicily, but after a few years she wearied of him and returned to her brother.

In the spring of A.D. 66, history further tells us, Bernice was in Jerusalem. It was during the Jewish War, and she performed the one redeeming act in her infamous career. She and other leading Jews went before Cestius to complain of the iniquities of the brutal Florus.

She has been depicted as going before him barefooted and with her hair disheveled. But Florus, we are told, paid no attention to the once proud Bernice, and even in her presence he scourged and murdered Jews. Bernice was reaping what she had sown when she had sat watching others unjustly accuse Paul.

Other scandals filled Bernice's life. She became the mistress of Titus while she was in Rome and lived in his palace there before he became emperor. Like her sister, she then disappeared into the obscure pages of history as one of the most shameless women of her time.

But Paul rose up stronger. He preached an even more triumphant message. The epistles he wrote in prison were more profound in doctrine and reached more people than had his earlier writings.

He died a martyr's death at Rome later on, but even in death his triumph was great, for he could declare, "I have fought a good fight, I have finished my course, I have kept the faith" (II Tim. 4:7).

But Bernice and Drusilla never experienced anything but wordly pleasures, for which they paid a heavy price.

They come into Bible history for one reason alone, because they were present and occupied influential positions at the trials of the courageous and earnest Christian, Paul. Though he introduced them to the regenerating power of Christ, they quickly retreated into the darkness of their own sensual and selfish lives.

EUNICE and LOIS

II TIM. 1:5   **II TIM. 1:5**

The careful training given to Timothy by his mother Eunice and his grandmother Lois emphasizes the importance of training in life of a child.

THE MOTHER AND GRANDMOTHER OF TIMOTHY

TIMOTHY the son, Eunice the mother, and Lois the grandmother represent the strongest spiritual trio stemming from the maternal line of any family group in the New Testament. The sublime faith of the mother and grandmother seems to have prepared the son for that greatest of all compliments, which Paul later bestowed when he called him "my dearly beloved son" (II Tim. 1:2).

Only because of the early training that he had received from his mother and grandmother could Timothy earn this fond term from the childless and wifeless Paul. The latter loved Timothy as if he were his own son and spoke of him always with genuine pride.

Only one verse in the Bible gives us an inescapable clue to the character of Timothy's mother Eunice and his grandmother Lois. Paul himself, writing that verse in his second epistle to his apostle Timothy, says, "When I call to remembrance the unfeigned faith that is in thee, which dwelt first in thy grandmother Lois, and thy mother Eunice; and I am persuaded that in thee also" (II Tim. 1:5).

Here is our complete Bible biography of these two women, who stand triumphantly alongside other great women of the New Testament. Their immortality comes entirely through their son and grandson, who was associated with Paul during a longer period than that of his other companions and was with him in both his outward labors and his intimate thoughts. Paul sent Timothy on the most delicate missions and put him over his most important congregations.

Eunice and Lois had prepared him for such responsibilities. Their home was at Lystra, a city in the Roman province of Galatia. Timothy's father was a Greek, while his mother was a Jewess. We do not even have the father's name. Probably he had died during his son's infancy.

No doubt his mother, like the young widow today, had to go forth and earn her living outside her home. Maybe she gleaned as did Ruth. Maybe she wove tents as did Priscilla. Maybe she worked in a dye and textile business, such as Lydia owned. This is supposition, of course. But the conspicuous part that the grandmother played is an indication the mother had to be away from home a great deal. In fact, the word "grandmother" appears in the Bible but once, and that is in connection with Lois. We can be sure she was a believing woman, as are most consecrated grandmothers.

Eunice and Lois seem to step right from the pages of the Bible and tell us that nothing is more important in a mother's life than the early training of her child. No record is given of the conversion to the faith of this mother and grandmother, but such records are not necessary. The imperishable record of their son and grandson is sufficient.

Just suppose Timothy had not had the home training that he received up until the age of fifteen years, when Paul converted him in Lystra in about A.D. 45. On his second visit to Lystra, just after his separation from Barnabas, the hand of providence seemed to lead him to Timothy. Though Paul had lost a brother in Barnabas, he had gained a son in Timothy.

The young Timothy now left his mother and grandmother and went forth with Paul and Silas to preach the gospel. We can imagine the sadness that this mother and grandmother experienced as they bade their beloved Timothy good-by. But like Hannah of old, when she left her young Samuel in the House of the Lord at Shiloh, they could relinquish their earthly affection for Timothy and say also, "I have lent him to the Lord; as long as he liveth he shall be lent to the Lord" (I Sam. 1:28).

We can be sure that Eunice and Lois knew well such stories from the Old Testament, then called the Books of Law and the Prophets, and that they had steeped Timothy in a knowledge of all the great judges, such as Samuel, and the most loved prophets, such as Jeremiah, and also the wisdom in Psalms and Proverbs.

You can almost hear them repeating some of them, such as "Train up a child in the way he should go: and when he is old, he will not depart from it" (Prov. 22:6). Or "She that bare thee shall rejoice" (Prov. 23:25). Another might have been, "I have taught thee in the way of wisdom; I have led thee in right paths" (Prov. 4:11).

Eunice and Lois had sent forth their son Timothy, a man of eminent unselfishness, one who had the capacity for generous devotion, one who was warmhearted and loyal, one with charm and gentleness, one who had tenderness and patience, and one who was willing to sacrifice himself without reservation to the cause of Christ. These were qualities such as only a consecrated mother and grandmother could bestow upon a son.

And Paul knew better than any other that the religious faith of Lois and Eunice had been handed down to Timothy in overflowing measure. Paul best expresses this when he says, "And that from a child thou hast known the holy scriptures, which are able to make thee wise unto salvation through faith which is in Christ Jesus" (II Tim. 3:15). What more lasting memorial could a great apostle bestow indirectly upon a mother and grandmother.

Also Paul wrote to Timothy, "But continue thou in the things which thou hast learned and hast been assured of, knowing of whom thou hast learned them" (II Tim. 3:14). These inspiring words have instilled in Christians everywhere a desire to delve more deeply into the character of Eunice and Lois.

In Paul's epistles to Timothy there are passages which seem to list the qualities of Timothy himself, for example, "But thou, O man of God, flee these things; and follow after righteousness, godliness, faith, love, patience, meekness" (I Tim. 6:11). These seemed to be the qualities trained in him by his mother and grandmother.

They had taught him not only these things but also a right sense of values, and he could understand with Paul, "For the love of money is the root of all evil: which while some coveted after, they have erred from the faith, and pierced themselves through with many sorrows" (I Tim. 6:10).

These words of Paul seem to flow like a clear spring of water as he reminded Timothy of his charge. Paul's words fell on an understanding heart, for at a young age Timothy had been grounded in upright living by his mother Eunice and his grandmother Lois.

Alphabetical Listing
of Named Women

ABI (II Kings 18:2), daughter of Zechariah, wife of Ahaz, and mother of Hezekiah, King of Judah.

Following her name and that of her son is the significant phrase, "And he did that which was right in the sight of the Lord," a phrase repeated often in Kings and Chronicles in the lists of queen-mothers.

It is a credit to Abi that her son removed the high places of sacrifice and broke images, because he trusted in the Lord God of Israel.

Abi's husband, Ahaz, eleventh king of Judah, was a wicked king who despoiled the Temple and set up altars for idol worship. The fact that her son destroyed these sheds some light on the mother's character.

She is called Abijah in II Chronicles 29:1.

ABIAH (I Chron. 2:24), wife of Hezron, who was a grandson of Judah and Tamar and founder of the family of Hezronites. She also was the mother of Ashur and the grandmother of Tekoa, neither of whom bore any special distinction. Probably Abiah's name is mentioned (I Chron. 2:24) largely because of the importance of the Judah-Tamar line, from which Christ is descended.

ABIGAIL 1, widow of Nabal, a drunkard. She became one of David's wives. (See Section I, "Searching Studies.")

ABIGAIL 2 (II Sam. 17:25; I Chron. 2:16, 17), sister of David by the same mother. Also mother of Amasa, at one time commander in David's army. Her husband was Jether, an Ishmaelite. He also is called Ithra. In I Chronicles 2:16 she is called David's sister, along with Zeruiah, while in the other passage she is called the daughter of Nahash. The text has been corrupted, but Nahash probably was another name for Jesse.

Abigail's son Amasa was made captain of the host by Absalom instead of Joab, son of her sister Zeruiah. But Amasa was tardy in his movements, and troops were reluctant to follow him. His cousin Joab smote him while in the act of saluting him.

ABIHAIL 1 (I Chron. 2:29), wife of Abishur, descendant of Hezron of Judah, and mother of Ahban and Molid. Her name bears little significance except to carry through the genealogy of a long line of priests.

ABIHAIL 2 (II Chron. 11:18), daughter of Eliab, David's brother, and wife of Rehoboam. The text, however, leaves some question as to this identity. It all depends upon its interpretation. Abihail could be either a wife of Rehoboam, king of Judah, or the mother of his wife Mahalath. Probably the latter is correct. If so, she was the wife of Jerimoth, a son of David and a daughter of David's eldest brother Eliab. Frequent intermarriage like this was common in David's time.

ABIJAH (II Chron. 29:1), same as Abi, mother of Hezekiah. See Abi.

ABISHAG (I Kings 1:3, 15; 2:17, 21, 22), a maid from the town of Shunem, obtained to minister to King David in his old age. A search was made for a damsel who would be ravishingly beautiful, and Abishag was brought to David in his declining activity to act in the double capacity of nurse and concubine.

In his feebleness she gave to him of her warm, superabundant vitality. In the Septuagint translation we find the phrase, "and let her excite him and lie with him." This was a mode of medical treatment in the East and had been recommended by King David's physicians as a means of increasing his waning vitality.

Abishag was with David when Bath-sheba and Nathan went before him to plead with him to make Solomon king, and could have been an important witness had this intercession of Bath-sheba and Nathan been questioned.

Later, when Adonijah, David's son by Haggith, sought the hand of Abishag in marriage, he appealed to Bath-sheba, queen-mother, for help, hoping she would influence her son Solomon. But the latter saw in this a plot to get the throne. Solomon had Adonijah put to death. His request for Abishag in marriage had cost him his life.

ABITAL (II Sam. 3:4; I Chron. 3:3), one of King David's wives, and mother of Shephatiah, who was born in Hebron. She is one of the six wives of David listed together in II Samuel 3:3, 4, 5. Others are Ahinoam, Abigail, Maacah, Haggith, and Eglah. But David had eight wives in all and concubines. The other wives were Michal and Bath-sheba, and the best known concubine was Abishag, sometimes listed as a wife.

ACHSAH (Josh. 15:16, 17; Judg. 1:12, 13; I Chron. 2:49), daughter of Caleb, prince of the tribe of Judah, who received Hebron as an inheritance for himself and his descendants. He had been one of twelve men sent by Moses to explore the land of Canaan and one of two who kept their faith in the Lord.

After the Israelites had received their portion of inheritance, Caleb declared that the man who should take Kirjath-sepher, or Debir, could have his daughter Achsah as his wife. Evidently she was a beautiful and highly prized daughter and was won by Othniel, probably her father's half-brother. She rode forth to meet him on an ass, and as she came to him, she urged him to ask her father to give him a field.

When her father had given her a southland which was dry, she asked him also for springs of water. Her father gave her the upper and lower springs.

Achsah was not an only child. She had three brothers (I Chron. 4:15), but her father shared with her as he had with his sons.

ADAH 1 (Gen. 4:19, 20, 23), one of two wives of Lamech. Her name in Hebrew means pleasure and beauty, an index probably to her character.

She is the first woman after Eve mentioned by name and the mother of Jabal, founder of nomadic ways, and Jubal, founder of music.

Her name and that of her sister, Zillah, when spoken together form a musical combination. Her story comes in one of the oldest folk songs in the Old Testament, and is often referred to as the "Song of Lamech."

As the two wives of Lamech, Adah and her sister are the first women in the Bible mentioned as being part of a polygamous household.

Adah and her sister also are the first women on record to be told by their husband that he had slain a man in self-defense and that he expected to avenge himself "seventy and sevenfold" (Gen. 4:24).

Interesting it is, too, that she was a part of the first household in the Bible to take part in the development of man from a cultureless existence. As the mother of Jubal, she became the first woman to inspire music, both of harp and organ.

Her husband, a primitive poet, probably tested his first verses out on her and Zillah when he said, "Hear my voice; . . . hearken unto my spech."

Her husband belonged to the seventh generation of the descendants of Eve.

ADAH 2 (Gen. 36:2, 4, 10, 12, 16), one of the Canaanite wives of Esau and probably the same person as Bashemath 1, for she is identified in Genesis 26:34 and 36:2 as the daughter of Elon. She could have been a sister of Bashemath. Though there is some confusion, most authorities are of the opinion that Adah and Bashemath are the same.

Adah was the mother of Eliphaz, Esau's first-born (Gen. 36:15), from whose line came four dukes, Teman, Omar, Zepho, and Kenaz (Gen. 36:15).

She and Esau's other wives were mothers of the Edomites, regarded in the Mosaic Law as brothers of the Israelites. Adah was a cousin of Esau through the Abraham-Hagar line (Gen. 28:9) and became a "grief of mind" to Esau's parents, Isaac and Rebekah.

Adah went with her husband to reside at Mount Seir (Gen. 36:8) when he migrated from the land of Canaan, on account of his brother Jacob, as there was not sufficient pasturage for their numerous herds. There she probably lived in a cave, natural or excavated.

AGAR (Gal. 4:24-25), the Greek name for Sarah's handmaid Hagar. Paul employs the reference allegorically, using Agar and Sarah to represent two covenants. This phrase on Agar appears: "The one from the mount Sinai, which gendereth to bondage, which is Agar. For this Agar is mount Sinai in Arabia, and answereth to Jerusalem which now is, and is in bondage with her children." See Hagar also.

AHINOAM 1 (I Sam. 14:50), wife of Saul, first king of Israel, and daughter of Ahimaaz.

At the time she became first queen of Israel there was neither a palace nor a capital. Since Saul was a military leader, it is easy to suppose that Ahinoam often carried on the home without him, probably near a battlefield.

No doubt she was beset with many problems. When Saul's mind became embittered by his jealousy of David, she probably had to minister to him in what finally led to a mental breakdown, and a probable suicide, for he fell on his own sword.

Ahinoam had one consolation, a noble son Jonathan, whose unselfish friendship for David has become proverbial and who is commemorated in David's Elegy, in which he says the love of Jonathan for him passed the love of women (II Sam. 1:26). Jonathan may have inherited his noble qualities from his mother. Certainly he did not inherit them from his father Saul.

Ahinoam was also the mother of Merab, first promised to David as a wife by Saul, and also of a second daughter Michal, who became

David's first wife. In addition to Jonathan, Ahinoam had two other sons, Ishui and Melchishua.

AHINOAM 2 (I Sam. 25:43; 27:3; 30:5; II Sam. 2:2; 3:2; and I Chron. 3:1), a Jezreelitess, who was one of David's eight wives. After Saul had given Michal, David's first wife, to another, David took Ahinoam for his wife.

She and another wife Abigail, widow of the drunkard Nabal, were captured by the Amalekites at Ziklag, but David and 600 of his men went forth to bring them back. He recovered Ahinoam and also Abigail.

After the death of Saul, David took Ahinoam and Abigail to reside at Hebron. There she probably saw her husband anointed king.

She is the mother of David's son Amnon. This son dishonored Tamar by David's wife Maacah (II Sam. 13:14) and was murdered for this deed by Tamar's half-brother Absalom.

Is Amnon's wickedness an indication of this Ahinoam's character?

AHLAI (I Chron. 2:31), a daughter of Sheshan, a descendant of Pharez, elder son of Judah by Tamar. The text is confused. In I Chronicles 2:31, she is the only one of Sheshan's children who is named, but verse 34 speaks of Sheshan's daughters.

Ahlai's name has little importance except in relationship to Pharez, son of Tamar, who herself appears in Matthew's genealogy of Christ.

AHOLAH (Ezek. 23:4, 5, 36, 44), a feminine name used symbolically by Ezekiel to designate Samaria, the capital of the northern kingdom of Israel, larger than the southern kingdom, of which Jerusalem was the capital. Therefore, Aholah is designated as the elder sister. Her name appears with that of Aholibah, representing Jerusalem. In this allegory the two women are depicted as common harlots, who rival each other in their lewd practices.

In his imagery, Ezekiel makes the point that Aholah (Samaria) went awhoring after the heathen (the Assyrians) and became polluted with their idols. In other words, Aholah (Samaria) committed spiritual adultery.

In using Aholah, the harlot, to symbolize the evil of Samaria, Ezekiel was pointing out that a holy God demanded holiness of his people, that lewdness must cease and there must come in its place a moral and spiritual rebirth which would bring about a better world than that represented by the unholy Aholah (Samaria).

AHOLIBAH (Ezek. 23:4, 11, 22, 36, 44), the name of a whore in Ezekiel's allegory of the two kingdoms of Israel, the northern and southern, which had gone "awhoring" (after idols) of their heathen neighbors.

Aholibah represents Jerusalem, capital of the southern kingdom. Her evil was like that of her lewd sister, Aholah, representing Samaria. Both had gone awhoring after idols, had defiled God's sanctuary and profaned His sabbaths.

Aholibah is vividly portrayed in Ezekiel's imagery. He delivers the message that God would employ the Chaldeans to destroy the princes and priests of Judah for violating their covenants with Him. As the whore Aholibah finally must pay for her unholiness, so must Jerusalem suffer the penalty of turning from God.

AHOLIBAMAH (Gen. 36:2, 5, 14, 18, 25), one of Esau's wives and often regarded as the same as Judith, mentioned in Genesis 26:34. In this passage she is identified as the daughter of Elon the Hittite, but in Genesis 36:2 she is identified as the daughter of Anah, the daughter of Zibeon, and again in 36:25 as the daughter of Anah.

Aholibamah (also spelled in some translations as Oholibamah) is not mentioned under either of these names in the earlier texts of Esau's wives (Gen. 26:34 or 28:9). Various explanations have been made regarding this. Authorities who compiled the *International*

Standard Bible Encyclopedia believe there is some error in the text. The least we can say is that it is most confusing the way it stands.

Aholibamah had three children by Esau, namely, Jeush, Jaalam and Korah, who were born in the land of Canaan (Gen. 36:5). All of these children are referred to as dukes in Genesis 36:18.

Aholibamah was one of several of Esau's wives. She became a mother of the tribe of Edomites, never a righteous people like the Israelites.

ANAH (Gen. 36:2, 14, 18, 25), a daughter of Zibeon and mother of Aholibamah (Oholibamah), one of the wives of Esau. She is the only named mother of any of Esau's wives.

As the mother of Aholibamah, she was grandmother of Esau's children, Jeush, Jaalam and Korah, born in the land of Canaan (Gen. 36:5). We can assume that she was a contemporary with Rebekah, though not a friend, because Rebekah greatly objected to the marriage of her son Esau with the Hittite line, descended from Hagar.

ANNA, first woman to acclaim Christ. (See Section I, "Searching Studies.")

APPHIA (Philemon, verse 2), a Christian of Colossae, ancient Phrygian city, now a part of Turkey. She is thought to have been stoned to death in the reign of Nero.

Since the second century it has been assumed that she was the mother of Archippus and the wife of Philemon, a minister who opened his home to the early Christian Church. (See Harper's *Bible Dictionary* on Philemon.)

Apphia was supposed to have lost her life along with her son and husband and their slave, Onesimus. The latter met Paul in Rome and bore the Epistle of Philemon back to Colossae, and with it a salutation to Apphia and other members of her family.

ASENATH (Gen. 41:45, 50; 46:20), wife of Joseph and daughter of Potipherah, a priest of the great national temple of the sun at On or Heliopolis, seven miles northeast of modern Cairo.

The three times that Asenath's name is mentioned the same phrase appears, "daughter of Potipherah priest of On," "sacred city of the Sun-Worshipers." Priests of On were sages; hence the byword, "the wisdom of the Egyptians" (Acts 7:22).

Among the honors conferred on Joseph by King Pharaoh for interpreting a puzzling dream was the hand of Asenath. He probably thought she would be a factor in helping him forget his own people, the Israelites.

Asenath bore Joseph two sons before the years of famine in Egypt. He gave to both of them Hebrew, not Egyptian, names. The first was Manasseh, meaning "God hath removed me from all my troubles and from my father's house." The second was Ephraim, meaning "God hath made me fruitful in the land of my affliction."

Asenath's Egyptian sons were adopted by her father-in-law Jacob. Upon Ephraim, the younger, he conferred the family blessing.

One tradition says that Asenath renounced her sun-gods and worshiped Jehovah. She is the heroine of a remarkable Jewish and Christian romance that can be traced to the fifth century A.D.

ATARAH (I Chron. 2:26), the second wife of Jerahmeel, grandson of Pharez, also mother of Onam. Though Jerahmeel's first wife had five children, this wife is not named, and Atarah is only among those in a group of introductory genealogies.

ATHALIAH, daughter of Jezebel and Ahab and only ruling queen of Judah. (See Section I, "Searching Studies.")

AZUBAH 1 (I Chron. 2:18, 19), first wife of Caleb, one of the descendants of Judah. By him she had three sons, Jesher, Shobab, and Ardon. When she died he took another wife, Ephrath.

AZUBAH 2 (I Kings 22:42; II Chron. 20:31), daughter of Shilhi, wife of King Asa, third king of Judah and mother of Jehoshaphat.

Evidently she was a godly mother because she belongs in that group of queen-mothers in Kings and Chronicles whose biographies begin, "And his mother's name was," and he did "that which was right in the sight of the Lord" (II Chron. 20:32), emphasizing the importance of the mother in the life of a son.

Her husband King Asa reigned forty years and was regarded as a good king. In all probability this queen wife and mother was a woman who leaned on God, for righteousness seemed to surround her.

BAARA (I Chron. 8:8), one of the wives of Shaharaim, in a long list of introductory genealogies of the sons of Benjamin. She was a Moabitess, whom the Benjaminite took to wife when he went into the land of Moab.

BASHEMATH 1 (Gen. 26:34), the daughter of Elon the Hittite, and the first of two of Esau's wives. In Genesis 36:2 she is called Adah. She became his wife when he was forty years old and turned out to be a "grief of mind" to Esau's parents, Isaac and Rebekah.

Tradition has it that Esau had hunted, eaten, and drunk for years with sons of Elon, his wife's brothers, also had sworn, sacrificed, and vowed to their false gods of the fields and the groves. Having outdone her brothers in his debaucheries, Esau finally had brought Bashemath, a Canaanite, and Judith, daughter of Beeri, another Canaanite, into the covenanted camp of his father.

The record of Bashemath's marriage to Esau comes at a significant place. The next verse begins the story of the blessing and how Jacob obtained it. A long space of years had passed, however, probably about thirty-seven. Esau had had time to repent of his errors and to return to the godly way of life. But he did not. He continued in the path of the godless; and it is probable that this wife was one of the reasons for his turning away from God.

BASHEMATH 2 (Gen. 36:3, 4, 10, 13, 17), a second wife of Esau bearing the name of Bashemath. She was the daughter of Ishmael and sister of Nebajoth and in Genesis 28:9 her name is given as Mahalath. Esau probably married her after his marriage to the first two Hittite wives recorded in Genesis 26:34. This second Bashemath or Mahalath was the mother of Reuel.

BASMATH (I Kings 4:15), a daughter of Solomon, sometimes called Basemeth. She became the wife of Ahimaaz, one of her father's twelve commissary officers.

BATH-SHEBA, wife of David and mother of Solomon. (See Section I, "Searching Studies.")

BATH-SHUA (I Chron. 3:5), same as Bath-sheba, mother of Solomon. It appears with this spelling in only this one place.

BERNICE, who with her brother Agrippa II heard Paul in the judgment hall in Caesarea. (See Section I, "Searching Studies.")

BILHAH (Gen. 29:29; 30:3, 4, 5, 7; 35:22, 25; 37:2; 46:25; I Chron. 7:13), Rachel's handmaid given to her by her father Laban at the time of her marriage with Jacob.

Rachel, being childless while her sister Leah had had four sons, gave her handmaid Bilhah to Jacob for a wife. Bilhah thus became the mother of two of the tribes of Israel. Later Leah followed this example and gave her maid Zilpah to Jacob as a secondary wife.

When Bilhah gave birth to her first son Dan, Rachel said, "God hath judged me, and hath also heard my voice, and hath given me a son" (Gen. 30:6). When the second son Naphtali was born to

Bilhah, Rachel said, "With great wrestlings have I wrestled with my sister, and I have prevailed" (Gen. 30:8).

About twenty years later Bilhah and her sons left Padan-aram, with Jacob, who placed her and her sister and their sons at the front of the caravan.

When Rachel and Leah's father Laban overtook the party to search for his images, he came into the tent of Bilhah but did not find them there, for her mistress Rachel had secreted them in her own saddle-bag.

When the party met Jacob's brother Esau near Shechem, Bilhah and her two sons made obeisance to him, along with other members of Jacob's party.

In Genesis 35:22 it is recorded that "when Israel dwelt in that land, . . . Reuben went and lay with Bilhah his father's concubine: and Israel heard it." This verse appears in the text rather abruptly and may have been dependent upon some local tradition. (See *Interpreter's Bible* on Genesis, p. 742).

Among the descendants of Bilhah's first son Dan was Samson, described as a Danite (Judg. 13:2).

The tribe which descended from Bilhah's second son Naphtali became very large; at the first census in the wilderness its fighting men were 53,400 (Num. 2:29, 30). The territory allotted to them was in north Palestine.

BITHIAH (I Chron. 4:18), daughter of one of the Pharaohs, who married Mered, descendant of Judah. Scholars have been unable to determine whether this Pharaoh was an Egyptian king or a Hebrew who bore the name of Pharaoh. (The name of Bithiah, it is conceded, seems to mean one who has become converted to the worship of God.) This would favor the supposition that as the daughter of an Egyptian king she had been converted to faith in God. The text is somewhat confused, but in all probability Bithiah was a woman of some distinction.

CANDACE (Acts 8:27), a term applied to ruling queens of Meroe, capital of the country that later became the kingdom of Ethiopia, at the junction of the Nile and Atbara. Candace was a hereditary appellation used in the same manner as was the term "Pharaoh," applying to the older Egyptian kings.

This Candace of Acts ruled in Ethiopia in the time of Paul and the evangelist Philip. She is mentioned because the eunuch who had charge of her treasury and went from Meroe to Jerusalem to worship declared that he believed Jesus Christ was the son of God.

Candace's eunuch was baptized by Philip and took back Christ's message to Ethiopia. It is probable that Candace was the first in high circles in Ethiopia to hear the triumphant message of Jesus Christ.

CHLOE (I Cor. 1:11), a woman, apparently of Corinth, in the time of Paul, in whose household were those who told Paul of strife among religious leaders in the early Christian Church, probably at Corinth.

Paul bade those who had disagreed to have no divisions among them, but to be "perfectly joined together in the same mind and in the same judgment" (I Cor. 1:10).

Chloe may have been a Christian or a pagan, and those from her household who went to Paul may have been her close friends or her slaves. That is unimportant. What is important is that members of her household brought to Paul rumors of dissension among these first Christians.

CLAUDIA (II Tim. 4:21), a woman in the Christian Church at Rome, who sent her greetings through Paul to Timothy. Scholars have made several conjectures about this Claudia.

She appears in the same passage with Pudens and Linus. Some scholars are of the opinion that she was a wife of Pudens and a mother of Linus, bishop of Rome, who was mentioned by Irenaeus, Greek Church father, and Eusebius, "father of church history."

Martial, Latin poet born in Spain, but a citizen of Rome from about A.D. 64 to 98, writes in an epigram of Claudia and Pudens. Some scholars conclude that they are identical with the Claudia and Pudens mentioned in Timothy, though others question why the name of Linus comes between them.

H. S. Jacobs, writing in the *International Standard Bible Encyclopedia* (p. 666), says that the Apostolica Constitutions (VII, 21) name Claudia as the mother of Linus. He further comments that a passage in the Agricola by Tacitus, Roman historian, and "an inscription found in Chichester, England, have been used in favor of the further statement that this Claudia was a daughter of a British King, Cogidubnus." But Lightfoot in *The Apostolic Fathers* argues against the theory that Claudia and Pudens were husband and wife and that Linus was their son.

Some authorities, with little justification, have identified this Claudia with Pilate's wife, to whom tradition has given the name of Claudia.

COZBI (Num. 25:15, 18), a Midianitish woman slain at Shittim by Phinehas, son of Eleazar and grandson of Aaron. Phinehas was commended for the act in Psalms 106:30, 31. He thrust a javelin through Cozbi's stomach after Moses had given orders publicly to execute chiefs of the people, guilty of whoredoms in Baal-peor worship.

Cozbi was a princess, daughter of Zur, head of a chief house in Midian. And she had influenced Zimri, son of Salu, prince of a chief house among the Simeonites. Her influence for evil was greater because of her prominence and because she had beguiled a Hebrew of prominence.

At the same time that Phinehas slew her, he also slew Zimri. Together they had entered the camp where the Israelites were worshiping and praying to Yahweh, because of a plague sent down upon them. Phinehas, zealous as he was, believed that his act of doing away with the wicked pair would terminate a plague then raging as a judgment against the idolatries and impurities into which the Midianitish women were leading the Hebrews.

The slaying of Cozbi and her accomplice Zimri is thought to have stayed the plague of whoredom and idolatry with foreign daughters. But 23,000 died from the plague caused by this evil (I Cor. 10:8).

Cozbi's name means deceitful. She is the only woman in the Bible of whom it is written that a javelin was thrust "through her belly" (Num. 25:8).

DAMARIS (Acts 17:34), a woman of Athens, who believed in the message of Paul. That one word "believe" presents a whole sermon in itself. Paul had just preached to the Athenians on Mars Hill, but many of them did not believe, for many were ignorant of God. But Damaris and a man, Dionysius, had the spiritual receptivity to receive Paul's message based on the theme, "For in him we live, and move, and have our being" (Acts 17:28).

Damaris must have been a woman of distinction or she would not have been singled out with Dionysius, one of the judges of the great court.

In all probability she was one of the Hetairai, constituting a highly intellectual class of women who associated with philosophers and statesmen. This may be the reason she was in the audience when Paul delivered his address on Mars Hill.

We learn from Acts 17:18 that he had spoken before certain Epicurean and Stoic philosophers, who "took him, and brought him unto Aeropagus."

Some commentators have suggested that Damaris was the wife of Dionysius; however, this is rather improbable for the Greek wife lived in seclusion. The Hetairai were the only free women in Athens. If Damaris had been a wife, her presence would not have been recognized in that concourse on Mars Hill. If the wife of Dionysius, she would have been, according to oriental custom, mentioned as such. Instead of "a woman named Damaris," we would have "and his wife Damaris." Or more likely still, her name would have been omitted.

DEBORAH 1 (Gen. 35:8), Rebekah's nurse, who had come with her from Mesopotamia to the land of Canaan and had afterwards been taken into the family of Jacob and Rachel. Her death is recorded at Beth-el while the family was on its way from Mesopotamia into the land of Canaan.

Deborah, who evidently was held in great reverence by the family which she had served for two generations, was buried at Beth-el under an oak, the name of which was Allon-bachuth, meaning "terebinth of weeping."

Some scholars (see Zondervan's *Commentary on the Whole Bible*, p. 37, col. 2), suppose Deborah might have attained "the great age of 180." In these early patriarchal families old nurses such as she were honored as foster-mothers.

Commentators have theorized that, had Deborah lived, Rachel also might have lived (see *Interpreter's Bible* on Genesis, p. 739, col. 2). In the very next verses after Deborah's death we learn that Rachel gave birth to Benjamin and died in childbirth (Gen. 35:19).

Humble though Deborah's role was, her place in the life of Jacob's family is not to be underestimated, for not only is her name recorded but she was buried in a place of holy associations.

DEBORAH 2, a "judge" and prophetess, who summoned Barak to undertake the contest with Sisera. She went with the former to the field of battle. (See Section I, "Searching Studies.")

DELILAH, the Philistine woman from the Valley of Sorek who lured Samson to ruin. (See Section I, "Searching Studies.")

DINAH, daughter of Leah and Jacob, who was dishonored by Shechem. (See Section I, "Searching Studies.")

DORCAS, a woman of good deeds, also called Tabitha. Peter raised her from the dead. (See Section I, "Searching Studies.")

DRUSILLA, wife of Felix, Roman procurator at Caesarea when Paul appeared in the judgment hall there. (See Section I, "Searching Studies.")

EGLAH (II Sam. 3:5; I Chron. 3:3), one of David's eight wives, about whom the least is known. She is merely identified as a wife of David and mother of Ithream. There have been many conjectures about her. One is that Eglah is another name for Michal, David's first wife.

ELISABETH, mother of John the Baptist and cousin of Mary, Mother of Jesus. (See Section I, "Searching Studies.")

ELISHEBA (Exod. 6:23), wife of Aaron, first head of the Hebrew priesthood. She became the ancestress of the entire Levitical priesthood.

Elisheba was the daughter of Amminadab and sister of Naashon, prince of the tribe of Judah. She bore Aaron four sons, Nadab, Abihu, Eleazar, and Ithamar. From her latter two sons descended the long line of priests who ministered in the sanctuary and taught the people the law of God. Her other two sons, Nadab and Abihu, offered "strange fire before the Lord, which he commanded them not ... and they died before the Lord" (Lev. 10:1, 2). Probably these sons disobeyed God when they drank strong wine before entering the tabernacle (Lev. 10:9).

But Elisheba's third son Eleazar became chief of the Levites and second only to his father Aaron in authority of the priesthood. After

[261]

his father's death he held his office during the remainder of Moses' life and the leadership of Joshua. Also he played a prominent part in dividing Canaan by lot among the several tribes.

Upon Elisheba's youngest son Ithamar fell the duty of enumerating materials gathered for the tabernacle (Exod. 38:21).

Her name means "God is an oath," a probable indication of her strong belief in God.

EPHAH (I Chron. 2:46), one of the concubines of the Caleb who represented the tribe of Judah as its prince, who counseled Moses in the invasion of the Promised Land, and who received Hebron as an inheritance for himself and his descendants. By Caleb she had three children, Haran, Moza, and Gazez.

EPHRATAH (I Chron. 2:50; 4:4), same as Ephrath.

EPHRATH (I Chron. 2:19), mother of Hur and one of the wives of Caleb, of the Tribe of Judah. She became Caleb's wife after his wife Azubah had died and after his three sons by Jerioth had been born. Ephrath's name appears in a long genealogy, significant to the early Hebrews because they felt that their strength and virtue derived from the line from which they had sprung.

ESTHER, a Jewess, who became the wife of Ahasuerus, king of Persia. (See Section I, "Searching Studies.") She is also called Hadassah.

EUNICE, daughter of Lois and mother of Timothy. (See Section I, "Searching Studies.")

EUODIAS (Phil. 4:2), eminent in the church at Philippi and probably a deaconess. In this Macedonian country where she lived, woman's social position was higher than it was in most parts of the civilized world.

Of her and Syntyche, Paul says, "They labored with me in the gospel." Of all the individuals whose names appear in the Pauline writings, of only one, aside from these two, did Paul say "labored with me in the gospel." That other person was Timothy.

It appears that Euodias and Syntyche did not agree about a matter in the church and Paul entreated them to be of the "same mind in the Lord." Furthermore, he told them to "Rejoice in the Lord alway: and again I say, Rejoice" (Phil. 4:4). Only in this epistle does Paul give special instructions to women who labored with him in the gospel.

We know that Euodias and Syntyche were worthy of help because Paul says of them that their names "are in the book of life," indicating that they were spiritual laborers.

And so it was he entreated others to help bring about a reconciliation between them. Shortly after his words to Euodias and her companion, Paul gave one of his most beautiful messages: "Whatsoever things are true, whatsoever things are honest, whatsoever things are just, whatsoever things are pure, whatsoever things are lovely, whatsoever things are of good report; if there be any virtue, and if there be any praise, think on these things" (Phil. 4:8). Euodias probably brought this message to other women in the early Church.

EVE, the name given by Adam to the first woman. (See Section I, "Searching Studies.")

GOMER (Hos. 1:3), wife or concubine of the prophet Hosea, who became notorious for her infidelity and impurity. She was a daughter of Diblaim (the name means "grape-cakes"), or a daughter of sensuality.

She had three children, first Jezreel, a son, whose name meant "God soweth." Then there was born a daughter Lo-ruhamah, whose name meant "She will not be shown compassion." Finally there was another son, Lo-ammi, whose name signified "Not my people."

Gomer supposedly was a whore, and these children, especially the latter two, were not thought to be Hosea's. Probably Hosea did not find out about her harlotry until either right before or after the birth of their first child, thought to have been Hosea's own. It is questionable whether the other two were his children.

Gomer's story has had many interpretations. Some scholars think that Hosea told this story as the outcome of the sufferings of his own heart; otherwise he could not have written it so effectively. A large number of scholars regard the story as a parable or an allegory. If so, Hosea used the idea of his own marriage relationship with Gomer to picture the relationship of Yahweh to the people of Israel, comparing God to a loving husband and Israel to an unfaithful wife. Israel, like Gomer, had been unfaithful to the true God when it turned to Baal worship.

The last part of the story, dealing with the purchase back of Gomer as a slave from her paramour, has been interpreted by some scholars to mean the spiritual adultery and desolation of Israel following the death of Jeroboam and during the overthrow of Samaria in 722 B.C.

HADASSAH (Esther 2:7), the Hebrew name for Esther, cousin of Mordecai, who became the wife of King Ahasuerus (Xerxes). Many Jewish women's organizations are called Hadassah societies after this woman who saved her people, then refugees in Persia. Out of the story of Hadassah comes the Purim Festival, celebrated the fourteenth and fifteenth of March.

HAGAR (Gen. 16:1, 3, 4, 8, 15, 16; 21:9, 14, 17; 25:12), Sarah's Egyptian handmaid, obtained probably while she and Abraham were in Egypt. The maid became the mother, through Abraham, of Ishmael, from which came the tribe of Ishmaelites, who were nomads of northern Arabia.

When Sarah was 76 years old (according to the way of reckoning time then) and had failed to conceive the heir God had promised, she followed a custom of the times, that of giving her maid Hagar to her husband. And Hagar became the earthly channel for what Sarah thought was the Heir of Promise.

When Hagar had been raised to the place of secondary wife by her mistress, her pride became inflated and she was insolent to Sarah. Her actions caused Sarah to complain to her husband, who told her to do with her maid as she pleased. Upon being reprimanded by Sarah, Hagar fled to the wilderness.

The angel of the Lord found Hagar by a fountain of water and inquired of her what had happened. Hagar announced that she was fleeing from her mistress. The angel then announced to Hagar that she would conceive by Abraham and that her seed would be multiplied for posterity. Hagar's child was born and named Ishmael.

About 14 years later the angel told Abraham that Sarah would bear a son in her old age, and that she would be a mother of nations. This Heir of Promise, Isaac, was born when Hagar's son Ishmael was about 14 years old. Sarah weaned her child when he was about three years of age and celebrated the weaning with a festival. But Hagar and her son Ishmael stood off mocking Sarah's child.

Sarah said to Abraham, "Cast out this bondwoman and her son: for the son of this bondwoman shall not be heir with my son" (Gen. 21:10). Abraham yielded after an angel had told him that Isaac was the son through whom God's promises would be fulfilled.

Early one morning Abraham arose and placed a goatskin of water upon Hagar's shoulder and sent her with Ishmael into the wilderness. After the water was gone, Hagar cast her son under a shrub to die and lifted up her voice and wept.

When God heard Ishmael crying, he told Hagar to fear not, but to arise, for he would make of Ishmael a great nation. Then she opened her eyes and saw a well of water and gave her son a drink.

The child grew and dwelt in the wilderness of Paran. The final account in Genesis states that "his mother took him a wife out of the land of Egypt."

The concluding Biblical record of Hagar is in Galatians 4:24-25, where she is referred to as Agar. Paul speaks of her, a bondwoman, and Sarah, a freewoman, saying: "Which things are an allegory: for these are the two covenants; the one from the mount Sinai, which gendereth to bondage, which is Agar. For this Agar is mount Sinai in Arabia, and answereth to Jerusalem which now is, and is in bondage with her children." The allegory compares the child of the flesh and the child of the spirit.

Many traditions have arisen around the name of Hagar. One is that after Sarah's death Abraham took Hagar for a wife. Abraham's second wife was Keturah, meaning "separation."

Other traditions center around Hagar and Mecca and the holy well of Zem-Zem, in the sacred area surrounding the Kaaba, or holy building. In the cornerstone here is said to be the original Koran of the Mohammedans. At this well Hagar and her son were supposed to have quenched their thirst.

From the Arabs of the Hagar-Abraham line, Mohammed was descended, say Mohammedans. The strength of Islam, still mighty on three continents, is said to be bound up with the name of Hagar.

HAGGITH (II Sam. 3:4; I Kings 1:5, 11; 2:13; I Chron. 3:2), the fifth wife of David and mother of his fourth son Adonijah. In the five places that Haggith is mentioned, it is always as the mother of Adonijah.

Immediately after the name of Haggith in I Kings 1:5, is the passage that Adonijah was a man who "exalted himself, saying, I will be king."

Haggith is mentioned another time when Nathan spoke to Bathsheba, mother of Solomon, saying, "Has thou not heard that Adonijah the son of Haggith doth reign, and David our lord knoweth it not?" (I Kings 1:11). Solomon took this attempt to be a plot to seize the throne, and because of it Haggith's son, Adonijah, was put to death.

Finally, in Chronicles the name of "Haggith, mother of Adonijah" is again recorded. Are not the son's selfish attempts to push himself a reflection of the character of his mother, who has no identity except through her son?

HAMMOLEKETH (I Chron. 7:18), mother of Ishod, Abiezer, and Mahalah. From the line of Abiezer sprang the great judge Gideon. It is thought that Hammoleketh ruled over a portion of the land belonging to Gilead, hence her name, which translated from the Hebrew means a queen of Israel.

This woman lived in the middle of the fourteenth century before Christ and was the daughter of Machir and sister of Gilead, grandson of Manasseh.

HAMUTAL (II Kings 23:31; 24:18; Jer. 52:1), daughter of Jeremiah of Libnah, wife of the godly Josiah, but mother of two ungodly king sons, Jehoahaz and Zedekiah. The former reigned three months, and his tendencies were evil rather than good. The latter reigned eleven years, and neither he nor his people gave heed to the word of God.

The great prophet Jeremiah, in his denunciation of the wickedness of Hamutal's son Zedekiah, placed emphasis on the fact that "his mother's name was Hamutal. . . . And he did that which was evil in the eyes of the Lord" (Jer. 52:1-2).

This mother's first king son Jehoahaz, after being deposed, was taken in chains to Riblah by Necho, king of Egypt, and afterwards into Egypt. Her other king son saw his own sons put to death, had his own eyes put out, was bound in fetters himself and carried to Babylon.

Is the character of these sons a reflection of the mother?

HANNAH, godly mother of Samuel. (See Section I, "Searching Studies.")

HAZELELPONI (I Chron. 4:3), one of those women in the background, merely appearing in the genealogies of Judah. She is identified as the daughter of Etam and the sister of Jezreel, Ishma, and Idbash. She lived in the latter part of the thirteenth century before Christ.

HELAH (I Chron. 4:5, 7), one of two wives of Ashur, father of Tekoa, and mentioned in the posterity of Judah. She had three sons by him, Zereth, Jezoar, and Ethnan.

HEPH-ZIBAH (II Kings 21:1), wife of King Hezekiah, a godly king, and mother of Manasseh, ungodly king, who reigned over Judah fifty-five years, a longer period than that of any king.

Though Heph-zibah's husband had cleansed the Temple, reorganized the religious services and its officers, built water conduits, and made other reforms, her son was an exact opposite in his leadership of the people. He undid the good work of his father and built altars to Baal. The Bible says he did that which was "evil in the sight of the Lord, after the abominations of the heathen" (II Kings 21:2). Though prophets warned him, he continued in his evil ways.

HERODIAS, wife of Herod. She brought about the beheading of John the Baptist. (See Section I, "Searching Studies.")

HODESH (I Chron. 8:9), wife of Shaharaim, a Benjamite. This is probably another name for Baara mentioned in I Chronicles 8:8.

HODIAH (I Chron. 4:19), a question mark with scholars. According to the *International Standard Bible Encyclopedia,* the reference in the passage to "his wife" is wrong. But Young's *Concordance* concedes that Hodiah is the same as Jehudijah (I Chron. 4:18). If so, Hodiah had three sons, Jered, the father of Gedor; Heber, the father of Socho; and Jekuthiel, the father of Zanoah.

HOGLAH, one of Zelophehad's five daughters. (See Section I, "Searching Studies," under "Daughters of Zelophehad.")

HULDAH, a woman in the time of King Josiah, who prophesied. (See Section I, "Searching Studies.")

HUSHIM (I Chron. 8:8, 11), one of the two wives of Shaharaim, a Benjamite who went to Moab.

Hushim, like Ruth, was a Moabitess and by the Benjamite had two sons, Abitub and Elpaal.

ISCAH (Gen. 11:29), a daughter of Abraham's younger brother Haran, and a sister of Lot and Milcah.

JAEL (Judg. 4:17, 18, 21, 22; 5:6, 24), the wife of the Kenite Heber, and slayer of Sisera, Canaanite chieftain of the twelfth century B.C. Her tribe were itinerant metal-smiths. This probably explains the friendly relationship between her husband and Jabin, Canaanite king. Doubtless he had something to do with the making of Jabins' 900 chariots of iron, which Sisera had used in battle.

When the Israelites defeated Sisera at "Taanach by the waters of Megiddo," he fled by foot to save himself. He came to the "oaks of the wanderers," at the foot of Mount Tabor, where the tribe of Heber lived. And when he accepted the invitation to go into Jael's tent, he thought he was with friends or at least a family that was neutral. (Jael's tribe of Kenites were not Israelites, but Midianites, descendants of Moses' father-in-law.)

Jael received Sisera hospitably, and when he asked her for water to quench his thirst she opened a bottle of milk and gave him a drink. Then she covered him.

He asked her to stand in the door of the tent and if any man came inquiring if a man were there to answer "No."

Wearied from battle, Sisera soon fell asleep. While he was in this torpid state, Jael took a workman's hammer and a long tent peg and drove it through Sisera's temple. She then went to meet Barak, the Israelite general, to claim credit for her deed.

Though such a deed violated the ancient code of hospitality, Jael is commended in the ancient Song of Deborah for the murder of Sisera. It is difficult to picture Jael as a rude and coarse woman, though her deed reveals hardness of character. However, it found approval in these ancient times before just and wise laws had been established.

The most striking scene resulting from Jael's murder of Sisera is that of his mother watching for her son to return. But he already had been murdered by Jael.

Jael's act suggests that of Judith in the Apocrypha, who drove a sword through Holofernes' throat as he slept.

The poetic account of Jael's deed, found in Deborah's Song of Victory (Judg. 5:24-27), is a part of one of the oldest Hebrew songs of victory on record, probably antedated only by Miriam's Song of Triumph. A prose account of Jael's deed appears in Judges 4:19-22.

JECHOLIAH (II Kings 15:2; II Chron. 26:3), the wife of Amaziah, king of Judah, who brought back idols of the Edomites and set them up for his gods. Her son was Azariah (or Uzziah), king of Judah.

There is no record of her, except her name and the fact that her son "did that which was right in the sight of the Lord" (II Kings 15:3). In Chronicles we find the significant phrase after this mother's name that her son prospered "as long as he sought the Lord" (II Chron. 26:5).

He developed Judah's agricultural resources, raised a large army, and supplied Jerusalem with military defenses. But then he violated the priestly code and was stricken with leprosy.

JEDIDAH (II Kings 22:1), mother of Josiah, daughter of Adaiah of Boscath, and the wife of Amon. Her husband, a wicked king, was murdered in his palace by servants and succeeded by his eight-year-old son, who ruled Judah well for thirty-one years. In a later part of his reign Josiah ordered the repairing and beautifying of the house of the Lord, during which time was found the Book of the Law, the brilliant work of a group of prophets and priests who had recorded the Yahwistic spiritual ideals. Josiah used these laws as an instrument of reform.

It was probably his mother who guided Josiah during his youthful years and influenced him to be a much better king than were his predecessors. Right after his name and his mother's name again follows the meaningful sentence, "And he did that which was right in the sight of the Lord" (II Kings 22:2).

JEHOADDAN (II Kings 14:2; II Chron. 25:1), wife of Joash, who had been rescued at the age of six by Jehosheba, stepdaughter of Athaliah and wife of the high priest, Jehoiada, when Athaliah had sought to destroy all members of the royal family.

While suffering from a disease, Jehoaddan's husband was slain in his bed. He was then succeeded by their son, Amaziah, who started with a righteous rule but later brought back idols of the Edomites and set them up for his gods. He ruled twenty-nine years and, like his father, was murdered.

JEHOSHEBA (II Kings 11:2), in II Chronicles 22:11 also spelled Jehoshabeath. She was the daughter of King Jehoram by a secondary wife—not Athaliah—a half-sister of King Ahaziah (II Kings 11:2), and wife of the high priest of the lord, Jehoiada, during the reigns of Ahaziah and his mother, Queen Athaliah.

This courageous woman, Jehosheba, stole her nephew Joash from among the king's sons, either from among the corpses, where he lay only injured, or from his nursery. She hid him with his nurse in a bedchamber from the wrath of her stepmother Athaliah.

Such a bedchamber in the East of ancient time probably was a small closet or lumber room into which were flung during the day when not in use, mattresses and other bedding materials spread on the floors or divans of the sitting rooms. This room was thought to be in the Temple for the use of the priests. Jehosheba's husband, the high priest, had full charge over the Temple.

Later Jehosheba kept the little Joash in the main part of the Temple for six years (II Kings 11:3). The hiding of the youth, who was to be eighth king of Judah, is reminiscent of the hiding of Moses by his mother Jochebed and his sister Miriam. In his seventh year the young Joash was brought out by Jehosheba's husband, Jehoiada, before the civil and military leaders and displayed in the court, where he was anointed and crowned king.

He owed his life to his courageous aunt, who had had faith enough to hide him from Queen Athaliah for six years.

JEHUDIJAH (I Chron. 4:18), one of a long genealogical list of names. In the King James Version it reads "And his wife Jehudijah bare Jered the father of Gedor, Heber the father of Socho, and Jekuthiel the father of Zanoah."

In the Revised Standard Version the passage reads, "And his Jewish wife bore. . . ."

The *International Standard Encyclopedia* translates the term Jehudijah, also Hajehudijah, to mean "The Jewess."

JEMIMA (Job 42:14), the eldest of Job's three daughters born after his restoration to health and prosperity. His other sons and daughters had been killed (Job 1:18, 19).

Her name, meaning "daylight," is significant since she was born after her father's great trials.

In all the land, it is related in Job 42:15, were no women found so fair as Jemima and her two sisters, Kezia and Keren-happuch. Their father gave them, along with their brothers, an inheritance, an unusual favor for daughters in these times. According to the Jewish law, daughters inherited if there were no sons. Job showed his integrity as a man and his wisdom as a father in providing justly for his fair daughters.

Jemima's home was "in the land of Uz." She lived in that early patriarchal age, long before Israel became a nation with religious, social, and political organizations.

Though her father was a man of God, her mother is regarded as a woman with an unsympathetic disposition and lacking in spiritual qualities.

See also Kezia and Keren-happuch.

JERIOTH (I Chron. 2:18), a wife or concubine of Caleb, son of Hezron. However, scholars are not of the same opinion about this. J. H. Michaelis regards this as another name for Azubah. One scholar interprets the passage to read, "Caleb begat children of Azubah his wife, Jerioth," while another has it read "Caleb begat children of Azubah his wife, the daughter of Jerioth." The Revised Standard Version has the passage read, "Caleb the son of Hezron had children by his wife Azubah, and by Jerioth."

JERUSHA (II Kings 15:33; II Chron. 27:1), another of the queen-mothers listed in Kings and Chronicles. She was the daughter of Zadok, priest in the time of David, the wife of Uzziah, a leper, and the mother of Jotham. The latter two were kings of Judah.

Reared in a godly household, she probably held before her son high standards and he "did that which was right in the sight of the Lord."

He built "the high gate at the house of the Lord," cities in the mountains of Judah, and castles and towers in the forests. It is recorded that this mother's son "became mighty, because he prepared his ways before the Lord" (II Chron. 27:6).

JEZEBEL 1, daughter of the king of the Zidonians and heathen wife of Ahab, king of Israel. (See Section I, "Searching Studies.")

[273]

JEZEBEL 2 (Rev. 2:20) is, according to most reliable authorities, a symbolic name.

In Thyatira, during the time of the early Christian Church, there may have been a woman by this name, who did not believe in one God. Some scholars conjecture that she was the wife of one of the elders in the early Church.

Because her influence was dangerous among some of the newer and weaker Christians, she might have been referred to as "that woman Jezebel." In her idolatry probably she resembled the wicked Queen Jezebel of Israel.

Calling herself a prophetess, this Jezebel in Revelation sought to seduce people to practice immorality and to eat things sacrificed to idols.

JOANNA (Luke 8:3; 24:10), wife of Chuza, the house-steward of Herod the Tetrarch. In Luke 8:1-3 she appears as one of the certain women who had been healed, either of a sickness or of an evil spirit.

It is thought by some scholars that the centurion mentioned in Matthew 8:5-13 and Luke 7:1-10 might have been Joanna's husband Chuza. If so, she may have been led to attach herself to Jesus through the restoration of her servant's health, or even his life. Consequently she gave of herself and her substance to Jesus and His disciples.

In the last mention of Joanna, in Luke 24:10, she is one of the women who went to the sepulcher to embalm the body of Jesus. She, with Mary Magdalene, the mother of James, and other women, later told the apostles that Christ had arisen.

Though the mention of her is brief, one is convinced of the genuineness of her conversion, the depth of her love for Jesus, and the faithfulness of her stewardship.

The knowledge she gained as she accompanied Jesus and His disciples and other women on preaching tours, gives her a firm place in this missionary group.

Her husband, as head of Herod the Tetrarch's household, also had charge of his personal estate. Some scholars venture that he was the nobleman of John 4:46-53.

JOCHEBED, mother of Moses, Miriam, and Aaron. (See Section I, "Searching Studies.")

JUDAH (Jer. 3:7, 8, 10), an allegorical reference to the country of Judah. Three times Jeremiah refers to "her treacherous sister Judah."

JUDITH (Gen. 26:34), the daughter of Beeri and one of the Hittite wives of Esau, who grieved and vexed Isaac and Rebekah, Esau's parents. They grieved because their son had married a foreign woman and not one of their own people.

Some authorities are of the opinion that Judith is the same as Aholibamah (Oholibamah) mentioned in Genesis 36:5, but other authorities do not agree with this. If so, she had three children by Esau—Jeush, Jaalam, and Korah—who were born in the land of Canaan.

Esau's marriage at age forty to this woman from a land that worshiped idols is said to have been one of the reasons why Esau, though the elder son of Isaac and Rebekah, lost the blessing to his twin brother Jacob, born second and regarded as the younger. The account of the loss of the blessing of his father Isaac appears immediately after Esau's marriage to his Hittite wives. The marriage comes in Genesis 26:34, and the loss of the birthright in Genesis 27:1.

Because Judith did not worship the one God, she did not occupy as high a place in patriarchal history as did her sisters-in-law, Rachel and Leah, Jacob's wives.

The Bible shows that Esau, though born into a godly family, turned to the more material path, and that his Hittite wives led him completely away from God.

JULIA (Rom. 16:15), one of the early Christian women in Rome, to whom Paul sent salutations. He referred to her and others, concluding his salutations with the phrase, "and all the saints with them," making us know that Julia was a saintly woman, if we may judge by the friends with which she surrounded herself in the early Christian Church of Rome.

KEREN-HAPPUCH (Job 42:14), Job's third daughter, whose name meant "horn of antimony," an eye paint that was used as a beautifier by oriental women, to make their eyes large and lustrous. She was born after her father's great trials, when his wealth, health, and honor had been restored.

Her mother's name is not recorded. We only know her as Job's wife, one who urged her husband, in the midst of his trials, "to curse God and die."

Keren-happuch's story appears in a book of the Bible known not only for its spiritual but for its literary heights.

Like her two sisters, Keren-happuch inherited property from her father, as did also her two brothers. This was unusual in these early times, when the inheritances usually went only to the sons.

Keren-happuch and the sisters, Kezia and Jemima, were regarded as their father's crowning blessing after all of his trials.

KETURAH (Gen. 25:1, 4; I Chron. 1:32, 33), second wife of Abraham, after the death of his beloved Sarah. Six sons were born to Keturah and Abraham: Zimran, Jokshan, Medan, Midian, Ishbak, and Shuah. From these sons descended six Arabian tribes of southern and eastern Palestine. The best-known tribe bearing the name of one of Keturah's children were the Midianites. We come upon them first as camel-riding merchants traveling from Gideon to Egypt with gum, balm, and myrrh. These same Midianites sold Joseph to the Ishmaelites for twenty sheckels of silver.

Keturah's sons were not joint heirs with Sarah's son Isaac, who received his father's blessing and became heir to all his large holdings. In order that they might not interfere with Isaac, legitimate Son of Promise, Abraham made special gifts to his younger sons by Keturah and sent them away, just as he had sent Ishmael away.

KEZIA (Job 42:14), second daughter of Job. She is sometimes referred to also as "Cassia," a word linked with the fragrance of a flower. She and her sisters, Jemima, the elder, and Keren-happuch, the younger, were born after their father's great afflictions.

She lived in a far-off patriarchal age when life was much like that described in the Book of Genesis. Relationships between people were both elemental and primitive.

Like her two sisters, Kezia inherited land and property at her father's death, along with her brothers (Job 42:15).

Scripture says, "And in all the land were no women found so fair as the daughters of Job" (Job 42:15).

See Jemima and Keren-happuch also.

LEAH, sister of Rachel and wife of Jacob. (See Section I, "Searching Studies.")

LOIS, grandmother of Timothy. (See Section I, "Searching Studies," on Eunice and Lois.)

LO-RUHAMAH (Hos. 1:6, 8), daughter of Gomer, whose name literally means, "she will not be shown compassion." She was thought to have been born of adultery while Gomer was married to the prophet Hosea. Following the story of her birth is the phrase, "For I will no more have mercy upon the house of Israel."

Most scholars concede that this is an allegory and that the Lo-ruhamah illustration signifies that God would not have mercy on Israel but would utterly destroy her.

LYDIA, businesswoman of Philippi and the first Christian convert in Europe. (See Section I, "Searching Studies.")

MAACAH, same as Maachah.

MAACHAH 1 (Gen. 22:24), daughter of Abraham's brother Nahor by his concubine Reumah, and one of the first-named women in the Bible.

Young's *Concordance* identifies this Maachah as a son, but the *International Standard Bible Encyclopedia* refers to the name as that of a daughter.

MAACHAH 2 (II Sam. 3:3; I Chron. 3:2), a daughter of Talmai, king of Geshur, and one of David's eight wives and mother of his beloved son Absalom, born when David was at Hebron. She was also the mother of David's daughter Tamar.

Little else is known about Maachah except through her son Absalom, who killed his half-brother Ammon to avenge the ruined honor of Tamar.

Maachah's son Absalom was of faultless form and had extremely beautiful long hair, so thick that it later cost him his life. He was riding upon a mule, and when the mule went under the thick bows of a great tree his hair caught in the limbs, and he was left hanging by his long hair, of which he was proud. Though he had organized a plot to seize the throne from his father, David had given orders that Absalom was not to be injured. But three darts were shot through him as he hung by his hair, helpless.

When David heard of the death of this son by Maachah, he said, "O my son Absalom, my son, my son Absalom! would God I had died for thee, O Absalom, my son, my son!" (II Sam. 18:33). See also Tamar 2.

MAACHAH 3 (I Kings 15:2; II Chron. 11:20, 21, 22), daughter or granddaughter of Absalom, no doubt named for his own mother Maachah, and probably a woman of great beauty and charm.

She was a wife of King Rehoboam, successor to his father King

Solomon. And he loved her above all his wives and concubines. This was a great distinction, for he had seventy-eight official and unofficial wives, which meant keen competition for his favor. All who came to court probably sought the good will of Queen Maachah, for she would have the ear of the king on important matters.

Though Queen Maachah had power, she did not exercise it for good. Her husband's reign was marked by apostasy and calamity. Rehoboam "forsook the law of the Lord, and all Israel with him."

Though her husband had twenty-eight sons and sixty daughters by his seventy-eight wives and concubines, he made her son Abijah his successor. Evidence shows that the hands that held the reins of government were none other than those of Maachah, his favorite wife.

Like father, like son. Her son "walked in all the sins of his father, which he had done before him: and his heart was not perfect with the Lord his God."

It is quite evident that Maachah never came to love God and remained an idol worshiper to the end of her life, influencing both her husband and her son to worship idols instead of God.

MAACHAH 4 (I Kings 15:10, 13; II Chron. 15:16), mother of Asa, though some authorities say she was his grandmother and thus identical with Maachah 3, above (see Harper's *Bible Dictionary* on Asa, p. 45). As queen-mother she erected an image for an Asherah (pagan goddess). Asa, third king of Judah, removed her as queen. He destroyed her idol in a grove and burned it by the brook of Kidron.

She is called Michaiah in II Chronicles 13:2, but this is probably a textual corruption (see *Westminster Dictionary of the Bible*).

There is some confusion in the text on Maachah 3 and Maachah 4. Josephus (*Antiquities* VIII 10.1) says that Maachah was the granddaughter of Absalom and that her mother was Tamar. The Septuagint says that Asa's mother was named Ana, but there is little support for this.

MAACHAH 5 (I Chron. 2:48), one of Caleb's concubines. Her children were Sheber, Tirhanah, Shaaph and Sheva. She probably was the mother of Caleb's daughter Achsah, though the text is a bit obscure on this point. This Maachah is one of several of the concubines of Caleb, who was made a descendant of Judah through his father Hezron.

MAACHAH 6 (I Chron. 7:15, 16), the wife of Machir and mother of Peresh and Sheresh. She also was a daughter-in-law of Manasseh, son of Joseph.

MAACHAH 7 (I Chron. 8:29; 9:35), wife of Jehiel, "father" of Gibeon, and an ancestress of King Saul.

MAHALAH (I Chron. 7:18), daughter of Hammoleketh. She is identified as a granddaughter of Manasseh, Joseph's first-born.

MAHALATH 1 (Gen. 28:9), one of the wives of Esau, a daughter of Ishmael and sister of Nebajoth. Mahalath seems to bear no connection with the first two of Esau's wives, mentioned in Genesis 26:34. One of these was Judith, daughter of Beeri the Hittite, and the other, Bashemath, was the daughter of Elon the Hittite. Mahalath is clearly identified in Genesis 28:9 as the daughter of Ishmael, son of Hagar, secondary wife of Abraham. Esau took this wife from his father's family when he saw that his foreign wives were not pleasing to his father Isaac and his mother Rebekah.

There is some confusion about the names of Esau's three wives. In Genesis 36:2, 3 Judith is called Aholibamah, Bashemath is called Adah, and Mahalath is called Bashemath.

MAHALATH 2 (II Chron. 11:18), granddaughter of David and one of the eighteen wives of King Rehoboam. He also had sixty concubines.

MAHLAH (Num. 26:33; 27:1; 36:11; Josh. 17:3), one of five daughters of Zelophehad. (See Section I, "Searching Studies," "Daughters of Zelophehad.")

MARA (Ruth 1:20)—meaning "bitterness"—another name for Naomi. Coming back to her native Beth-lehem from Moab, Naomi said, "Call me not Naomi, call me Mara: for the Almighty hath dealt very bitterly with me. I went out full, and the Lord hath brought me home again empty."

MARTHA, the woman to whom Jesus first declared "I am the resurrection, and the life." (See Section I, "Searching Studies.")

MARY 1, Mother of Jesus. (See Section I, "Searching Studies.")

MARY MAGDALENE 2, first to report to the disciples the miracle of the Resurrection. (See Section I, "Searching Studies.")

MARY OF BETHANY 3, sister of Martha and Lazarus. (See Section I, "Searching Studies," "Martha and Mary.")

MARY 4, wife of Cleophas, mother of James and Joses. (See Section I, "Searching Studies," "Mary, Mother of James and Joses.")

MARY 5, mother of John Mark. (See Section I, "Searching Studies," "Mary, Mother of James and Joses, and Mary, Mother of John Mark.")

MARY 6 (Rom. 16:6), mentioned by Paul: "Greet Mary, who bestowed much labour on us." Is it not enough to know that she was a woman who bestowed much labor in the building of the early Church? Is it not enough that Paul himself singled her out among a handful of women at Rome, who were workers in the Christian movement?

MATRED (Gen. 36:39; I Chron. 1:50), mother-in-law of Hadar or Hadad, last of the old kings of Edom, through her daughter Mehetabel. Matred lived about 1500 B.C. in the city of Pau, about which little is known.

The Septuagint designates Matred as a male, son of Mezahab, instead of daughter.

MEHETABEL (Gen. 36:39; I Chron. 1:50), daughter of Matred and wife of Hadar or Hadad, last of the old kings of Edom.

MERAB (I Sam. 14:49; 18:17, 19), King Saul's eldest daughter, who had been promised to David for his prowess in slaying the Philistine Goliath. But Merab was not given to David as had been promised (I Sam. 17:25). In the meantime David was entertained in court and received such adulation from the crowd that King Saul became jealous of him.

For the hand of his daughter Merab he incited David to more dangerous deeds of valor against the Philistines. By this time King Saul's other daughter, Michal, had shown a fondness for David, and matters were complicated.

Merab finally was given to Adriel, the Meholathite. The passage in II Sam. 21:8 which seems to designate Michal rather than Merab as the mother of the five sons of Adriel, is thought by scholars to be a scribal error. These five sons, along with the sons of Saul's concubine Rizpah, were put to death and their bodies were left on the gallows for several months until the rains fell. (See Section I, "Searching Studies," "Rizpah.")

Scholars assume that Merab died comparatively young, leaving her five sons, who were cared for by her sister Michal. In later years they became identified as Michal's own children, when in reality they were Merab's children.

MESHULLEMETH (II Kings 21:19), wife of Manasseh and mother of Amon, both kings of Judah. There follows after her name the fact that her son "did that which was evil in the sight of the Lord."

She was the daughter of Haruz of Jotbah and lived in about 670 B.C.

MICHAIAH (II Chron. 13:2), same as Maachah 3.

MICHAL, daughter of King Saul, and David's first wife. (See Section I, "Searching Studies.")

MILCAH 1 (Gen. 11:29; 22:20, 23; 24:15, 24, 47), daughter of Haran and wife of Nahor, brother of Abraham. She had eight sons, Huz, Buz, Kemuel, Chesed, Hazo, Pildash, Jidlaph and Bethuel. The latter was the father of Rebekah, which means that this Milcah was Rebekah's grandmother.

MILCAH 2 (Num. 26:33; 27:1; 36:11; Josh. 17:3), one of five of Zelophehad's daughters. (See Section I, "Searching Studies," "Daughters of Zelophehad.")

MIRIAM 1, sister of Moses, who led the women of Israel in that oldest of national anthems, "Sing Unto the Lord." (See Section I, "Searching Studies.")

MIRIAM 2 (I Chron. 4:17). There is some difference of opinion about this Miriam among scholars. The *Westminster Dictionary* (p. 400) calls this Miriam a man, but Young's *Concordance* (p. 664) lists her as a daughter of Ezra of the tribe of Judah.

NAAMAH 1 (Gen. 4:22), first daughter in Bible mentioned by name. Her parents were Lamech, primitive poet, and Zillah, one of his two wives. Her brother was Tubal-Cain, founder of the ancient craft of the metalsmith.

Whether she was as gifted as was her father, her brother, and her cousins, Jubal, founder of music, and Jabel, founder of nomadic ways, we are not told.

NAAMAH 2 (I Kings 14:21, 31; II Chron. 12:13), one of Solomon's many wives, who became the mother of King Rehoboam, last king of the united monarchy of David and Solomon and first ruler of the southern kingdom of Judah. She was probably from the royal line of Ammonites, inveterate enemies of Israel, and a force for spiritual corruption. She was abhorrent to the people of Israel and had an evil influence over Solomon. He did build a magnificent temple to the worship of God, but at the same time he erected on the hill which was before Jerusalem a high place for Naamah's god Moloch.

Naamah's son King Rehoboam lived and died a monument of his father's sin and of his mother's hatred for the God of the Israelites.

NAARAH (I Chron. 4:5, 6), one of two wives of Ashur and mother of four sons, Ahuzam, Hepher, Temeni, and Haahashtari.

NAOMI (Ruth 1:2, 3, 8, 11, 19, 20, 21, 22; also Ruth 2:1, 2, 6, 20, 22; 3:1; 4:3, 5, 9, 14, 16, 17), wife of Elimelech, an Israelite, and mother of Mahlon and Chilion. One of her daughters-in-law was Ruth, the Moabitess, who first was married to Mahlon in the land of Moab but later became the wife of Boaz. The other daughter-in-law was Orpah, wife of Chilion.

After her two sons died, Naomi returned to Beth-lehem-Judah, the land of her people, which she and her husband and sons had left during a famine. Ruth returned with her, but Orpah kissed her mother-in-law at the city gate and turned back to Moab. Naomi and Ruth pressed on together to Beth-lehem.

When Naomi returned to her people, she said, "Call me not Naomi, call me Mara" (Ruth 1:20), which meant "bitterness," for the Almighty had dealt bitterly with her during her ten years' absence, she told her friends. She had gone forth from Beth-lehem with a husband and two sons but had returned husbandless, childless, and penniless.

By gleaning in the fields of her father-in-law's kinsman Boaz, Ruth supported her mother-in-law. Later Naomi counseled with Ruth how to win Boaz as a husband, for according to the levirate law of that time she could become his wife, as he was a near kinsman.

Naomi rejoiced to see Boaz later marry Ruth. To them was born Obed, a child who became a "restorer" of Naomi's life and a "nourisher" of her old age. Neighbors now said to Naomi, "Thy daughter in law, which loveth thee, which is better to thee than seven sons, hath born him" (Ruth 4:15).

Ruth's pledge of devotion to Naomi, as they left Moab for Beth-lehem, is unsurpassed in all literature. Naomi must have been lovable to have had Ruth speak to her these immortal words: "Intreat me not to leave thee, or to return from following after thee: for whither thou goest, I will go; and where thou lodgest, I will lodge: thy people shall be my people, and thy God my God: Where thou diest, will I die, and there will I be buried" (Ruth 1:16-17).

NEHUSHTA (II Kings 24:8), daughter-in-law of a king, sister-in-law of two kings, wife of a king, and mother of a king. She lived during the last years of the kingdom of Judah, when there is little mention made of women, because they were overwhelmed by sorrows of the nation.

She was the daughter of Elnathan, prominent man of Jerusalem, who probably was a friend and counselor of King Josiah and of the prophets Jeremiah and Zephaniah.

Probably Nehushta's life looked very bright before her father-in-law King Josiah was slain in battle with an Egyptian army.

Nehushta's husband, probably Jehoiakim, Josiah's oldest son, desired an alliance with Egypt. Those who were opposed to such an alliance made Josiah's second son, Jehoahaz II, the king.

He was quickly dethroned by a strong Egyptian army and taken captive to Egypt. There he died, and Jehoiakim began to reign.

He was in opposition to the prophet Jeremiah and one of his acts was to destroy the prophet's scroll on which his prophecy was written (Jer. 36:23). Nehushta's father tried to prevent her husband from doing this, but the king had the precious scroll cut and committed to the flames.

This ungodly king died on his sickbed, and his and Nehushta's son Jehoiachin became the next king. But Nehushta was queen-mother only three months and ten days.

In 598 B.C. King Nebuchadnezzar subdued Jehoiachin's kingdom, captured Jerusalem, and deported many important people to Babylon. Nehushta was taken captive by the king of Babylon, along with the king and his wives, officers, princes, artisans, and servants. Doubtless she saw fire consume every possession she had. Her brother-in-law, Zedekiah, was now set up as a vassal king at Jerusalem by Nebuchadnezzar, but after reigning eleven years he was captured, his sons were killed, and his eyes were put out.

It is thought that the years of Nehushta's captivity may have been brightened by favors from Babylonian monarchs, for her son, Jehoiachin, finally was honored by having a chief place among the captive kings and a daily allowance from King Evil-merodach (II Kings 25:27-30).

Nehushta's life doubtless was affected by the prophet Ezekiel, who taught the people that they must recognize Jehovah as God, because unbelief and adherence to false prophets had been the reason for Jerusalem's destruction, and Nehushta had witnessed this.

We have no evidence of what kind of woman she was during the reigns of the kings in her family. But all of them, except her father-in-law Josiah, were weak and wicked, and Israel suffered accordingly. She certainly did not prove herself to be a woman with an influence for good.

NOADIAH (Neh. 6:14), a false prophetess, who with Sanballat, Samaritan leader, and Tobiah, Ammonite governor, made insidious attempts to prevent Nehemiah, a Jew of the captivity, from rebuilding the walls of Jerusalem in about 445 B.C.

She and her allies used various stratagems to intimidate him. For example, they told him that during the night his enemies would kill him. They advised him to shut himself up in the house of God. He declined such advice, exclaiming, "My God, think thou upon Tobiah and Sanballat according to these their works, and on the prophetess Noadiah, and the rest of the prophets, that would have put me in fear."

Despite the stratagems of this false prophetess and her friends, the Jerusalem wall was finished, and those who saw it perceived that it was the work of God.

NOAH (Num. 26:33; 27:1; 36:11; Josh. 17:3), one of the five daughters of Zelophehad. (See Section I, "Searching Studies," "Daughters of Zelophehad.")

OHOLIBAMAH, one of Esau's wives. See Aholibamah.

ORPAH (Ruth 1:4, 14), sister-in-law of Ruth, and wife of Chilion, son of Naomi.

As Ruth and Naomi stood ready to depart for the latter's native Beth-lehem-Judah, Orpah wept as she bade them good-by. She kissed her mother-in-law and turned back to Moab. Her record ends there, while Ruth's journey into great things begins after she becomes a believer in Naomi's God.

[287]

Though Orpah had been closely associated with four who had worshiped God—her husband, her brother-in-law Mahlon, her father-in-law Elimelech, and her mother-in-law Naomi—like Lot's wife, she turned back to her own way of life and worshiped the gods of Moab.

Orpah showed spiritual indifference, preferring her own rich and highly prosperous Moab to the uncertainties and poverties that lay ahead of the widow Naomi in Beth-lehem-Judah.

Orpah typifies the normal young woman who selfishly pursues her own way, thinking little of older people and drawing away quickly from sacrifices she can avoid.

PENINNAH (I Sam. 1:2, 4), one of the two wives of Elkanah. She taunted his other wife Hannah, mother of Samuel. No mention is made of Peninnah save that she bore children and lived in the town of Ramah and vexed Hannah when the family made annual trips together to Shiloh for the feast.

It is Peninnah, not Hannah, who appears to have had an unpleasant disposition and gloried in the fact that she could have children while Hannah had none. But to Hannah later were born Samuel and other children.

PERSIS (Rom. 16:12), a woman in the early Roman Church, whom Paul called beloved, for she "laboured much in the Lord." He sent salutations to her along with other devout and zealous Christian women in the early Church at Rome.

PHANUEL (Luke 2:36). A question mark centers around whether this is a man or a woman. Young's *Concordance* calls her the Asherite mother of Anna, the prophetess, who was the first to proclaim Jesus as the Christ, when His parents brought Him into the Temple.

Harper's *Bible Dictionary,* the *Westminster Dictionary,* and other authorities call Phanuel a father of Anna. Others, like the *Inter-*

national Standard Bible Encyclopedia, merely refer to Phanuel as a parent of Anna.

PHEBE, deaconess in the church at Cenchrea. (See Section I, "Searching Studies.")

PRISCA, same as Priscilla.

PRISCILLA, wife of Aquila and helper of Paul. (See Section I, "Searching Studies.")

PUAH (Exod. 1:15), midwife in the time of Moses, probably a director of a group of midwives. Naturally, a nation with almost two million people would need many midwives, but only Puah's and Shiprah's names are listed. They were probably the principal women and had under them many midwives, to whom it was decreed by the Pharaoh of Egypt that they must destroy all Hebrew male children when they were born.

The Hebrews were increasing so rapidly that the new Pharaoh was alarmed at their growing power.

Puah was told that when she saw a Hebrew mother giving birth to a baby, "if it be a son, then ye shall kill him: but if it be a daughter, then she shall live" (Exod. 1:16). But Puah had the courage to disobey the mandate of a cruel tyrant and to save "the men children alive."

For her courage, we are told God rewarded Puah by enabling the Hebrews to have even more children and stronger ones than before.

It is also recorded, "because the midwives feared God, that he made them houses" (Exod. 1:21). Dr. Lee Anna Starr, in her scholarly work *The Bible Status of Woman,* interprets this to mean "he elevated them to the headship of their father's houses."

RACHEL, wife of Jacob and sister of Leah. (See Section I, "Searching Studies.")

RAHAB 1, harlot who aided Israel spies. (See Section I, "Searching Studies.")

RAHAB 2 (Matt. 1:5), wife of Salmon and mother of Boaz. There is a difference of opinion among scholars whether this was the same Rahab as the harlot who harbored two spies. (See Section I, "Searching Studies") or another. In the King James Version it is spelled Rachab. In the Revised Standard Version it is Rahab.

REBECCA, same as Rebekah. (See Section I, "Searching Studies.")

REUMAH (Gen. 22:24), concubine of Abraham's brother Nahor and mother of Tebah, Gaham, Thahash, and Maachah. She is the first concubine, whose name is recorded in the Bible and so designated. In reality, Hagar became the concubine of Abraham, but she is referred to as Sarah's handmaid.

RHODA (Acts 12:13), a maidservant in the Jerusalem house of Mary, mother of Mark, who was the first to hear Peter knock at the gate after his miraculous escape from prison. Many had gathered to pray for him. Rhoda, knowing that they were now on their knees in Mary's upper room praying for Peter, gladly ran to tell them, before admitting him.

When she announced to them that Peter now stood at the gate, they said to Rhoda, "Thou art mad" (Acts 12:15). But she affirmed that Peter was there. His continued knocking brought others to the door, and when they saw Peter they knew that their prayers had been answered. An angel of the Lord appeared in the prison and Peter's chains had fallen miraculously from off his hands.

Rhoda demonstrated that she was a spiritual ally to the woman she served. Also, she was willing to serve late, for it was now long after midnight when Peter knocked and the Christians were still gathered at Mary's house.

Rhoda showed that she was intensely interested in Peter's need and anxiety and that she rejoiced in his freedom. Thus she served not only her mistress but the larger fellowship of the Church as well.

RIZPAH, concubine of Saul, who had two sons by him. After they had been hanged, she watched over their dead bodies for several months. (See Section I, "Searching Studies.")

RUTH, Moabite daughter-in-law of Naomi and married first to her son, Mahlon and afterwards to the landowner Boaz, in Beth· lehem. Through the latter, Ruth became the mother of Obed, ancestor of Christ. (See Section I, "Searching Studies.")

SALOME 1, wife of Zebedee and mother of the apostles James and John. (See Section I, "Searching Studies.")

SALOME 2 is not actually named in the Bible text but is only identified as the daughter of Herodias. But Josephus calls Herodias' daughter Salome, and because of the Richard Strauss opera also by that name, tradition has given Herodias' daughter the name of Salome.

SAPPHIRA, wife of Ananias. Both were members of the early Christian community at Jerusalem. (See Section I, "Searching Studies.")

SARAH 1, wife of Abraham and mother of Isaac. (See Section I, "Searching Studies.")

SARAH 2 (Gen. 46:17; Num. 26:46; I Chron. 7:30), daughter of Asher and granddaughter of Jacob by his wife Leah's handmaid Zilpah. In the Genesis and Chronicles account she is called Serah, but in the Numbers account, Sarah.

SARAI, the original name of Sarah, Abraham's wife, who became the mother of Isaac. When God changed her husband's name from Abram to Abraham, he changed her name from Sarai to Sarah (Gen. 17:15), and announced that he would bless her and make her "a mother of nations."

SERAH, see Sarah 2 (Gen. 46:17; I Chron. 7:30).

SHELOMITH 1 (Lev. 24:11), prominent figure in the story of the stoning of her son for blasphemy. She was the daughter of Dibri of the tribe of Dan. Hers had evidently been a mixed marriage with an Egyptian during the period the Israelites were in Egypt. Real problems arose when the latter made their exit from Egypt.

In Leviticus 24:10 we are told that an Israelite woman's son, whose father was an Egyptian, went out among the children of Israel, and that he and a man of Israel quarreled together in camp.

In the next passage, where it is related that the son blasphemed the name of the Lord, Shelomith is called by name, an indication that she was a well-known woman.

Half-Egyptian and half-Israelite, her son evidently had quarreled with the Israelite in camp and had vented his rage in some shocking manner. Often the Egyptians cursed their idols when failing to obtain the object of their petitions.

After Shelomith's son had blasphemed the God of his opponent, he was put in custody and then Moses ordered that he be stoned to death by the congregation.

The youth's actions stirred Moses to enact a new law, stating "He that blasphemeth the name of the Lord, he shall surely be put to death, and all the congregation shall certainly stone him: as well the stranger, as he that is born in the land, when he blasphemeth the name of the Lord, shall be put to death" (Lev. 24:16).

In the last sentence of Leviticus 24:23 there is the confirmation that Shelomith's son was stoned to death. A hard trial this was for a mother, but it illustrates the problems that arose in these mixed marriages, when God was not worshiped by both parents and the love of Him was not instilled in the offspring.

The rabbis have a tradition that Shelomith was a handsome and virtuous woman, with whom an Egyptian overseer of the Hebrews became enamored, and that during her husband's absence he stole by night into her house. When she found she was with child by the Egyptian, her husband put her out and struck at the Egyptian.

Moses, passing by, so continues the tradition, took the part of the Israelite and killed the Egyptian. The brothers of Shelomith called her husband to account for abandoning her. Moses again interfered, but the husband asked him whether he would kill him, as yesterday he had killed the Egyptian. And so it was Moses fled from the land of Midian.

The rabbis' story of Moses and Shelomith's husband, based purely on tradition, is recorded in Sarah Josepha Hale's *Biography of Distinguished Women.*

SHELOMITH 2 (I Chron. 3:19), a daughter of Zerubbabel, who was an ancestor of Christ (Matt. 1:12; Luke 3:27). It is easy to assume she was a godly woman.

Her father, successor to Jehoiachin (Jeconiah), served as head of the civil administration for exiles returning from Babylon to Jerusalem in about 520 B.C., and had reared an altar and restored the worship. He held office as Persian governor under Darius when the second Temple was built at Jerusalem. It has been called Zerubbabel's Temple.

The daughter of a man in such a conspicuous religious position no doubt lived close to God herself.

Her brothers were Meshullam and Hananiah.

SHELOMITH 3 (II Chron. 11:20), probably a daughter of Maachah and King Rehoboam.

Shelomith is named with three other children, Abijah, Attai, and Ziza, and is not referred to as a daughter. The name could be that of a son.

The name Shelomith appears in the Bible seven times; of these, only two are positively identified as women.

SHERAH (I Chron. 7:24), a daughter of the little-known Beriah, descendant of Ephraim. She is mentioned as having built "Beth-horon the nether, and the upper, and Uzzen-sherah," ancient border towns between Benjamin and Ephraim and belonging to the latter tribe. The towns now occupying their sites dominate one of the most historic roads in history.

Sherah lived about 1450 B.C. and must have accomplished a great deal as a builder to have had even this identification in Chronicles.

SHIMEATH (II Kings 12:21; II Chron. 24:26), Ammonite mother of Jozachar, one of the servants who conspired against King Joash of Judah and slew him on his bed as he lay ill.

In the account in Kings there is no definite way to determine whether Shimeath was the father or mother of Zabad, except that the Chronicler later carefully identifies Shimeath as an "Ammon-itess."

In Kings, Shimeath's son is called Jozachar, while the Chronicler names the son of Shimeath as Zabad.

The evil influence of the Ammonite mother is here again brought into the foreground.

SHIMRITH (II Chron. 24:26), same as Shomer.

SHIPHRAH (Exod. 1:15), midwife of the time of Moses. She and another midwife, Puah, in all probability were directors of a corps of midwives. The new Pharaoh of Egypt, fearful of the increasing power of the Hebrews, called the two principal midwives in and ordered them to destroy all Hebrew male children when they ministered to their mothers at birth.

To Shiphrah and Puah he issued the order that, when they saw a Hebrew mother giving birth to a child they were to kill the newborn baby, if it were a son.

Shiphrah, like Puah, refused to murder these Hebrew male children, excusing herself later to Pharaoh by saying that the Hebrew women were lively and delivered their own children before the midwife arrived.

Because of the courage of Shiphrah, God made "houses" for Shiphrah and Puah. Probably this means that He gave them the headships to their families, or built up the numbers of their own families.

SHOMER (II Kings 12:21), same as Shimrith. She was the Moabite mother of Jehozabad, one of two servants who slew King Joash of Judah as he lay ill in bed. She is called Shimrith in II Chronicles 24:26.

SHUA (I Chron. 7:32), daughter of Heber, a Benjamite and a sister of three brothers, Japhlet, Shomer, and Hotham.

SUSANNA (Luke 8:3), one of those who ministered to Jesus of her substance. She is named with Joanna, wife of Herod's steward, and others.

In Luke 8:2 she is mentioned among "certain women, which had been healed of evil spirits and infirmities."

Because Susanna had been cured of disease, she joyfully ministered of her substance and helped to spread the good news of Christ's gospel.

SYNTYCHE (Phil. 4:2), member of the early Church at Philippi, whom Paul besought along, with Euodias, another woman member, to be of the same mind. Evidently they had disagreed, and he realized that this would hinder them in their gospel work.

Syntyche probably was one of the first teachers in the early Church, or she may have been a deaconess. Paul says her name had been entered in the "book of life," indicating that she was concerned with spiritual things.

In his message to the Philippians, Paul entreated other members of the church to help her and Euodias to make up their differences. And he entreated them all to "Rejoice in the Lord."

In this same letter Paul gave rules for living, themes for thought, and a message of victory over anxiety, making the Philippians understand that there was no time for bickering, and that such conduct did not become a Christian.

See also Euodias.

TABITHA, same as Dorcas. (See Section I, "Searching Studies," "Dorcas.")

TAHPENES (I Kings 11:19, 20), a queen of Pharaoh of Egypt in the time of David. Her sister was given by Pharaoh as a wife to Hadad, Edomite king. The latter had found favor in Pharaoh's sight.

Queen Tahpenes became the foster-mother of Genubath, son of her sister and Hadad, bringing him up in her own palace. The sister's name is not given. It might be inferred that the mother died at childbirth and Queen Tahpenes reared the child with her own sons.

TAMAR 1, mother of Pharez and ancestor of King David. (See Section I, "Searching Studies.")

TAMAR 2 (II Sam. 13:1, 2, 4, 5, 6, 7, 8, 10, 19, 20, 22, 32; I Chron. 3:9), a daughter of David and Maacah and full sister of Absalom. Amnon, her half-brother by her father David and another wife, Ahinoam, fell in love with Tamar and tricked her into his house.

Feigning illness, he begged his father, who visited him, to allow his sister Tamar to come and prepare some special food for him. She came and prepared cakes, probably in an outer room, but Amnon refused to eat. Ordering all his attendants to retire, he called Tamar into his chamber and invited her to come and lie with him.

Tamar told him that this was folly, that she would be shamed and he would be regarded as one of the fools in Israel. But Amnon did not listen to her but "forced her, and lay with her" (II Sam. 13:14).

Then Amnon's love for Tamar gave way to brutal hatred and he ordered her to leave his house. Tamar remonstrated, telling him that this wrong would be greater than that already done to her. Amnon called his servants and forced her outside and had the door bolted behind her.

Though she departed in the dress of a princess, Amnon's servants had treated her as a common woman. She then put ashes on her head, a mark of grief and humiliation, laid her hand over her head, and went forth into the streets crying.

Soon she came to Absalom, her own brother, who took her to his house, where she remained. When David failed to punish his son Amnon for the crime, Absalom took the matter into his own hands and had Amnon murdered.

TAMAR 3 (II Sam. 14:27), daughter of Absalom, probably named for his sister Tamar, who had been wronged by their half-brother Amnon. Absalom had had Amnon murdered because of his crime.

This Tamar is described as a "woman of a fair countenance."

TAPHATH (I Kings 4:11), one of the daughters of Solomon. She was married to the son (not named) of Abinadab, one of Solomon's officers in charge of the region of Dor.

THAMAR (Matt. 1:3), an ancestress of Jesus, same as Tamar 1.

TIMNA (Gen. 36:12), concubine of Esau's son Eliphaz and mother of Amalek. In Genesis 36:22 and I Chronicles 1:39, Timna is referred to as a sister of Lotan. They were children of Seir the Horite.

Timna bore a daughter who was given her name, and who, in I Chronicles 1:35-37, is reckoned as one of the sons of Eliphaz.

The word "concubine," which was applied to Timna, did not in Old Testament times have the meaning it has today. It was frequently applied to a woman who, before her marriage, had been a slave. This seems to have been its meaning in the case of Timna. Her people, the Horites, were the original inhabitants of Mount Seir. When the Edomites waged war against them and seized their territory (Deut. 2:12, 22), Timna may have been captured and enslaved. When she wedded Eliphaz, she would have been a secondary wife or concubine.

TIRZAH (Num. 26:33; 27:1; 36:11; Josh. 17:3), one of five daughters of Zelophehad. (See Section I, "Searching Studies," "Daughters of Zelophehad.")

TRYPHENA (Rom. 16:12), one of the early workers in the Church at Rome, to whom Paul sent salutations, because she had served the Church so faithfully.

TRYPHOSA (Rom. 16:12), an early worker in the first Christian Church at Rome whose name is linked with Tryphena's. Paul sent salutations to her because she "laboured in the Lord."

Probably she was one of the leaders or Paul would not have singled her out. Without her and other devout workers in the first Christian Church in Rome, the great Christian message would have died, but these zealous few, of whom Tryphosa was one, kept it alive.

VASHTI (Esther 1:9, 11, 12, 15, 16, 17, 19; 2:1, 4, 17), the beautiful wife of Ahasuerus (or Artaxerxes), king of Persia, who gained her fame by disobeying her husband.

At this time her husband was the most powerful monarch of the world. His kingdom stretched from "India to Ethiopia." Queen Vashti lived in a palace so magnificent that detailed description is given of its marble pillars, beds of gold and silver, and drinking vessels of gold (Esther 1:6, 7). And Vashti herself is described as "fair to look on" (Esther 1:11), one in whose beauty the king took great pride.

At his palace at Shushan Ahasuerus had a great feast for the governors of his provinces. It lasted seven days, and every man drank "according to his pleasure." At the same time Queen Vashti gave a feast for the women.

On the seventh day, when the king's heart was merry with wine, he commanded Vashti to be brought before him "with the crown royal" on her head, to show the people and princes her beauty. When she refused to come (Esther 1:12), she became one of the first queens in Bible history of whom it is recorded that she dared to disobey her husband, a king.

Much discussion has centered around the reason for her refusal. Some commentators contend that the queen was a modest woman, that the king had drunk too much to know what he had asked, and that he wanted to parade his queen before his guests in an immodest pose. Others commentators contend that such a reason for Vashti's disobedience is without real foundation. The king had sent seven chamberlains to her, and his orders did not fail to recognize Vashti's high dignity. The *Interpreters' Bible* expresses the opinion that "Vashti's insolence is a literary excuse for the subsequent elevation of Esther." At any rate, her courage must have been as great as her beauty or she could not have braved the displeasure of her husband.

In his wrath, the king referred the matter to his wise men, who were learned in the law. He feared that other wives would show the same kind of disobedience to their husbands. He was advised to repudiate his wife by a royal decree, and a new law was issued expressly for her disobedience.

Vashti was dethroned and later her place was taken by Esther, cousin and adopted daughter of Mordecai, the Jew.

ZEBUDAH (II Kings 23:36), mother of Jehoiakim, who reigned in Jerusalem eleven years, shortly before its fall. Right after his mother's name and the fact that she was daughter of Pedaiah of Rumah there appears the phrase, "and he did that which was evil in the sight of the Lord."

ZERESH (Esther 5:10, 14; 6:13), wife of Haman, prime minister and favorite of King Ahasuerus of Persia. The monarch had commanded that those who dwelt in the gates of the palace should bow down to Haman, but Mordecai, cousin of Queen Esther, refused to do so.

One day, when returning from the palace, Haman saw Mordecai who did not rise for him. When Haman told his wife, Zeresh, and friends about his troubles with Mordecai, they said, "Let a gallows be made of fifty cubits high, and tomorrow speak thou unto the king that Mordecai may be hanged thereon" (Esther 5:14).

Despite her designing, Zeresh did warn her husband: "If Mordecai be of the seed of the Jews, before whom thou hast begun to fall, thou shalt not prevail against him, but shalt surely fall before him" (Esther 6:13).

Her prediction was fulfilled completely when her husband Haman and their ten sons were hanged on the gallows he had erected for Mordecai.

She who had fostered her husband's vanity and foolish ambition was now to see him hang, and was powerless to aid him.

ZERUAH (I Kings 11:26), described as a "widow woman" at the time of the birth of her son Jeroboam, who became king of the ten tribes of Israel which revolted against Solomon's son and successor, Rehoboam.

Zeruah's son is described as Solomon's servant, and it may be assumed that his mother was in the employ of Solomon. Her husband Nebat had been an official under Solomon, and her son became an overseer of heavy work.

But her son made Israel to sin. His rule resulted in a lowering of the spiritual tone of northern Israel. The idolatry that he established was one of the things that caused the ten tribes to be carried into captivity.

We have no indication of the character of this mother Zeruah, except through her son, who later fought a great battle against Solomon's own grandson and successor Abijam.

In the Septuagint Zeruah is called a harlot, and not by the name of Zeruah. Because her son broke up the kingdom and set up idolatrous worship, she probably was hated by the Israelites. And because she was a widow at the time of her son's birth, she no doubt was the one who molded his life in a pattern of idolatry.

ZERUIAH (I Sam. 26:6; II Sam. 2:13, 18; 3:39; 8:16; 14:1; 16:9, 10; 17:25; 18:2; 19:21, 22; 21:17; 23:18, 37; I Kings 1:7; 2:5, 22; I Chron. 2:16; 11:6, 39; 18:12, 15; 26:28; 27:24). The fact that her name appears twenty-five times besides that of her sons is sufficient proof that she was a mother of distinction who had a marked influence over the lives of her sons.

She was a half-sister of David and a sister of Abigail 2. Her husband, according to II Samuel 2:32, was buried in a sepulcher at Beth-lehem.

The most famous of her three sons, Joab, became commander-in-chief of his uncle David's army and was loyally devoted to him.

Her son Abishai was a close companion in David's military adventure. The third son, Asahel, was slain by Abner, their commander, in self-defense.

Joab and Abishai are referred to all through Scripture as the "sons of Zeruiah." This latter fact, says David Francis Roberts in the In-

ternational Standard Bible Encyclopedia (p. 3148), "is explained by some as pointing to a type of marriage by which the children belong to their mother's clan; by others as being due to her husband's early death, and again as a proof of the mother in the case being the stronger personality."

Though she was David's sister, probably, like her sister Abigail, she was not a daughter of Jesse but a daughter of Jesse's wife by an earlier marriage with Nahash.

ZIBIAH (II Kings 12:1; II Chron. 24:1), wife of Ahaziah and mother of Jehoash or Joash, one of the kings of Judah. As a young child Joash was rescued from the murderous plot of Athaliah by his aunt and hidden in the Temple until he was seven years old. He was then proclaimed rightful king by his uncle, the high priest Jehoiada, and Athaliah was slain.

In Chronicles we learn that Zibiah's son reigned forty years and it is said of him, "His mother's name was Zibiah of Beer-sheba. And Jehoash did that which was right in the sight of the Lord all his days wherein Jehoiada the priest instructed him" (II Kings 12:1-2). This indicates the influence of his mother, who probably taught him to listen to the counsels of the priest.

ZILLAH (Gen. 4:19, 22, 23), one of two wives of Lamech, a primitive poet. Her name, meaning shadow of darkness, appears with that of Lamech's other wife, Adah. They were the first two wives on record in a polygamous household.

Zillah is the mother of Naamah, first daughter mentioned in the Bible, and also the mother of Tubal-cain, who founded the ancient craft of traveling metalsmiths and ironmakers.

She and her sister Adah are the first wives on record to have their husband tell them he had killed a man. Probably he had begun to put his trust, not in God, but in weapons and implements invented by Zillah's son, for he told Zillah and Adah that he would avenge himself "seventy and sevenfold" (Gen. 4:24).

Zillah, on the one hand, could take pride in a son who invented weapons of metal but, on the other hand, probably became the first mother on record to question the base use made by her husband of their son's invention.

ZILPAH (Gen. 29:24; 30:9, 10; 35:26; 37:2; 46:18), Leah's handmaid, whom her father Laban gave to her as a part of her dowry when she became the wife of Jacob. Through Jacob, Zilpah became the mother of two of the tribes of Israel. Leah followed the example of her sister Rachel, who had given her handmaid Bilhah to Jacob for a secondary wife.

When Zilpah's first son was born, Leah said, "A troop cometh: and she called his name Gad" (Gen. 30:11). When Zilpah's second son was born, Leah said, "Happy am I, for the daughters will call me blessed: and she called his name Asher" (Gen. 30:13). Both sons were born at Padan-aram.

Zilpah and her two sons accompanied Jacob when he left Laban's service to return to Canaan. She and her sons and Bilhah and her sons were placed in the front of the caravan. When they were overtaken by Laban at Mount Gilead, Zilpah's tent was searched by him to ascertain if his lost images were secreted there (Gen. 31:33).

When Jacob and his wives and children met Esau near Shechem, Zilpah and her two sons were introduced to him and made obeisance to him (Gen. 33:6).

The Gadites, originating from Zilpah's son Gad, at the time the first census was made in the wilderness numbered 45,650 who were capable of bearing arms (Num. 1:24-25). Moses assigned to them territory east of the Jordan.

The tribe of which Zilpah's second son Asher was the progenitor numbered 41,500 (Num. 1:40-41).

ZIPPORAH, one of the seven shepherdess daughters of Jethro She became the wife of Moses and bore him two sons. (See Section I, "Searching Studies.")

Chronological Listings
of Nameless Women
in the Background

*

Daughters
Wives
Mothers
Widows
Other Unnamed Women

*

In this section are all the nameless women, with the exception of those in the foreground who were included in Section I, "Searching Studies," namely Lot's wife, Potiphar's wife, the daughters of Zelophehad, Jephthah's daughter, Ichabod's mother, the woman of Endor, the two mothers of Solomon's Time, the widow of Zarephath, the Shunammite, the virtuous woman, the woman of Samaria, the Syro-Phoenician woman, who was also called the Canaanite woman, the three sick women, and Pilate's wife.

In the following section on the nameless women in the background appear more than one hundred sketches. It is impossible to count these women, because often the sketches include a group of them, as in the case of the wise-hearted women who spun fine linen for the tabernacle, or the women of Midian taken captive by the Israelites. We have no record of how many there were. And some of the women in the following section, such as the ten wise and foolish virgins, have a symbolical meaning.

The nameless women have been placed in five divisions: Daughters, Wives, Mothers, Widows, and Other Unnamed Women. The order in which these women appear in each division is chronological.

*

DAUGHTERS

The word "daughter" appears in the Bible more than two hundred times and "daughter-in-law" twenty times. The word "granddaughter" does not appear at all, though "grandmother" is mentioned once (II Tim. 1:5).

The term "daughter" is often used in Scripture in its literal sense. It is also used in a general sense, as "daughters of my people," "daughters of music," and "daughter of the eye." Mention is made of "daughter of unclean spirit" (Mark 7:25-27). Sometimes it is used to designate the inhabitants of a place, as daughters of Babylon, the Chaldeans, Edom, Egypt, Gallim, Jerusalem, Judah, Tarshish, Tyre, Zidon, Zion, Israel, Moab, Shiloh, and so on.

The word "daughter" appears for the first time in Genesis 5:4 and refers to the daughters of Adam.

Daughters are not mentioned as often by name as sons, because they were not so highly prized as were sons. Sometimes a father might sell his daughter as a bondwoman (Exod. 21:7), but not to a foreigner (Exod. 21:8).

Chastity was expected of all the daughters of Israel. In Leviticus 21:9 a penalty of burning was placed upon the priest's daughter who played the harlot.

The most famous named daughters in the Bible are the daughters of Zelophehad, who declared their rights (see Section I, "Searching Studies"). The most famous nameless daughter of the Old Testament is Jephthah's daughter (see Section I, "Searching Studies"). The most famous nameless daughter of the New Testament is Jairus' twelve-year-old daughter, who along with other nameless but significant daughters is mentioned in pages that follow.

ADAM'S DAUGHTERS

Adam's daughters (Gen. 5:4) belong to the second generation in the antediluvian genealogy.

SETH'S DAUGHTERS

Seth's daughters (Gen. 5:7) were granddaughters of Adam.

ENOS' DAUGHTERS

Enos' daughters (Gen. 5:10) were great-granddaughters of Adam.

CAINAN'S DAUGHTERS

Cainan's daughters (Gen. 5:13) belong to the fifth generation in the antediluvian genealogy.

MAHALALEEL'S DAUGHTERS

Mahalaleel's daughters (Gen. 5:16) belong to the sixth generation of the antediluvian genealogy.

JARED'S DAUGHTERS

Jared's daughters (Gen. 5:19) are the seventh generation in the family of Adam.

ENOCH'S DAUGHTERS

Enoch's daughters (Gen. 5:22) are the eighth generation in the genealogy of Adam.

DAUGHTERS

METHUSELAH'S DAUGHTERS

Methuselah's daughters (Gen. 5:26) were sisters of Lamech.

LAMECH'S DAUGHTERS

Lamech's daughters (Gen. 5:30) were the sisters of Noah and the tenth generation of Adam's family.

DAUGHTERS OF MEN

A curious passage (Gen. 6:2) tells of the marriage of the "sons of God" with the "daughters of men." Do we have here the echo of that ancient tradition that once the gods and men intermarried and from the union the great heroes of the past were born?

The close position of this statement concerning "the sons of God" and the "daughters of men" with the account of the great growth of evil in the world has led some to hold that these "daughters of men" were women from the unrighteous line of the murderous Cain, while the "sons of God" were men from the more upright family of Seth.

SHEM'S DAUGHTERS

Shem's daughters (Gen. 11:11). Among others in this long genealogical list of Genesis who "begat daughters" were Salah, Eber, Peleg, Reu, Serug, and Nahor, and finally we have the line of Abram and Nahor, who took as wives Sarai (Sarah) and Milcah.

LOT'S DAUGHTERS

Lot's daughters (Gen. 19:8, 15, 30-38) were guilty of incest with their father. Lot was forewarned by angels, who came to him at Sodom, to take his wife and two daughters and leave the city lest they be consumed by its approaching destruction. The wife looked back and was turned to a pillar of salt, but the daughters went on with their father, living first in the mountains of Zoar and later in caves.

Later, while their father was under the influence of wine, the daughters became guilty of incest with him. It was the elder daughter who suggested to the other that they make their father drink wine and then lie with him, "that we may preserve the seed of our father." The next night she suggested that the other sister lie with him.

Both daughters had a child by their father. The elder daughter's son was Moab, father of the Moabites. The younger daughter's son was Ben-ammi, father of the Ammonites.

The evil influence in Lot's family came because he had selfishly chosen the more fertile valleys from his uncle Abraham. In those valleys dwelt people of low character, who set a bad example for the family. Lot's wife was a native of this area and her evil influence carried on into the daughters.

PHARAOH'S DAUGHTER

Pharaoh's daughter (Exod. 2:5, 7, 8, 9, 10; Acts 7:21; Heb. 11:24) had much to do with shaping the future of Israel, because she had compassion on the baby Moses. Under a cruel decree of her father, one of the Pharaohs of Egypt, probably Ramses II, the child would have been destroyed. Because the Hebrews were increasing so rapidly in Egypt, Pharaoh had ordered that all male children be done away with at birth.

Jochebed, Moses' mother, managed to hide her son for three months after his birth, but when she could hide him no longer, by a supreme venture of faith she planned a way by which she might save him.

First she wove carefully an ark of bulrushes and placed her baby in it by the banks of the river Nile, where Pharaoh's daughter and her attendants often came to bathe. The mother had her daughter Miriam stand by to watch the baby until Pharaoh's daughter arrived.

The plan worked. Pharaoh's daughter, without knowing she was a part of the divine will, came upon the child. Her gentleness braved the harsh law of her father, and this gentleness made her great.

When the child Miriam said to her, "Shall I go and call to thee a nurse of the Hebrew women?" Pharaoh's daughter replied, "Go." And Miriam brought the child's own mother. Moses was taken into the imperial household and showered with love and all the luxuries of a palace. The child's own mother remained with the little Moses until after he was weaned, though her identity remained unknown.

As he grew older, Pharaoh's daughter gave him the finest education that Egypt afforded. She no doubt had professors to teach him hieroglyphics, also geography, medicine, music, and other subjects. All the while his Egyptian foster-mother protected the Hebrew child from the terror of her father's policy against the Hebrews.

Various names have been given to Pharaoh's daughter. She is Thermuthis in Josephus' *Antiquities,* Myrrina in the Alexandrian Chronicle, and Mercis in Artaphanes (quoted by Eusebius). But in Biblical history she is unnamed and is only identified as Pharaoh's daughter, woman of compassion, who saved for the Hebrew nation, and the whole world for that matter, the man who became the great lawgiver and led the Israelites from slavery in Egypt to nationhood in Canaan.

THE MIDIAN PRIEST'S DAUGHTERS

The Midian priest's daughters (Exod. 2:16, 20) were the seven shepherdess daughters of Jethro, who lived in the Midian wilderness. Zipporah, who became the wife of Moses, was one of these daughters. The others are not named. When the seven shepherdesses came to the well to fill the troughs for their father's flocks, the shepherds drove them away. Only one, Moses, who had come from Egypt into this land south of the Dead Sea, was courteous and helped them water their father's flocks.

When the seven daughters returned to their father Reuel, who is also called Jethro, the Midian priest, he asked them, "How is it that ye are come so soon today?" (Exod. 2:18). After they explained to him how an Egyptian had helped them water their flocks, he told his seven daughters to invite him in to eat bread, and to dwell with them. After that Jethro gave Zipporah, one of the seven, to Moses as his wife.

The seven daughters, tending and watering flocks, present a charming pastoral picture and point up women's service, even in the nomadic tribes of the Arabian desert in this time of about 1550 B.C.

PUTIEL'S DAUGHTERS

Putiel's daughters (Exod. 6:25). One of them married Eleazar, Aaron's son, and became the mother of Phinehas, who slew Zimro and Cozbi and was commended for the act because this pair had been guilty of whoredoms in Baal-peor worship.

Putiel's daughter is probably given a place in the record to show the influence of Jehovah in the life of a mother and how she passed this on to her son, who helped to destroy pagan worship.

THE PRIEST'S DAUGHTER

The priest's daughter (Lev. 21:9) was forbidden to play the whore, for she would profane her father, from whose family was expected a double degree of purity. The penalty was burning with fire.

JEPHTHAH'S DAUGHTER

Jephthah's daughter (Judg. 11:34, 35, 40). (See Section I, "Searching Studies.")

DAUGHTERS

IBZAN'S DAUGHTERS

Ibzan's daughters (Judg. 12:9) were thirty in number. Their father was a judge of Israel for seven years after Jephthah. He also had thirty sons and took for them wives from outside his native town. This record gives some idea of the size of Israel's early families.

DAUGHTERS OF ELKANAH

The daughters of Elkanah (I Sam. 1:4) were the half-sisters of Samuel. Their mother was Peninnah. They went into the temple at Shiloh and their father gave to them a portion for the offering there.

DAUGHTERS OF HANNAH

The two daughters of Hannah (I Sam. 2:21) were younger sisters of Samuel's. They had three brothers besides Samuel.

DAUGHTERS OF THE PHILISTINES

Daughters of the Philistines (II Sam. 1:20) are referred to as daughters of the uncircumcised, with whom the Israelites were not allowed to intermarry. See also Ezekiel 16:57.

MACHIR'S DAUGHTER

Machir's daughter (I Chron. 2:21) was Hezron's wife and the mother of Segub. Her brother was Gilead and her grandfather was Manasseh.

SHESHAN'S DAUGHTER

Sheshan's daughter (I Chron. 2:35) was given by her father to his servant Jarha and by him she bore Attai. She was a descendant of Tamar and Judah and lived in about the fourteenth century B.C.

It was not unusual in these times for a father to give his daughter to a worthy foreign slave. This would enable the daughter's husband to be legally adopted into the tribe, as well as to become heir to the property. It is probable there were no sons; and through the daughter the line was established.

For a father to give his daughter to a slave was not far different from a wife's giving her slave to her husband as a secondary wife, as was the case when Sarah gave Hagar to Abraham, and Rachel gave Bilhah to Jacob, and Leah gave Zilpah to him, all for the perpetuation of the family line.

DAUGHTERS OF SHIMEI

Daughters of Shimei (I Chron. 4:27) were six in number.

DAUGHTERS OF HEMAN

Daughters of Heman (I Chron. 25:5) were three. With their fourteen brothers they assisted their father, a singer in David's reign, with cymbals, psalteries, and harps for the service in the house of the Lord.

BARZILLAI'S DAUGHTER

One of Barzillai's daughters (Ezra 2:61; Neh. 7:63), when married, took not her husband's name but kept her own name. Like the daughters of Zelophehad, she probably inherited from her father a large estate, and kept it in her father's name and also retained that name herself. Her father is referred to merely as a Gileadite. The daughter had married a priest.

FOREIGN DAUGHTERS

Foreign daughters (Ezra 9:2). Ezra, the head of the priesthood, mourned because the people of Israel had taken to themselves foreign daughters, thus forsaking the commandments of the Lord.

SHALLUM'S DAUGHTERS

Shallum's daughters (Neh. 3:12) evidently belonged to a family of some wealth and social prestige, for their grandfather Halohesh was ruler over half of Jerusalem. They are mentioned as helpers in the rebuilding of the walls of Jerusalem, after Nehemiah had made a secret survey of the walls and had secured the co-operation of the citizens in an assembly, asking their help.

Shallum's daughters are mentioned probably to show that as women of means they set a noble example in menial service. Probably they also exhibited unusual enthusiasm in the rebuilding of the walls and may have given of their means as well. They are the only women mentioned in this large undertaking that brought in priests, goldsmiths, and others who repaired the tower and gardens as well as the walls, after the fall of Jerusalem.

DAUGHTER OF SANBALLAT

The daughter of Sanballat the Horonite (Neh. 13:28) became the wife of Joiada, priest of Jerusalem in the regime of Nehemiah. Sanballat was an influential Samaritan who had opposed the rebuilding of the walls of Jerusalem.

When Nehemiah demanded of Joiada that he give up his Samaritan wife or relinquish his priestly office, Joiada refused. The governor accordingly expelled him from Jerusalem, chasing him out of his presence, as the Biblical narrative informs us.

When Sanballat heard of it, he told his son-in-law not to move hastily but to keep his daughter as his wife. Sanballat would build Joiada a temple of his own, so that he might be not only a priest, and a high priest, but also his daughter's husband at the same time.

Thus was built the temple on Mount Gerizim, which became the center of Samaritan life and worship. It was concerning Mount Gerizim that the woman of Samaria at the well spoke when she said to Jesus, "Our fathers worshipped in this mountain; and ye say, that in Jerusalem is the place where men ought to worship" (John 4:20).

Many times the name of Sanballat appears as Bab Sin-uballit ("may sin give him life") in the contract tablets from the time of Nebuchadnezzar, Nabonidus, and Darius Hystaspis. (See *International Standard Bible Encyclopedia* on Sanballat, p. 2681.)

KING'S DAUGHTER

The king's daughter (Ps. 45) refers to a foreign princess who was to be married to a king of Israel. There have been many conjectures about who this woman was, but none of them has been satisfactory.

Escorted by virgins and wearing wrought gold, she is led to the nuptial chamber within the palace. And she comes to the king with "gladness and rejoicing."

The psalter tells her to forget her people and her father's house, becoming not like Jezebel, who clung to the gods of her own people, but like Ruth, who told Naomi, "Thy people shall be my people, and thy God my God" (Ruth 1:16).

In the closing part, the poet speaks of the children of the marriage, who will keep alive the royal line and cause the king's daughter to be remembered in all generations.

The king has been interpreted by Christians to mean the Messiah and the bride, Israel or the Church.

DAUGHTERS AS CORNER STONES

Daughters as corner stones (Ps. 144:12) emphasizes the Israelite' worship of chastity in women. Here the Psalmist, thanking God for His mercy, asks Him that "our daughters may be as corner stones, polished after the similitude of a palace." Many times in the Hebrew Scriptures is this ideal prominent.

DAUGHTERS OF ZION

Daughters of Zion (Isa. 3:16-26) is one of the most meaningful of the many phrases that appear in the Bible concerning daughters of a region. Here the young Isaiah makes a public utterance against the women of Jerusalem for their wanton haughtiness, their wasteful extravagance, their love of show, their self-indulgence, vice, and pride.

Because of the failure of the daughters of Zion to uphold the finest ideals of womanhood, the prophet says that the Lord will take away the bravery of their tinkly ornaments (anklets) about their feet, and their cauls (net works), and their round tires like moons (crescents), chains (or ear pendants), bracelets, mufflers, bonnets (head tires), ornaments of the legs (ankle chains), headbands, the tablets (or smelling boxes), earrings, rings, and nose jewels. Also listed among the luxuries to be taken away are the changeable suits of apparel (festal robes), the mantles, wimples (probably shawls), crisping pins, glasses (hand mirrors), and the fine linens, hoods (or turbans), and the veils.

Isaiah predicts that the husbands of these women shall fall by the sword, and Jerusalem's gates shall "lament and mourn."

KING'S DAUGHTERS

The king's daughters (Jer. 41:10) were the daughters of King Zedekiah, who were taken away from Mizpah by Ishmael as captives and were later recovered by Johanan. Through the line of the eldest daughter, the dynasty of David was perpetuated through the captivity.

KING'S DAUGHTER OF THE SOUTH

King's daughter of the South (Dan. 11:6) probably refers to Berenice I, daughter of Ptolemy Philadelphus of Egypt, about the middle of the third century B.C. Daniel here is telling of the conflict between kings of the south and kings of the north, the Ptolemies and the Seleucidae.

DAUGHTER OF JAIRUS

The daughter of Jairus (Matt. 9:18-25; Mark 5:35-43; Luke 8: 41-56) was raised from the dead by Jesus. Jairus, her father, was a ruler of a synagogue elected by elders of the community, and it was his duty to look after the order of the divine service. His office was one of the most respected in the community and no doubt his only child of twelve years was loved by all his people.

One day as she lay at the point of death, her father hastened to Jesus, then at Capernaum, beseeching Him to heal her. But as the anxious father spoke with Jesus, a woman who had had an issue of blood for twelve years touched the Master's garment, and the multitude thronged about Him.

This pause must have been a great test of Jairus' patience and faith, for he knew how necessary it was that Jesus hasten to his daughter's bedside. While Jesus paused to speak to the woman, messengers came from Jairus' house saying, "Thy daughter is dead" (Mark 5:35). Until then he had besought Jesus to heal his sick child, but now she lay dead. To the mourning Jairus, Jesus spoke the confident words, "Be not afraid, only believe" (Mark 5:36).

When Jesus had healed the woman with the issue of blood, he

hastened on to the house of Jairus, taking with Him Peter and James and John. Upon entering the house, Jesus found it filled with noisy mourners. Even the flute-players had gathered to play for the last rites of the dead (Matt. 9:23). But Jesus rebuked the mourners, saying, "The damsel is not dead, but sleepeth" (Matt. 9:24; Mark 5:39; Luke 8:52).

Then He went in to where the sick child lay, taking with Him His three disciples. He said to her, "Talitha cumi; which is, being interpreted, Damsel, I say unto thee, arise" (Mark 5:41).

The Gospel writer, Mark, in his graphic way tells us, "And straightway the damsel arose, and walked." And Luke, the physician, makes this comment, "And her spirit came again, and she arose straightway: . . . And her parents were astonished" (Luke 8:55, 56).

In their astonishment, the joyous parents forgot that their daughter needed food, but Jesus did not forget. Turning to them, He commanded that something be given her to eat (Mark 5:43). Her hunger, a natural condition after a long illness, also made Jairus and his wife more aware that their only daughter was not only alive again but fully restored to health.

Though Jesus told her parents to tell no one what had transpired in this room of death, Matthew reports that "the fame hereof went abroad into all that land" (Matt. 9:26).

HERODIAS' DAUGHTER

Herodias' daughter (Matt. 14:6; Mark 6:22) is given no name in the Bible, but Josephus says her name was Salome. The famous opera *Salome* by Richard Strauss is based on the life of this daughter. She danced before her stepfather Herod Antipas and pleased him so well that he said to her, "Ask of me whatsoever thou wilt, and I will give it thee" (Mark. 6:22). The daughter went to her mother and said, "What shall I ask?" And the mother made the ghastly request for the head of John the Baptist because he had objected to her divorce from the girl's father and her marriage to his half-brother. The head was brought to the girl on a platter. Her own father was Herod Philip, who was a half-uncle of her mother's and a son of Herod the Great, who sought to destroy the child Jesus.

DAUGHTER WITH AN UNCLEAN SPIRIT

The daughter with an unclean spirit (Mark 7:25) was the daughter of the Syro-Phoenician woman, also called the Canaanite woman. The unclean spirit no doubt refers to a demon affliction of the girl. She was healed instantaneously by Jesus, though He did not even see her. (See Section I, "Searching Studies," on her mother "The Syro-Phoenician Woman.")

ABRAHAM'S DAUGHTER

Abraham's daughter (Luke 13:16) refers in a general sense to a woman descendant of Abraham. No daughters of Abraham are listed in the Genesis account, by either his first wife Sarah or his second wife Keturah.

DAUGHTERS OF JERUSALEM

Daughters of Jerusalem (Luke 23:28) are the women with Jesus as He journeys to the cross. The Master looks up from His own wretchedness to see these women weeping for Him, but He sorrowfully tells them that they are to be more pitied than He. Jerusalem, which should be a city of light, prefers darkness; and darkness, He predicts, will soon envelop the city.

He foresees how hard the lot will be for women, especially those with children. The childless woman, upon whom they have looked with sympathy, may now be more fortunate than they. At least she will not have to see her babies die of famine, or her little ones dashed against the wall by cruel invaders.

Weeping, these daughters of Jerusalem walked the Via Dolorosa with Jesus to Calvary; and in due course, what He had told them came to pass.

PHILIP'S DAUGHTERS

Philip's daughters (Acts 21:9) were the four unmarried daughters of the evangelist Philip. They seem to have had the honor of knowing and working for and with the great Christian men and women of their time in Jerusalem, Samaria, and Caesarea. Their father helped to administer the business affairs of the apostles and the growing Church in Jerusalem and to distribute relief to the poor.

They probably assisted him in the latter and were with him when he preached and healed at Samaria and when he led Simon the sorcerer to become an active believer in Christ.

Their mission as prophetesses is mentioned in the narrative telling that "Paul's company" entered the house of Philip at Caesarea on the Mediterranean. Luke probably stopped at their house also, and it is thought he may have written parts of his Gospel and the Book of Acts there.

Because of their association with the greatest Christian leaders of their time and their own rare spiritual endowments, they became il lumined expounders of God's words.

WIVES

*

The words "wife" or "wives" appears in the Bible close to 400 times. Among the most evil wives are Potiphar's wife, who tried to tempt Joseph; Lot's wife, who looked back on the iniquity of Sodom and was turned to a pillar of salt; Ahab's wife, Jezebel, who brought her pagan worship into Samaria; and Herod's wife, Herodias, who brought about the beheading of John the Baptist.

The men of Israel were forbidden to covet a neighbor's wife (Exod. 20:17). In the New Testament a man was told to have his own wife (I Cor. 7:2).

The wife was bound by the law as long as her husband lived, but if he died she was at liberty to be married again (I Cor. 7:39). One of the most important chapters regarding wives appears in I Corinthians 7.

In I Timothy 3:11 we learn that wives must be grave, not slanderers, sober, faithful in all things. In I Peter 3:1-6 we also have some rules of behavior for wives. The relationship of husbands and wives is discussed in Ephesians 5:21-33.

In Psalm 128:3 we are told a wife "shall be as a fruitful vine by the sides of thine house."

CAIN'S WIFE

Cain's wife (Gen. 4:17). "And Cain knew his wife; and she conceived, and bare Enoch."

NOAH'S WIFE

Noah's wife (Gen. 6:18; 7:7, 13; 8:16, 18), in the five times that she is mentioned, is merely among those present, with the sons and sons' wives of Noah. In the first three instances, the sons come first, but in the last two the wife is listed first. There is no record of her, except that as the wife of the hero of the flood, she went with him into the ark made of gopher wood covered inside and out with pitch.

Noah's wife became the first woman on record to make a home on a houseboat in the midst of flood waters. Like her husband, who was a just man and walked with God, probably she too had a deep consciousness of God. Her character is reflected in her family line, which continued strong for 350 years after the flood.

It is interesting to note that Noah's wife played no part in his experience when he discovered the art of making wine and became drunk. He was found drunk by his sons. Probably his wife, had she been living, could have saved him this embarrassment, for this is the only blot on Noah's career.

NOAH'S SONS' WIVES

Noah's sons' wives (Gen. 7:7, 13; 8:18). Noah's sons, Shem, Ham, and Japheth, all had wives who went with Noah and his wife into the ark, where they dwelt during the flood along with their mother-in-law. These wives and their mother-in-law are the only women of whom we have any record who survived the flood. After that had subsided, the wives went with their husbands and their mother-in-law to the spot where Noah had built an altar unto the Lord. These wives are the mothers of the descendants of Noah mentioned in Genesis 10.

LOT'S WIFE

Lot's wife (Gen. 19:26; Luke 17:32). (See Section I, "Searching Studies.")

JUDAH'S WIFE
Judah's wife (Gen. 38:2-5, 12), a daughter of a Canaanite, Shuah of Adullam, bore her husband three sons, Er, Onan and Shelah. Her two elder sons, Onan and Er, both of whom had been married to Tamar, were slain by divine judgment for their sins. When Tamar later heard of the death of her mother-in-law, Judah's wife, she disguised herself and stood by the road at sheep-shearing season, and Judah went in unto her and had twins by her.

POTIPHAR'S WIFE
Potiphar's wife (Gen. 39:7, 8, 9, 12, 19). (See Section I, "Searching Studies.")

ETHIOPIAN WIFE OF MOSES
The Ethiopian woman (Num. 12:1) was the second wife of Moses. Because she was of a different race his sister Miriam and his brother Aaron rebelled against Moses. A few scholars regard this as referring to his first wife Zipporah, daughter of the Midian priest Jethro.

GIDEON'S WIVES
Gideon's wives (Judg. 8:30) were many, for he sired seventy sons, it is recorded. This remarkable military leader of about 1256 B.C., who delivered Israel from Midian, was succeeded not by a son of his wives but by Abimelech, a son of his concubine from Shechem.

GILEAD'S WIFE
Gilead's wife (Judg. 11:2) is mentioned in the narrative of Jephthah, who was not her son but the son of a harlot. She bore Gilead

several sons, and when they grew up, they thrust Jephthah out and told him that he could not inherit in their father's house because he was born of a "strange woman."

MANOAH'S WIFE

Manoah's wife (Judg. 13:2, 11, 19, 20, 21, 22, 23) was Samson's mother. She bore no name of her own in the record but is introduced as the wife of a certain Manoah of Zorah, of the family of Danites, and seems to have been a stronger character than her husband. The remarkable thing about her life is that she was told not to drink wine or any strong drink or to eat any unclean thing, for her child would be dedicated to the sacred calling of a Nazarite.

When the angel appeared before her, she was reverent and silent and obedient to the voice and filled with faith, but her husband became fearful and pessimistic, saying, "We shall surely die, because we have seen God" (Judg. 13:22). But Manoah's wife remained unshaken in her faith. Together, however, they offered up a burnt sacrifice to God in grateful praise. She taught her son that no intoxicating drink should enter his lips and no razor should touch his head, for his long-grown locks would speak outwardly of his sacred vow to God.

Manoah's wife is typical of the wife who has a simple, trusting confidence in God and of the mother who is willing to consecrate herself to all that is good. We can be sure she lived closely to God, for the angel of the Lord appeared both times to her, and each time she made haste and told her husband.

Manoah's wife appears twice in the narrative after Samson is grown. First she and Manoah are protesting because their son has chosen for his wife a woman in Timnath, of the daughter of the Philistines, out of whose hands, it had been foretold before his birth, he would begin to deliver the Israelites. But Samson informed his mother and father that this Philistine woman "pleaseth me well"

(Judg. 14:3). But they knew their son's marriage was not of the Lord.

Manoah's wife last appears on her way to Timnath to see her son married to the woman to whom she had objected (Judg. 14:5). The marriage turned out badly, as Manoah and his wife had predicted.

Though Samson was weak where women were concerned, he became one of the most eminent of the Hebrew "Judges." Can we not believe that it was to his mother's love and prayers, her dedication of her son to God even before his birth, that he owed his true greatness?

Was it not the godliness he had inherited from his mother that triumphed in the end? For even at the eleventh hour, when he tore the pillars from their position and brought down the roof upon his foes, the Philistines, did he not atone for all his wasted years? Despite his weakness in character, the New Testament named him one of those Hebrew heroes whose animating principle was faith, a faith such as his godly mother had possessed before her child was born (Heb. 11:32).

SAMSON'S WIFE

Samson's wife (Judg. 14:15, 16, 20; 15:1, 6) tried to entice her husband by weeping and in reality opened doors that ultimately led to his ruin. Samson met her at Timnath, several miles from Zorah, his birthplace, and came back and told his parents, "Get her for me; for she pleaseth me well" (Judg. 14:3). In these ancient times parents usually negotiated the marriage alliances of their sons. But Samson's parents, a godly pair, felt that the marriage of their son, an Israelite, with a Philistine was not of the Lord. Their son, a "Nazarite from the womb," was set apart from other men for a religious mission.

On his way to visit this Philistine girl at Timnath, Samson met a lion which he slew without a weapon. (This part of the story, as well as some other parts, belongs to what many scholars regard as folk tale.) About a year later Samson went down again, for the seven-day feast which preceded the actual marriage ceremony, and he saw that honeybees had gathered in the carcass of the animal he had slain. As riddles were popular entertainment at such marriage feasts, he made up one based on one of his own recent experiences, saying, "Out of the eater came forth meat, and out of the strong came forth sweetness" (Judg. 14:14).

After the guests had sought the answer and failed, they threatened to burn Samson's wife if she would not obtain an answer. With tears, she tried to entice her husband; on the seventh day of the feast he told her the answer. She immediately revealed it to her banqueting Philistine friends.

Just before the sun went down, when the seven days of betrothal would have ended in a formal marriage ceremony, the Philistines revealed to Samson the answer to his riddle. He was so angered that he went out and slew thirty men and took their coats and gave them to the friends of his wife who had expounded the riddle. Then he returned to his father's house.

To avoid embarrassment, Samson's parents-in-law gave their daughter to Samson's best man. But later Samson decided to return to his father-in-law's house to be with his wife; and he took along with him a kid, the usual gift. From his father-in-law, Samson learned that because of his angry withdrawal at the betrothal ceremonies, his betrothed wife had been given to another. Her younger sister was now offered to him instead.

Samson was so incensed that he caught 300 foxes, divided them into pairs, and tied the tails of each pair together with slow-burning firebrands. Then he turned the foxes loose in cornfields of the Philistines, who were so angered that they went to the house of Samson's wife and burned her and her father to death.

Infuriated, Samson entered upon an even greater slaughter of the Philistines.

Though Samson's wife's story has some crude and confusing angles, it furnishes an excellent example of what happens to a man when he chooses a wife from a godless people. This Philistine wife's unprincipled conduct was what actually started the young Samson on the path to disaster.

EPHRAIM LEVITE'S CONCUBINE

The Ephraim Levite's concubine (Judg. 19, 20) was the secondary wife of a priest living near Mount Ephraim, but her position was sanctioned according to the customs of the time. Some trouble arose between the concubine and her husband and she went home to her father's house in Beth-lehem and remained there four months. At length her husband came to Beth-lehem for her, and after being hospitably received, he departed with his concubine.

At nightfall they reached Gibeah, a town in the territory belonging to the tribe of Benjamin. There they were invited to lodge for the night at the house of an old man whom they met coming in from the fields. During the night a terrible crime was commited by "certain sons of Belial" (Judg. 19:22) against the Levite's concubine.

In order to spread the news of the outrage far and wide throughout Israel, the Levite took the dead body of his concubine and cut it in twelve pieces and sent them to all the tribes. Everyone that heard of the crime said, "There was no such deed done nor seen from the day that the children of Israel came up out of the land of Egypt unto this day" (Judg. 19:30).

A fierce and bloody war was waged against the tribe of Benjamin to avenge the outrage against the Ephraim Levite's concubine.

FOUR HUNDRED YOUNG WIVES

Four hundred young virgins from Jabesh-Gilead (Judg. 21:12-23) were brought into the camp at Shiloh and given as wives to the defeated Benjamites. This incident followed the war started over the Ephraim Levite's concubine, who had been ill-treated by the wicked Sons of Benjamin, who had no wives.

Grieved that the tribe of Benjamites was now nearly destroyed, the Israelites received them into their favor and found them wives from among their own daughters. After the Benjamites received the four hundred young virgins as wives, they went and repaired their cities and dwelt in them.

Here is a striking example of how good wives can be the civilizers of men, thus influencing them away from evil into that which is good.

DAVID'S TEN CONCUBINES

David's ten concubines (II Sam. 15:16; 16:22; 20:3) were left in charge of his household in Jerusalem when he and his servants fled from the city. Absalom, the son of King David, had rebelled against his father and induced a great portion of the Israelites to flock to his standard.

The new master of Jerusalem was Absalom. Ahithophel, David's counselor, whose wisdom was highly rated, but who was disloyal to him during the revolt of his son Absalom, said unto Absalom,

"Go in unto they father's concubines, which he hath left to keep the house; and all Israel shall hear that thou art abhorred of thy father: then shall the hands of all that are with thee be strong.

"So they spread Absalom a tent upon the top of the house; and Absalom went in unto his father's concubines in the sight of all Israel" (II Sam. 16:21,22).

Absalom was ultimately slain by Joab and his followers were dispersed. When David returned to Jerusalem, he placed the concubines in custody, supplied them with food, but went not in unto them. "So they were shut up unto the day of their death, living in widowhood" (II Sam. 20:3).

SOLOMON'S WIVES

Solomon's wives (I Kings 3:1; 7:8; 11:1-8) numbered 700. Solomon also had 300 concubines. His first wife was the daughter of Pharaoh, whom he married during the early part of his reign. At this time her country of Egypt was the wealthiest and most powerful in the world.

Solomon's marriage with the princess from such a country doubtless was a great event and probably took place after he had been crowned. Through this marriage with Pharaoh's daughter, Solomon won the Canaanitish city of Gezer, about midway between Jerusalem and Joppa.

For Pharaoh's daughter Solomon built a house in his palace court, immediately behind his magnificent royal palace. Like the latter, it was fashioned of costly dressed stones, and the foundation also was of huge costly stones. The large court around it was of hewed stones and a row of cedar beams (I Kings 7:8-12).

After this Solomon loved many foreign wives, Moabite, Ammonite, Edomite, Sidonian, and Hittite, all from nations with which he probably had entered into political alliances. In his marriages with many women, Solomon broke the Deuteronomic Code (Deut. 17:17).

His many foreign wives were his undoing. In his later years, they turned his heart away to other gods. He began to worship Ashtoreth, the goddess of the Sidonians, and Milcom, the "Abomination of the Ammonites." Blessed with great material possessions, Solomon had felt rich enough to patronize these gods of his foreign wives.

Doubtless all Solomon's wives lived in great luxury, for Solomon had 40,000 stalls of horses, countless chariots, an endless array of servants and cupbearers, and a rich cuisine; his drinking vessels were of gold. His splendor eclipsed that of all other potentates of the earth. His wives evidently were women who placed high value on his riches. There is no record of any one of them turning to the God of his father David.

TAHPENES' SISTER, HADAD'S WIFE

The sister of Tahpenes (I Kings 11:19, 20) was the wife of Hadad, son of the king of Edom. Tahpenes was queen consort of Pharaoh of Egypt and a contemporary of Solomon, king of Israel. Scripture tells us that when David and Joab were at Edom, every male Edomite was slain except a youth named Hadad and some of his father's servants. The young Hadad fled to Egypt, where he was favorably received by Pharaoh, who gave him the sister of his wife in marriage. She gave birth to Genubath, who was brought up by Tahpenes among Pharaoh's children. It might be inferred that this sister died in childbirth.

JEROBOAM'S WIFE

Jeroboam's wife (I Kings 14:2, 4, 5, 6, 17) was the queen who went to the prophet Ahijah to inquire whether her sick son would recover. Her husband, Jeroboam, first king of the northern kingdom of Israel, was an apostate who had led his people away from the faith and worship of their fathers. He had calf shrines built for heathen worship, but when his son became ill, he longed for help in his son's healing.

Guilty because of his treatment of the priests of the Lord, Jeroboam told his wife to disguise herself in the dress of an ordinary woman when she went to see the prophet. Jeroboam also directed his wife to take the sort of gifts that an ordinary woman might offer, such as ten loaves and cracknels (crisp biscuits and pork crisply fried) and a cruse of honey, for it was customary to take a gift, however small, when advice or God's word was sought from a prophet.

The queen did disguise herself, as her husband had advised, and went to Shiloh, but when she arrived there, the aged and blind prophet, forewarned by the Lord of her coming, said, "Come in, thou wife of Jeroboam; why feignest thou thyself to be another? for I am sent to thee with heavy tidings" (I Kings 14:6). He then proceeded to tell her to go back and tell her husband that, because he had made other gods and molten images, he had provoked God, and his house would be visited with evil.

The prophet further prophesied to Jeroboam's wife that when she returned home her child would die, but all Israel would mourn him. Her child would be the only one of the house, however, to be laid in a grave, because there was some good "toward the Lord" in him. Others of the house of Jeroboam would be eaten by dogs or by fowls of the air. Jeroboam's wife arose and departed and when she came to her threshold her child died, and they buried him, and all Israel mourned.

NAAMAN'S WIFE

Naaman's wife (II Kings 5:2) had waiting on her a little Israelite maid, who had been captured in a border skirmish. Though Naaman was the successful commander-in-chief of Ben-hadad and had received many military honors and known much good fortune, he was now afflicted with leprosy. Through the maid's sympathetic interest in Naaman's condition he learned of Elisha's healing power. She probably told Naaman's wife, who carried the information to her husband, after which he went to Elisha, and was healed, and accepted the God of Israel as the "only God in all the earth."

Though Naaman's wife is the background figure in the incident, at least she became a channel for God's healing, because she had the faith to listen to a little maid in her household, insignificant though she was.

MACHIR'S WIFE

Machir's wife (I Chron. 7:15) was in the line of Zelophehad, who had the five distinguished daughters who declared their property rights.

ARTAXERXES' QUEEN

The queen who sat beside Artaxerxes (Neh. 2:6) is only briefly mentioned when Nehemiah came before the king to ask for the commission to build again the wall of Jerusalem.

JOB'S WIFE

Job's wife (Job 2:9; 19:17; 31:10) has been called everything from the "adjutant of the devil" (St. Augustine) to the "faithful attendant upon her husband's misery" (William Blake). She is introduced after Job, one of the richest and greatest men of his time, has been bereft of his cattle, flocks, camels, and all his children. Moreover, he is suffering from a loathsome disease, probably leprosy.

As he sat on an ashheap outside the city walls, Job still did not blame God. His wife, probably not so faithful and certainly not so patient, cried out, "Dost thou still retain thine integrity? Curse God, and die" (Job 2:9). No doubt Job's wife regarded a quick death as better than long-drawn-out suffering. In those days sudden death was supposed to result from cursing God.

In this statement we see Job's wife as an ordinary, normal woman. Though a dutiful wife, she probably failed to suffer with her husband in his hour of agony and consequently failed to share with him the marvelous victory of trusting God in spite of not understanding Him.

There is another side, however, to Job's wife. She had endured her husband's affliction, even the loss of all their children and all their material possessions, and had survived these trials. Like her husband, she was bewildered amid so much calamity. Such a piece of advice as she gave him in his affliction could have been inspired by sympathy and love. Probably she would rather have seen him die than endure such great suffering.

In the next scene where she is depicted, we find her turning from her husband (Job 19:17), because his breath is so offensive on account of the disease from which he suffered.

Though Job's wife is not mentioned in the closing chapters, we learn in 42:14 that three daughters, Jemima, Kezia, and Keren-happuch, as well as sons, were later born to him. Probably Job's wife arose to new joy, just as he did, and regretted her own lack of faith when she had advised him to "curse God, and die."

ISAIAH'S WIFE

Isaiah's wife (Isa. 8:3). In the entire period of political decline which preceded the fall of Samaria in 722 B.C. and of Jerusalem in 586 B.C. only two prophetesses appear in the record: Huldah, and Isaiah's wife, whom he speaks of as a prophetess. In the case of Isaiah's wife, she was probably called a prophetess because she was the wife of a prophet, rather than one who prophesied herself.

Isaiah tells that he went unto her and she conceived. Their son was Maher-shalal-hash-baz, meaning "Hasten the spoil, rush on the prey." In Isaiah 7:3 another son of Isaiah is mentioned. He is Shear-jashub, and his name means "A remnant returns." The names stand for two of Isaiah's prophecies concerning Jerusalem.

WIVES WHO BURNED INCENSE TO GODS

Wives who burned incense to other gods (Jer. 44:15) were Hebrew women who had left Judah and had fled to Pathros, a province of the land of Egypt. They were rebuked by Jeremiah for their idolatrous worship. He forewarned them of the dreadful evils that would befall them if they persisted in their false worship.

These women presumptuously declared it was their intention to continue in the same course, to burn incense unto the queen of heaven, as their fathers had done before them. They saw no evil in such a practice (Jer. 44:19).

EZEKIEL'S WIFE

Ezekiel's wife (Ezek. 24:16, 17, 18) is referred to as the desire of his eyes. The wife of this prophet-priest of the sixth century B.C. was taken quite suddenly with a stroke. Ezekiel was warned that this would happen but was forbidden to perform the customary mourning rites.

He restrained his tears and went forth to preach, probably the morning after he had been told that he would lose his wife. In the evening she died. But that morning he spoke to his people on the coming destruction of Jerusalem, when they also would lose loved ones, but he told them that they too must abstain from any outward signs of mourning. Ezekiel's own great grief, only a few hours away, enabled him to speak with greater conviction to those who looked to him for spiritual guidance.

Doubtless Ezekiel's wife was a godly woman who had helped him serve his small, remote congregation. Their home was a little mud-brick house in a colony of exiles at Tel-abib on the Chebar, an important canal in the Euphrates irrigation system (Ezek. 3:15).

PETER'S WIFE

Peter's wife (Matt. 8:14; Mark 1:30; Luke 4:38; I Cor. 9:5) no doubt witnessed her mother's healing. Since Jesus probably used Peter's home as headquarters when in Capernaum his wife must have seen Jesus often. She is referred to as Simon's or Cephas' wife. She traveled with him as did the wives of other apostles.

WIFE WHO WAS TO BE SOLD FOR DEBT

The wife who was to be sold for debt (Matt. 18:25) appears in Jesus' parable of the unforgiving servant and illustrates the principle of the Lord's Prayer, "Forgive us our debts, as we forgive our debtors."

Here Jesus is comparing our heavenly Father to a king who wished to settle accounts with his servants. One was brought to him who owed him ten thousand talents (approximately ten million dollars). When the servant could not pay, the king ordered him to be sold, with his wife and children and all that he had. The servant begged the king to have patience with him, and the king, moved with compassion, loosed his servant and let him go.

But the servant went forth and cast into prison a fellow servant who owed him a very small debt. Then the king called back the servant he had forgiven of his large debt and asked why he had not showed the same compassion to his fellow servant that had been shown to him. The man was then jailed until he should pay all that he owed.

Jesus, concluding the parable, said, "So likewise shall my heavenly Father do also unto you, if ye from your hearts forgive not every one his brother their trespasses" (Matt. 18:35).

The Old Testament tells of selling people into slavery to pay a debt (Amos 2:6; 8:6; Neh. 5:4, 5), but this is the only reference of a woman's being sold, along with her children, to pay a debt.

PILATE'S WIFE

Pilate's Wife (Matt. 27:19). (See Section I, "Searching Studies.")

THE UNBELIEVING WIFE

The unbelieving wife (I Cor. 7:14), says Paul to the Corinthians, is sanctified by her husband. Though he is a Christian and she is not, his belief sanctifies the union. Paul goes on to say that the faith of one Christian parent gives to the children a near relationship to the Church, just as if both parents were Christians. The children are regarded not as aliens to the Christian faith but as sharers in it. Paul presumed that the believing parent will rear the child in the Christian principles.

He makes the same point in regard to husbands, saying that "The unbelieving husband is sanctified by the wife."

MOTHERS

A mother is the Bible's most honored woman, and great stress is laid upon the influence of mothers. The most significant phrase using the word "mother" is "And his mother was." It appears twenty times in II Kings and II Chronicles and underlines the importance attached to the mothers of kings.

Often the queen-mother is more honored than the queen-wife. Right after the names of great queen-mothers in Kings and Chronicles there usually occurs a phrase summarizing the spiritual and moral tone of the king's reign, "And he did that which was right in the sight of the Lord" or "And he did that which was evil in the sight of the Lord." The juxtaposition of the queen-mother's name and an evaluation of her son's reign seems significant.

The mother's influence is also stressed in Ezekiel 16:44, where appears the phrase "As is the mother, so is her daughter." The love of children was deep in the hearts of Hebrew women, and the mother was regarded with the deepest reverence. In one place in the Law the mother is even placed before the father as the object of filial reverence (Lev. 19:3). We find among some of the earliest laws of the Hebrews the obligation placed upon children to honor the mother as well as the father (Exod. 20:12).

The word "mother" or "mothers" appears in the Bible almost 300 times, while the word "mother-in-law" appears eleven times, and always in reference to Naomi, mother-in-law of Ruth.

Sometimes a nation is spoken of as a mother and the people as her children (Isa. 50:1, Jer. 50:12; Hos. 4:5). Large cities also are likened to mothers, as in II Samuel 20:19.

MOTHERS

THE CANAANITISH MOTHER OF SHAUL

The Canaanitish woman (Gen. 46:10; Exod. 6:15) was the mother of Shaul. Her husband was Simeon. The Israelites had been warned not to marry the daughters of the Canaanites (Gen. 24:3).

THE ARAMITESS

The Aramitess (I Chron. 7:14) was the mother of Machir, who became the father of Gilead. She was a native of Aram (Syria) and became the concubine of Manasseh, Joseph's eldest son.

SISERA'S MOTHER

Sisera's mother (Judg. 5:28) represents the aged mother, watching longingly for her warrior son to return from battle. Sisera, a Canaanite chieftain of the twelfth century B.C., had already been killed by Jael, the Kenite wife, who had driven a tent peg into his head while, wearied from battle, he lay sleeping.

After many of his men had perished in the floodwaters of the Kishon, Sisera had sought refuge in the tent of Jael and her husband Heber, the Kenite, thinking them friendly to him (Judg. 4:17).

Sisera's mother, we know, was a luxury-loving, materially minded woman. She does not appeal to God for her son's safe return. On the other hand, we see her sitting beside the latticed windows of her palace, and she is asking, "Why is his chariot so long in coming?" Her ladies-in-waiting comfort her by stories of the wild spoils of war. They tell her that her son, Sisera, is late because, like all sons of war, he has probably received a damsel or two. Also they picture to her the rich garments that her son will bring back, garments luxuriant in their colors and rich in their embroideries.

The story of Sisera's mother appears in Deborah's Song.

ABIMELECH'S CONCUBINE MOTHER

Abimelech's concubine mother (Judg. 9:1, 3) was a native of Shechem, where her Canaanite family evidently had great influence. She became the concubine of Gideon, who had many wives. Abimelech, her son by this union, became a cruel and unjust despot. Desiring his father's throne, he obtained it with assistance from his mother's relatives, killing seventy sons of his father on one stone at Ophrah, his mother's native city. Abimelech ruled three years, shedding much blood. He was finally mortally wounded by a woman.

MICAH'S MOTHER

Micah's mother (Judg. 17:2, 3, 4) had dedicated 1,100 shekels of silver to the making of graven images. Her son, Micah of Ephraim, stole the shekels, but when he heard his mother had cursed because of the loss, he returned them to her and confessed his guilt. She made restitution of the money to him, but took 200 shekels (probably from the original amount) and had images made at a foundry.

There seems to be spiritual confusion in the mind of this mother, who in one breath blessed the Lord and in the next told her son that she had set aside the shekels for him and had planned that part be used for the making of graven images. She appeared to want to honor God but was ignorant as to the meaning of faith in the one God.

Though Micah's mother does not appear in the text after this incident, we learn how her influence in idolatry carried on. Her son built a shrine or house of gods, probably a miniature copy of the temple at Shiloh, and set it up in his home. He placed there the graven images and secured a priest to stay in his home, administer the shrine, and educate his son for the priesthood.

But the graven and molten images were stolen by migrating

Danites, who also persuaded Micah's priest to leave with them. And they took to Shiloh the images which Micah's mother had given him and competed with them against the house of the Lord.

ICHABOD'S MOTHER

Ichabod's mother (I Sam. 4:19-22). (See Section I, "Searching Studies.")

DAVID'S MOTHER

David's mother (I Sam. 22:3, 4) and father took refuge in Moab. They remained with the king of Moab as his guests while David who was fleeing from Saul took refuge there also.

THE WISE WOMAN OF TEKOAH

The wise woman of Tekoah (II Sam. 14:1-20) was the mother of two sons. She was a dramatic actress as well as a sagacious woman. Dressed in mourning, she came up from her home in Tekoah to Jerusalem and feigned a story about her two sons, one of whom, she said, had been killed by the other as they fought together in the field, where there was no one to part them. Now her whole family wanted to put her guilty son to death. She begged David to have mercy on her son and David declared the young man would not be harmed.

Tekoah was twelve miles south of Jerusalem, far enough away so that her story could not be easily investigated. She had woven it together to be as much like the story of David's own sons, Absalom and Amnon, as she could make it and still not have him recognize immediately the real purpose of her mission.

Several years before, David had banished Absalom, his most beloved son, for the murder of Amnon.

Realizing that David now needed the company of his favorite son, the discerning Joab, commander-in-chief of David's army, had instructed the woman to come from Tekoah and make this appeal. Though in his heart David still loved Absalom, he probably had not recalled him because he dreaded public opinion.

To overcome David's scruples and help him see that mercy was reasonable in this case, the woman of Tekoah came with her story, and David soon saw that it paralleled that of his own two sons. When he asked if Joab had sent her, she revealed that he had put all these words into her mouth. Then in her argument she made it clear that Absalom had reason to complain that he was treated by his own father more sternly than her son, one of the humblest subjects in the realm.

She let him know that the nation could now say that the king gave more attention to her humble petition than to the wishes and desires of the whole kingdom. She argued with him also that the death of her own son would be only a private loss to her family, but the termination of Absalom's banishment was to the common interest of all Israel, who now looked to Absalom as David's successor on the throne.

This wise woman of Tekoah was successful in her mission. After she left, David sent Joab to Geshur to bring Absalom back to Jerusalem. The reconciliation came about because the woman of Tekoah had acted so well the feigned story of her two sons.

Evidently she was a devout woman, for she stressed that "as an angel of God, so is my lord the king to discern good and bad: therefore the Lord thy God will be with thee." Earlier she had spoken of her own "inheritance of God" coming through her son. Her devotion to God was what probably won King David's heart.

TWO MOTHERS OF SOLOMON'S TIME

Two mothers (I Kings 3:16-28). (See Section I, "Searching Studies.")

HIRAM'S MOTHER

Hiram's mother (I Kings 7:13, 14) is referred to in II Chronicles 2:14 as a widow and daughter of Dan. The son became the great architect, artisan and artist summoned from Tyre by King Solomon to cast the metals and other furnishings for his magnificent Temple at Jerusalem. Could it be that his mother is mentioned, both in Kings and in Chronicles, to stress the importance of a mother in a son's life, even in the directing of his talents for that which is beautiful and lasting?

The father is mentioned in both II Chronicles 2:14 and II Chronicles 4:16, and the *Westminster Dictionary* (p. 248) makes the point that this title of father "probably denotes a master workman or a counselor."

ELISHA'S MOTHER

Elisha's mother (I Kings 19:20) is mentioned when the young Elisha departed with the prophet Elijah. The older prophet had cast his mantle upon Elisha and the youth asked that he might return and kiss his mother, and then he said, "I will follow thee."

THE SHUNAMMITE MOTHER

The Shunammite (II Kings 4:8-37; 8:1-6). (See Section I, "Searching Studies.")

TWO MOTHERS WHO AGREED TO EAT THEIR SONS

Two mothers agreed to eat their sons (II Kings 6:26-30) during a great famine in Samaria, in the time of Elisha. They had become so desperately hungry that they made a pledge with each other that they would eat first one of their sons and then the other.

The king of Israel, passing by the city walls to look at his defenses, came upon one of the mothers crying against the walls. "Help, my lord, O king," she implored. When he asked what was her trouble, she told him, "This woman said unto me, Give thy son, that we may eat him today, and we will eat my son tomorrow. So we boiled my son, and did eat him: and I said unto her on the next day, Give thy son, that we may eat him: and she hath hid her son." When the king heard this story of two mothers, whose hunger had been so great that they were led to cannibalism, "he rent his clothes."

JABEZ' MOTHER

Jabez' mother (I Chron. 4:9) bore her son in sorrow and called him by a name meaning "sorrow." She gave to the world a son "more honourable than his brethren." He became a prayerful and pious man, who asked that God might keep him from evil. His prayer was answered. Doubtless the sorrow of Jabez' mother had drawn her closer to God.

It is probable that she was familiar with the story of how Jacob called the name of the place where God spoke with him Beth-el, and perpetuated the circumstances which marked her son's birth similarly.

Some scholars are of the opinion that Jabez was the son of Coz (I Chron. 4:8). If so, his mother also had other children.

If she lived to know of the achievements of her godly son, she must have felt compensated for all her sorrow. Jewish writers affirm that Jabez became an eminent doctor in the law. His reputation is thought to have drawn so many scribes around him that a town, probably in the territory of Judah, was called by his name (I Chron. 2:55).

LEMUEL'S MOTHER

Lemuel's mother (Prov. 31:1) has never been identified, nor has her son, but the counsel of the virtuous woman (see Section I, "Searching Studies") is credited to her.

MAHER-SHALAL-HASH-BAZ'S MOTHER
Maher-shalal-hash-baz's mother (Isa. 8:4) was the wife of the
great eight-century prophet Isaiah.

JEREMIAH'S MOTHER
Jeremiah's mother (Jer. 15:10) is mentioned in the prophet's
lament over the strife and contention in Jerusalem. He speaks as
though communing with his mother who has brought him into the
world. He rues his birth because of the distress and affliction of his
beloved country.

BELSHAZZAR'S MOTHER
Belshazzar's mother (Dan. 5:10, 11, 12) is referred to as queen
in Daniel 5:10. She was either the grandmother or, more probably,
the queen-mother during the reign of Belshazzar, last king of the
Neo-Babylonian Empire. Some scholars are of the opinion that she
was Nitocris, queen of Babylonia, to whom Herodotus ascribed many
civic improvements.

If so, Belshazzar's mother was regarded as the noblest and most
beautiful woman of her time. History records that during the in-
sanity of her husband, Nebuchadnezzar (Dan. 4:36), Nitocris did
much to beautify Babylon. She built beautiful bridges, wharves, tiled
embankments, and lakes and made improvements and enlargements
to the buildings. Years after Nebuchadnezzar's death she was an
influential force in the government.

Though in the three verses of the fifth chapter of Daniel Belshazzar's mother appears and disappears, like a face in a window, she
gives us much of herself in a single speech there. It came when
Belshazzar was celebrating a great feast.

The king, crazed with drink, earlier had shouted to his butlers to
bring the cups of the Lord's Temple which had been brought to

Babylon as plunder from Jerusalem. These sacred vessels were filled with wine and defiled by the lips of the drunken king and his thousand lords. At the height of the celebration an apparition, in the shape of the fingers of a man's hand, wrote upon the walls the words, "Mene, Mene, Tekel, Upharsin" (Dan. 5:25). None of the drunken guests could understand what they meant.

Then it was that Belshazzar's mother, learning that her son was troubled by this astonishing occurrence, came into the banquet hall. Not knowing how to interpret the strange words, she advised the king to call in Daniel, now an old man, who had served Nebuchadnezzar as an interpreter of dreams years before.

Daniel appeared and read the meaning of the words, which were, "God hath numbered thy kingdom, and finished it; thou art weighed in the balances, and art found wanting; thy kingdom is divided, and given to the Medes and Persians."

In that same night Belshazzar was slain, and Darius seized the kingdom. The queen-mother probably never saw Belshazzar again after her brief appearance in the banquet hall.

Her mention in the Bible came not because she had beautified Babylonia—if she was Nitocris—but because she knew the prophet Daniel, who foretold the coming of Christ.

Of one thing we can be certain: Belshazzar's mother was a woman who believed in the greatness of God, because in her speech in the banquet hall, when she advised the king to summon Daniel, she described him as a man "in whom is the spirit of the holy gods." And she wisely added, "And in the days of thy father light and understanding and wisdom, like the wisdom of the gods, was found in him."

PETER'S WIFE'S MOTHER

Peter's wife's mother (Matt. 8:14, 15; Mark 1:30, 31; Luke 4:38, 39). (See Section I, "Searching Studies," "Three Sick Women.")

MOTHERS

THE SYRO-PHOENICIAN WOMAN

The Syro-Phoenician woman, same as the Canaanite woman, was the mother of an afflicted daughter (Matt. 15:21-28; Mark 7:24-30). (See Section I, "Searching Studies.")

THE MOTHER WHOSE HOUR IS COME

The mother whose hour is come (John 16:20-22) is referred to by Jesus. He reminds His followers of the sorrow that comes to a woman in pains of labor before the birth of her child, and also of the great joy that follows when her child is born and she first sees it. Then she thinks not of the anguish, but of her joy. He tells His disciples they will be sorrowful, but their sorrow will be turned to joy at the Resurrection.

Jesus foretold the last days of the Temple at Jerusalem, and in reporting His message, the first three Gospel writers use exactly the same words: "Woe unto them that are with child, and to them that give suck in those days!" (Matt. 24:19; Mark 13:17; Luke 21:23).

His words point to the suffering of those living in Jerusalem when the Temple is destroyed.

THE MOTHER OF THE BLIND SON

The mother of the blind son (John 9:2, 3, 18, 20, 22, 23) figures in the story of Jesus' healing of her son. She testified to doubting Jews that her son was blind from birth. She does not appear alone, but always with her husband in the phrases "his parents" or "the parents."

When Jesus' disciples asked, "Master, who did sin, this man, or his parents, that he was born blind?" (John 9:2), they assumed a current idea of that period that every calamity is due to some sin.

Jesus replied with one of his positive statements: "Neither hath this man sinned, nor his parents; but that the works of God should be made manifest in him."

Then Jesus spat on the ground and made a paste of dust and spittle and put it on the son's eyes. One commentator suggests that this symbolized the creative act of Genesis 2:7. After Jesus had sealed the man's eyes he sent him to the pool of Siloam to wash away the clay.

After the man had received his sight, his parents were summoned before the Pharisees to testify that their son had been born blind and to explain how he had been healed. The parents declared that the man was their son, that he had been born blind, and that now he could see. More than this they would not say, for they feared displeasing the Pharisees and being put out of the synagogue. They said to the Jews: "He is of age; ask him" (John 9:23), meaning "Ask our son."

PAUL'S SISTER

Paul's sister (Acts 23:16) was the mother of a son, who seems to have resided with her, probably in Jerusalem. He gave information to the chief captain of the plot to kill Paul. It may be inferred that Paul's sister was connected with some of the more prominent families.

RUFUS' MOTHER

Rufus' mother (Rom. 16:13) was one of those to whom Paul sent salutations in his letter to the Romans, written from Corinth and probably carried by Phebe, a deaconess of the Church at Cenchrea near Corinth.

"Salute Rufus chosen in the Lord," Paul wrote, "and his mother and mine." The last phrase referred, of course, to his spiritual relationship in the early Christian Church with Rufus' mother. The phrase shows us that she was a spiritually minded woman, probably one of the most faithful workers in this early church.

In Paul's long list of salutations in this chapter, this is the only woman designated as a mother.

WIDOWS

Widows in the Old Testament are said to be under the special care of the Lord.

In Exodus 22:22 there is strong warning not to afflict the widow. The widow is referred to often in Deuteronomy (10:18; 14:29; 16:11; 24:17; 25:5, 6, 7, 8, 9, 10; and 27:19). The final passage gives strong warning that "Cursed be he that perverteth the judgment of the . . . widow." The passages in Deuteronomy 25 state clearly points in the old levirate law written for the protection of the widow.

Job (31:16, 22), in his distress, cried out, "If I have . . . caused the eyes of the widow to fail, . . . Then let mine arm fall from my shoulder blade, and mine arm be broken from the bone." In Psalms (146:9) is the comforting statement that "The Lord . . . relieveth . . . the widow," and there is a Proverb (15:25), "The Lord . . . will establish the border of the widow."

Isaiah (1:17) exhorts people to plead for the widow and cries out woe (10:2) unto them who make widows their prey. Jeremiah (7:6; 22:3; 49:11) and Zechariah (7:10) speak comfort for the widow. Finally, Malachi (3:5) says God will be a swift witness for those who oppress the widow.

In the New Testament Matthew (23:14), Mark (12:40), and Luke (20:47) speak woe unto those who devour widows' houses. The Grecians murmured because their widows were neglected (Acts 6:1).

Paul writing to Timothy (I Tim. 5:3, 4, 5, 6, 9, 10, 11, 12, 16) has much to say in behalf of the widow, and finally James (1:27)

[350]

says that "Pure religion and undefiled before God and the Father is this, To visit the . . . widows in their affliction."

WOMEN OF MIDIAN

Women of Midian (Num. 31:9), after their husbands had been slain, were taken as captives by the Israelites. With their children, their cattle, their flocks and goods, the women were taken as spoils of war to Moses and Eleazar, the priest in the camp on the plains of Moab before the congregation there.

Moses was "wroth" that these women of Midian had been saved because they came from a people who had committed trespasses against the Lord, and a plague had followed. He ordered that the women who had been married be killed, but that the virgins be saved and given as wives to the Israelites.

The lesson taught here is that the Israelites believed that victory in war belonged to Yahweh. Thus any booty, even women of the enemy, belonged to Him and must be divided according to His will.

This story again lets us see how women of antiquity were regarded not as persons but as things, just like cattle and flocks and household goods.

WIDOW OF ZAREPHATH

Widow of Zarephath (I Kings 17:8-24; Luke 4:25, 26). (See Section I, "Searching Studies.")

WIDOW WHOSE OIL WAS MULTIPLIED

The widow whose oil was multiplied (II Kings 4:1-8) appears early in the story of Elisha. It evinces the prophet's kindness for a poor widow. She had no claim to the compassion of the prophet, except that he had known her husband, who "did fear the Lord." Her husband had died with debts so heavy that his creditors had come and demanded that her two sons be given them as slaves, in payment of the debts.

Unless she could pay her debts she would have to part with her sons. Without fear she approached the prophet Elisha, who asked, "What shall I do for thee?" And when she told him her trouble, he then asked, "Tell me, what hast thou in the house?" When she told him that she had nothing but a pot of oil, he told her, "Go, borrow thee vessels abroad of all thy neighbors, even empty vessels; borrow not a few. And when thou art come in, thou shalt shut the door upon thee and upon thy sons, and shalt pour out into all those vessels, and thou shalt set aside that which is full."

The woman had to possess a childlike and trusting faith to carry out such orders. But it came to pass when the vessels were full that she said to her son, "Bring me yet a vessel. And he said unto her, There is not a vessel more. And the oil stayed."

When the widow came back to Elisha and told him what had happened, he directed her, "Go, sell the oil, and pay thy debt, and live thou and thy children of the rest." It was enough to give the poor widow permanent relief, and Elisha had provided for her future and given her the added blessing of keeping her sons by her side.

WIDOW WITH TWO MITES

The widow with two mites (Mark 12:41-44; Luke 21:1-4) has given us one of the most meaningful short stories in the Bible. During the last Passover week of Jesus' life on earth, this poor woman entered the Court of the Women in the Temple at Jerusalem and cast into the chest there her two mites, hardly enough to buy a loaf of bread.

Streams of visitors were in the Holy City through the seven days of the great annual Feast of the Jews, and this woman would have passed unnoticed, but devotion like hers could not escape Jesus' notice. Her sacrifice appealed to Him, and He preserved her story in the safekeeping of His praise. Both Mark and Luke relate it.

Luke tells that in praising her generosity Jesus said, "This poor widow hath cast in more than they all: For all these have of their abundance cast in unto the offerings of God: but she of her penury hath cast in all the living that she had" (21:3-4).

The cash value of her gift compared to the gifts of the wealthy was hardly enough to notice, but the devotion behind it was another matter. That devotion, beginning there and spreading throughout the world, has built hospitals and helped the needy, fed the hungry and encouraged the imprisoned. Today the world knows more about the poor widow than about the richest man in Jerusalem in her day.

WIDOW OF NAIN'S SON

The widow of Nain's son (Luke 7:11-19) was the first person Jesus raised from the dead. It was after He and his disciples and a multitude following Him had left Capernaum and had entered the village of Nain, which lies on the lower slopes of the Little Hermon.

When Jesus came to the gate of the city, "Behold, there was a dead man carried out, the only son of his mother, and she was a widow: and much people of the city was with her."

Luke goes on to relate that Jesus had compassion upon her, as He always did upon women in distress. No one asked Him for help, but walking up to the widow Jesus said, "Weep not." Such words were not a feeble effort to console her. They had a deeper meaning, as she was soon to learn.

He came and touched the bier of her son and spoke to him, "Young man, I say unto thee, Arise." And the young man who had been dead began to speak. Though Luke does not give us a definite picture of the mother or express how she felt when her son was raised from the dead, the one graphic stroke is sufficient: Jesus "delivered him to his mother."

The most amazing phase of the healing of the widow of Nain's son is that all who had witnessed this miracle "glorified God," saying a great prophet had come among them. And they recognized that Jesus was a far greater prophet than had been Elijah, who had raised from the dead the son of the widow of Zarephath. Elijah had raised her son after he had gone into a room alone and prayed for the boy. But Jesus healed the son of the widow of Nain instantaneously as a bewildered crowd looked on.

IMPORTUNATE WIDOW

The importunate widow (Luke 18:3, 5) appears in one of Jesus' parables. When the widow went to the judge begging him to avenge her of her adversary he refused. She continued to plead with the judge to help her. Finally he yielded to her plea for he feared that "by her continual coming she weary me."

Jesus used the parable of the importunate widow to teach his disciples the need for persistent prayer.

GREEK WIDOWS

Greek widows (Acts 6:1). Though the number of the disciples in Jerusalem had been multiplied, the Grecians complained against the Hebrews "because their widows were neglected in the daily ministration." The Greeks were regarded as inferior by the Hebrews. The complaint no doubt was well founded. Each party wanted its own poor cared for in the daily ministration of alms and foods.

TATTLERS AND BUSYBODIES

Tattlers and busybodies (I Tim. 5:13) refer to women in a religious order of widowhood. They seem to have some of the same duties as the men presbyters who served in the early Church. Paul, writing to Timothy on how to deal with various problems in the Church, says that it is better for these younger widows to marry again than to spend their time in idle chatter.

The ideal, however, was that these women serving in the Church not remarry. Though Paul does not impose a law, he points out a remedy for these younger widows (those up to age sixty), who engage in a lot of vain talk.

OTHER UNNAMED WOMEN

＊

The unity and fellowship of woman with man is stressed early in the Creation, and we become more and more certain of how man and woman were made for each other as the stories of women unfold.

Among some of the most interesting women in the Bible are these nameless ones. Though some of their stories are short, we soon discover that their roles were not as unimportant as they might at first seem. Every woman who appears in the Bible holds a significant place in the history of mankind.

In the section that follows are many of the unnamed women in the background whose lives had meaning and purpose in the Bible record.

The words "woman" and "women" appear in the Bible more than 400 times, and we find women in every role from poets to prophets.

WISE-HEARTED WOMEN

Wise-hearted women (Exod. 35:25) refers to the devout women who spun, "both of blue, and of purple, and of scarlet, and of fine linen" for the tabernacle. In the next verse we learn that all women "whose heart stirred them up in wisdom spun goats' hair." We get a picture of how, in this time of Moses, about fifteen centuries before Christ, women worked just as they do now to beautify their places of worship. These gifts that they made came from the heart and into them they put their best talents. This is the earliest record we have of the handwork of the women of Israel.

WOMEN ASSEMBLING AT TABERNACLE

Women assembling at the tabernacle (Exod. 38:8) are those who ministered at the door of the tent meeting place. In a description of the building of the tabernacle after the Israelites had come out of Egypt, we are told that near the altar there was a laver or vessel of metal made from the polished copper or bronze "looking glasses of the women assembling." These women who ministered at the door probably assisted the Levites in the preparations for the service. This is one of the earliest examples of women's ministry in the house of God.

WOMAN PATRIOT OF THEBEZ

The woman patriot of Thebez (Judg. 9:53) dropped a millstone from the city wall on the head of Abimelech and broke his skull. He was a king of many bloody deeds who had murdered his seventy half-brothers, sons of his father Gideon, in order to become king of Shechem.

After he had ruled for three years, an insurrection arose because Abimelech's throne had been founded in blood. He had a thousand men and women who had taken refuge in a tower at Shechem burned to death. Then he marched on the fortress at Thebez.

"A certain woman" there, knowing of Abimelech's terrible cruelty, became the heroine in battle. She mortally wounded him as he marched on the fortress at Thebez, but in order to avoid the shame of death at a woman's hand, Abimelech ordered his armor-bearer to take his sword and slay him. The armor-bearer did, and Abimelech, Gideon's evil son, died. Because of the woman's act her people were delivered and it appears that the land had peace for many years.

HARLOT OF GAZA

The harlot of Gaza (Judg. 16:1) is mentioned in the story of Samson. He went in unto her, and because he did, the Gazites knew where he was and lay waiting for him all night in front of the woman's house. When it was morning, they expected to kill him, but Samson arose at midnight, taking with him, in revenge, the doors of the gates of the city, together with the posts.

YOUNG MAIDENS GOING OUT TO DRAW WATER

Young maidens going out to draw water (I Sam. 9:11) were met by Saul as he, accompanied by one of his father's servants, went out to look for his father's asses that had been lost. He came upon these maidens, of whom he asked the way. They directed him to Samuel, the man of God, and they told him to make haste.

Insignificant though these maidens appear, they made it possible for Saul to find Samuel and through Samuel to find the way of God (I Sam. 9:27).

WOMEN WITH TABRETS

Women with tabrets (I Sam. 18:6) came out of all the cities of Israel singing and dancing. They came to meet King Saul and David after the latter had slain Goliath. Though they moved forward with joy, playing instruments of music, they angered Saul because they sang, "Saul hath slain his thousands, and David his ten thousands" (I Sam. 18:7). We see here how one untactful remark by a group of women can change the course of history. Though these women sang songs of victory, they aroused the envy of the victorious King Saul, and from this moment forward he hated David and began to plot against him.

OTHER UNNAMED WOMEN

WOMAN OF ENDOR
Woman of Endor (I Sam. 28:7-25). (See Section I, "Searching Studies.")

NURSE WHO LET CHILD FALL
The nurse who let the child fall (II Sam. 4:4) cared for Mephibosheth, Saul's grandson and Jonathan's son. Possibly Mephibosheth's mother was dead, for the nurse apparently had full charge of him when word came of the disaster at Jezreel and the approach of the Philistine army. She picked up the little prince, then about five years old, and in her haste to carry him to safety dropped him and lamed him. The text is a little obscure. He is mentioned as being lame before his fall and he was probably made lame again after his fall. The nurse took the lame prince to Lo-debar in the mountains of Gilead, where he was reared in the house of Machir, son of Ammiel (II Sam. 9:4).

THE WENCH
The wench of En-rogel (II Sam. 17:17) was a maidservant who formed a communication link between King David, who had fled from Jerusalem, and Jonathan, son of Abiathar, and Ahimaaz, the high priest, both of whom remained in Jerusalem. Absalom was then in rebellion against his father David, and this wench gave information to David's two men of Absalom's designs to seize the throne. Because of her information Absalom soon met his death at the hands of Joab, David's commander-in-chief. The word "wench" appears in the Bible only once.

THE BAHURIM WOMAN

The Bahurim woman (II Sam. 17:19) helped to save David's small forces in a battle with the larger forces of his son Absalom, who was plotting to seize the throne. In her yard was an empty cistern, where she hid two of David's messengers, Jonathan and Ahimaaz, on their way from Jerusalem to carry vital information to David and the party loyal to him during Absalom's rebellion.

The woman, living in the town of Bahurim, a village near the Mount of Olives on the road from Jerusalem to the Jordan, realized that David's men were being pursued by partisans of Absalom. So she seized a cloth from her house and covered the mouth of the well with it. Then she snatched a basket of corn from her doorway and spread it over the cloth. David's men remained safely hidden there.

All their pursuers saw was a heap of corn drying in the sun. When they asked the woman, nonchalantly standing in her yard, if she had seen two men running past that way, she replied that she had but they had long since gone on their way over the brook. Thus she sent the pursuers in the wrong direction, while David's messengers went on to where the king was and told him he must press on and cross the Jordan River.

An inconspicuous, faithful woman, through the simple act of covering a well with a cloth and a basket of corn, helped to save David and his army and the kingdom of Israel.

THE WISE WOMAN OF ABEL

The wise woman of Abel (II Sam. 20:16-22) was able to stop an assault on her city. Joab, David's commander-in-chief, had already battered her city wall and was ready to throw it down and massacre the people. This woman, who probably was a prophetess or one who held a position of high influence in her community, opened communication with Joab's officers and asked to see their commander. He was called, and she conferred with him.

Skillfully she began her plea for her city by citing its peculiar renown as a law-abiding servant of the kingdom. She reminded Joab that the ancient rule "to ask counsel at Abel" had settled quarrels for generations. A town that had been a peacemaker of a province for so long, she told Joab, was too valuable to be wiped out of existence.

Was it not better that he ask counsel at Abel first and batter i down afterward, if he must? She grew eloquent and cried, "I am one of them that are peaceable and faithful in Israel: thou seekest to destroy a city and a mother in Israel: why wilt thou swallow up the inheritance of the Lord?" What courage, what faith it took on this woman's part to make such a plea before a powerful commander-in-chief.

She was successful. The fierce soldier accepted her judgment as more just than his. He told her it was not his wish to slaughter and lay waste indiscriminately but explained to her that he was assaulting her city because of one man, Sheba, the Benjamite, who had organized a revolt and had retreated northward and entrenched himself in the walled city of Abel.

Joab had traced him from place to place and had finally located him in Abel, above the sources of the Jordan, under the very shadow of the Lebanon mountains. The people of Abel were in a sad plight, the innocent victims of one man, who had sought refuge inside their walls and had brought an avenging army knocking at their gates; and this wise woman had arisen as the defender of her people.

Who was this rebellious Benjamite that would hide behind their walls? Her answer was stern and swift. "Behold, his head shall be thrown to thee over the wall," she said to Joab. And she was in a position to make good her words.

She went before her people and told them the truth about the dangerous visitor. Sheba had no supporters among the people of Abel, and they were willing to wield the sword swiftly. The traitor's head was delivered to Joab's officer. The city of Abel was saved.

This woman proved how devout she was when she had the courage to cry to an enemy, "Why wilt thou swallow up the inheritance of the Lord?" (II Sam. 20:19). Wise, significant words in time of war!

PAGAN GODDESSES

Pagan goddesses appear in the Bible under a number of names. In only one instance does the word "goddess" occur in the Old Testament. That is in I Kings 11:5, 33, and determines the gender of Ashtoreth, the goddess of the Zidonians. This female deity was often represented as a virgin yet pregnant goddess. The pagan goddess' name is found in various forms some forty times in the Old Testament, especially in Kings and Chronicles.

In the New Testament the term "goddess" is applied to Diana, worshiped in the great temple at Ephesus (Acts 19:27, 35, 37).

THE LITTLE MAID

The little maid (II Kings 5:2, 4), though a minor character, was the channel for one of the great miracles of the Old Testament, the healing of Naaman by the great prophet Elisha. She was a young Hebrew girl in the retinue of Naaman's servants in the royal city of Damascus, having been taken by Naaman, commander of the army of Ben-hadad, king of Damascus, as one of the spoils of war in his raid into Israelite territory.

When the little maid saw that her master was suffering from leprosy, she expressed the wish to his wife that he could visit Elisha, the prophet-healer of the Israelites. The king of Syria, learning that there was a possibility that his army commander Naaman could be cured, sent a letter to the king of Israel, who in turn sent word to Elisha of Naaman's approaching visit to him.

Naaman departed in his chariot for Elisha's home in Israel, taking with him "ten talents of silver, and six thousand pieces of gold"

(II Kings 5:5), or the equivalent of about $80,000 for the great prophet, if he should be healed. In order to humble Naaman's pride and teach him that his healing could come only through God, Elisha refused to see Naaman personally but directed him to give himself seven baths in the river Jordan.

Naaman rode away enraged and humiliated, but after his temper cooled he tried Elisha's prescription, and when he came out of the water his flesh was like that of a little child. Turning back homeward with his gifts, which Elisha had refused to accept, Naaman took with him two mules' burden of earth, in order that he might build an altar to the Lord God of Israel in Syria.

All of these wonders came about through the lowly little maid, who exercised her simple faith and did not hesitate to help her master in his affliction.

THE WOMEN OF PROVERBS
(BOOK OF PROVERBS)

The strange woman (Prov. 2:16; 5:3, 20; 7:5; 20:16; 23:27, 33), who was a loose woman or a harlot, appears more often than any other. These passages are filled with grim warnings against her, for the strange woman's feet go down to death, her steps take hold on hell (5:5). Men are admonished not to come near the door of her house, but to rejoice with the wife of their youth. In the greatness of his folly, it says, a man can easily go astray, for "the lips of a strange woman drop as an honeycomb, and her mouth is smoother than oil" (5:3). She is unstable, sure to disappoint, and those who go before her will be filled with remorse. A man who goes to her is spiritually dead and will be held in spiritual bondage. "Drink waters out of thine own cistern, and running waters out of thine own well" (5:15), he is told, for such a woman is impure, and her sin is destructive. Even though a man go unto her quietly, God himself "pondereth all his goings" (5:21).

The wife of thy youth—rejoice with her (5:18).

The evil woman—lust not after her beauty or be taken by her eyelids (6:25).

The neighbor's wife—who touches her shall not be innocent (6:29).

The harlot—is subtle of heart, loud and stubborn; she lieth in wait at every corner (7:10, 11, 12); who keepeth company with her spendeth his substance (29:3).

The foolish woman—is clamorous, simple, and knoweth nothing (9:13).

The gracious woman—retaineth honor (11:16).

The fair woman without discretion—is as a jewel of gold in a swine's snout (11:22).

The wise woman—buildeth her house well (14:1).

The foolish woman—plucketh her house down. (14:1).

The wife—who findeth her findeth a good thing and obtaineth favor of God (18:22). The contentious wife is a continual dropping on a rainy day (19:13; 27:15). The prudent wife is from the Lord (19:14).

The brawling woman—better to dwell in the corner of the house-top than with her in a wide house (21:9; 25:24).

The angry woman—better to dwell in a wilderness than with her (21:19).

The contentious woman—and a continual dropping in a very rainy day are alike (27:15).

The adulterous woman—eateth and wipeth her mouth and says, "I have done no wickedness" (30:20).

The odious woman—when she is married is disquieting to the earth (30:21, 23).

The virtuous woman or the good wife—see Section I, "Searching Studies."

WOMAN WHOSE HEART IS SNARES AND NETS

The woman whose heart is snares and nets (Eccles. 7:26) is said to be more bitter than death. In other words, she is the evil woman, such as the harlot, whose hands are as bands that enclose a man. He who would please God should escape from such a woman, says the writer, "but the sinner shall be taken by her."

THE SHULAMITE SWEETHEART

The Shulamite sweetheart in the Song of Solomon has had many allegorical and mystical interpretations by scholars. She seems to represent a woman faithful to her pledged love amid the seductive temptations of an oriental court.

There are thought to be three chief speakers in the Song of Solomon: the country maid, her lover, and Solomon. The daughters of Jerusalem join in like a chorus in a Greek play.

In the period in which this poem was written, it was considered proper for a king to have a harem with many wives. Solomon's wives numbered 700. Emissaries of the king sought everywhere for beautiful women who were deemed worthy to be brought to the king. If one pleased the king, she was made a permanent member of his household.

This song depicts a country maiden in the north who attracted the king's emissaries. She came to Jerusalem under protest, and the king was pleased with her, but he did not wish to force her into his harem. On the other hand, he sought to woo her by offering her every possible inducement.

It is this wooing, and the Shulamite's refusal, because she is pledged to another, that constitutes the action for the Song. Even with all inducements, the country maid does not wish to become one of the king's many wives. She wishes to remain faithful to her own lover. Even though there are three attempts of the king to win the Shulamite, there is the final strong tribute to a faithful love.

The Song of Solomon is a beautiful composition. Pastoral scenes bound. Doves hide in the cleft of the rocks. Gazelles leap on the mountains. There are trees with fine foliage, flowers with bright hues and rich perfume. One seems to sense the balmy air of spring and walk amid terraced vineyards and tropical trees.

But the Song of Solomon is more than a beautiful poem. Written at a time when polygamy was a universal practice, some scholars regard it as a protest against polygamy. Here shines the purity and constancy of a woman's love, the kind of love that is not tempted by a king or his palace but endures amid the simpler things of life. Here speaks a voice in the midst of a corrupt age. It is lifted for the purity of life and right relationships, ordained by God, between one man and one woman.

Some scholars interpret the account of the Shulamite sweetheart as an allegory representing the mutual love of Jehovah and Israel under the symbolism of marriage. Christian scholars find it easy to follow this Jewish allegorical interpretation. The figure of wedlock is employed in the New Testament by both Paul and John to represent the intimate and vital union of Christ and His Church.

Other scholars consider the Song of Solomon as an anthology of love lyrics, still others as a drama of the period of Solomon. Many scholars interpret it in a mystical and allegorical sense.

VIRGIN PROPHESIED

Virgin prophesied (Isa. 7:14). Isaiah made this prophecy at least seven centuries before Christ, that a virgin would conceive and bear a son, and his name would be called Immanuel.

OTHER UNNAMED WOMEN

CARELESS WOMEN AT EASE
Careless women at ease (Isa. 32:19-12) are admonished to rise up
and hear God's voice and give ear unto His speech. And there is the
warning that "the vintage shall fail, the gathering shall not come,"
for those who are careless and indolent.

QUEEN OF HEAVEN
The queen of heaven (Jer. 7:18; 44:17, 18, 19) was an ancient
Semitic goddess in whose honor the Hebrews of Jeremiah's period
made cakes, burned incense, and poured out drink offerings. Probably she was the Phoenician or Canaanite goddess Ashtoreth or the
Babylonian Ishtar. Many figurines of these and other goddesses have
been dug up in archaeological explorations.

WOMEN WEEPING FOR TAMMUZ
The women weeping for Tammuz (Ezek. 8:14) sat at the north
gate of the Jerusalem Temple. Instead of weeping for the national
sins, these women wept for the dead god Tammuz, ancient god
of pasture and flocks, of the subterranean ocean, and of vegetation.

This incident is listed in Ezekiel's vision of "abominations" of
the people. God had declared that He would not pardon this and
other idolatrous worship.

WOMEN WHO SEW PILLOWS TO ARMHOLES
The women who sew pillows to armholes (Ezek. 13:18) were the
false prophetesses who made cushions to lean on, typifying the perfect tranquillity which they foretold to those consulting them. Their
pretended inspiration enhanced their guilt as prophetesses.

The translation of this phrase in the Revised Standard Version paints a slightly different picture, but the basic idea is the same. Instead of "women that sew pillows to all armholes" they are described as "women who sew magic bands upon all wrists." This refers to the amulets people bought from false prophetesses or sorceresses and wore to give them a sense of security. But the security was false.

The men who are said to have built a wall (Ezek. 13:10), and the women who sewed pillows or made magic arm bands—both alike promised a false peace and security.

WOMAN WITH LEAVEN

The woman with leaven (Matt. 13:33; Luke 13:21) appears in one of Jesus' parables about the kingdom of God. He likens the kingdom of God to leaven, "which a woman took, and hid in three measures of meal, till the whole was leavened." Three measures were probably more than a bushel, an enormous amount for bread, but the quantity probably was large in order to emphasize the mighty extent of God's rule. In this parable Jesus teaches that His gospel, though apparently small and weak, nevertheless possesses the power quietly to transform all of life.

Woman the loaf-giver as well as man the seed-sower are both needed to feed the hungry.

WOMAN WITH SEVEN HUSBANDS

The woman with seven husbands (Matt. 22:25-32; Mark 12:20-25) was married first to one, then another of seven brothers. As each one died, without leaving a child, she became the wife of another of the brothers. Her marriage was in keeping with the early levirate law, making it obligatory for a man to marry his brother's widow.

The Pharisees and Sadducees, desiring to place Jesus at a disadvantage, brought to Him this unusual but hypothetical case of the woman with seven husbands, asking him whose wife she would be if the husbands arose in the resurrection. And he told them that they knew not the Scriptures nor the power of God, for in heaven they neither marry nor are given in marriage, but are as angels in heaven.

TWO WOMEN AT THE MILL

Two women at the mill (Matt. 24:41; Luke 17:35) is a picture used by Jesus to make clear to His disciples how necessary it was to be ready for the day when the Son of man should be revealed. He said, "Two women shall be grinding together; the one shall be taken, and the other left."

Jesus used this story immediately after that of the two men in bed, one of whom shall be taken and the other left, and just before the story of the two men in the field, one of whom should be taken and the other left. The fate of everyone was dependent upon whether he or she was ready for the sudden and unexpected coming of the kingdom of God.

He wanted women to know, just as he wanted men to know, that none was exempt, not even women busy at their household tasks.

TEN WISE AND FOOLISH VIRGINS

Ten wise and foolish virgins (Matt. 25:1-3) are the subject of one of Jesus' parables illustrating the need for a vigilant and expectant attitude of faith. The virgins, in these times, were to light the way for the bridegroom when he appeared.

Jesus told of the five virgins who were wise and took along extra oil for their lamps, and of five who were foolish and took none. When the bridegroom tarried, they all slumbered, and at midnight, when it was announced that he was coming, the wise virgins arose and trimmed their lamps, but the foolish virgins said, "Our lamps are gone out." While the foolish ones went to buy more oil, the bridegroom came; and they that were ready went in and the door was shut, but the foolish virgins were too late.

In this parable Jesus points to the contrast between the preparedness of the spiritually faithful and the unreadiness of the faithless, and exhorts all to be ready. In this case the bridegroom is Christ Himself and this refers to His second coming.

The parable is set between two other parables concerning men and may contain a warning that women are expected to bear their full share of responsibility for the coming of the kingdom.

MAIDS AT THE HIGH PRIEST'S HOUSE

The maids at the high priest's house (Matt. 26:69-71; Mark 14:66-69; Luke 22:56-59; John 18:16, 17) are witnesses to Peter's denial of Jesus after Judas had betrayed Him and He had been led to the house of the high priest, Caiaphas, for trial.

Peter had boasted that he would never forsake Jesus, but when first one maid and then another recognized him in the courtyard and asked him if he were one of Jesus' disciples, he vehemently declared he was not.

In Matthew's and Mark's accounts two maids are mentioned, while in Luke's and John's there is only one maid. John adds the information that the maid was "the damsel that kept the door."

"MANY WOMEN WERE THERE"

"Many women were there [Matt. 27:55] beholding afar off, which followed Jesus from Galilee, ministering unto him." Though in the next paragraph Mary Magdalene, and Mary the mother of James and Joses, and the mother of Zebedee's children are named among the women there, we can be sure there were many nameless women with them.

They had followed Jesus to the cross because He had blessed

them and healed them, and their gratitude was great. They did little but watch, but their watching had meaning and purpose. They showed unflinching courage and extreme faithfulness in remaining close to Jesus throughout the long hours of His suffering upon the cross.

Evidently Matthew believes that women are guarantors of the tradition. They were with Jesus at the tomb and they would be with Him at the Resurrection. They were among His most faithful followers, and because they were present at the Crucifixion and saw the empty tomb they became transmitters of what happened to Jesus both at the cross and on the morning of the Resurrection.

THREE SICK WOMEN

Three sick women (Matthew, Mark, Luke). (See Section I, "Searching Studies.")

SINFUL WOMAN

The sinful woman (Luke 7:36-50) washed the feet of Jesus with her tears and anointed His feet with ointment. He had come to be entertained at the house of Simon, the Pharisee, when this unnamed woman entered with an alabaster box of ointment and stood at Jesus' feet weeping. She washed His feet with her tears, wiped them with the hair of her head, kissed His feet, and anointed them with the ointment.

Simon, the Pharisee, shocked that a woman who was a sinner should come to Jesus, said to himself: "This man, if he were a prophet, would have known who and what manner of woman this is that toucheth him: for she is a sinner."

Jesus then told Simon the parable of the creditor and his two debtors, one of whom owed five hundred pence and the other fifty. Because neither of them could pay their debts, the creditor forgave them both. Jesus asked Simon, "Which of them will love him most?" And Simon answered, "I suppose that he, to whom he forgave most."

Jesus then reminded Simon that he had not even offered Him the usual courtesy of water in which to wash His feet when He entered his house, but the woman had humbly served Him. He then made the point to Simon that "Her sins, which are many, are forgiven; for she loved much: but to whom little is forgiven, the same loveth little." And then Jesus turned to the woman and said, "Thy sins are forgiven. . . . Thy faith hath saved thee; go in peace."

WOMAN WHO LIFTED HER VOICE

The woman who lifted her voice (Luke 11:27, 28) was one of those emotional women who stood on the side listening to Jesus and who said to Him, "Blessed is the womb that bare thee, and the paps which thou hast sucked." But Jesus, practical in His religion, answered, "Blessed are they that hear the word of God, and keep it."

WOMAN WITH LOST PIECE OF SILVER

The woman with the lost piece of silver (Luke 15:8-10) appears in another of Jesus' parables in which women figure. It emphasizes diligence and repentance, fellowship and joy. The lost piece of silver probably refers to one of the coins worn on a woman's headdress. A woman could expect trouble with her husband if she lost them. Probably that is why this woman was sweeping so diligently, using her broom and a candle in all the dark corners of her house. The coin represented part of the wealth of her family. So do God's angels sweep this world for souls that have slipped away and fallen into the dirt. Jesus bids us go and seek them too. Just as the woman rejoiced with her neighbors when she had found her lost piece of silver, so do the angels of God rejoice over one sinner that repents.

OTHER UNNAMED WOMEN

WOMAN OF SAMARIA

Woman of Samaria (John 4:7-42). (See Section I, "Searching Studies.")

ADULTEROUS WOMAN

The woman taken in adultery (John 8:3-11) could have been stoned to death, according to the old Mosaic Law (Deut. 17:5, 6), but because Jesus forbade judgment against her, she was saved. The Pharisees were attempting to trap Jesus when they brought before Him the woman, whom they had found, they said, in the very act of adultery.

When she was brought before Jesus, He reached down and wrote on the ground, as if He did not hear them. He wished the Pharisees to know that He did not want to interfere in the local administration of the law, though He certainly did not regard adultery as a trivial matter. He only wished to give the woman's accusers time to realize that they only pretended zeal for the law.

After Jesus had shamed her accusers and they had gone, leaving Him alone with her, Jesus asked the most pertinent question of all, "Hath no man condemned thee?" In other words, where was the man, probably the one to whom she had been engaged, who had condemned her. When the woman replied, "No man, Lord," Jesus said, "Neither do I condemn thee: go, and sin no more." In this incident He raised new standards for marriage, that men as well as women are expected to keep their vows of marriage loyalty.

This woman who had been brought before Jesus was probably not a continual sinner but a young woman, and this, no doubt, was her first offense. Jesus did not condone her wrongdoing, but gave her another chance, if she would sin no more.

HONORABLE AND DEVOUT WOMEN

Honorable and devout women (Acts 13:50) of Pisidian Antioch, incited by the Jews against Paul and Barnabas, joined with the magistrates to expel these successful missionaries from their city. This event shows the influential position of women in Asia Minor.

A CERTAIN DAMSEL

A "certain damsel" (Acts 16:16) was a slave girl who encountered Paul while he was in Philippi. In all probability she was a clairvoyant who was "possessed of a spirit of divination," and "brought her masters much gain by soothsaying." But Christianity opposed this form of spiritualism. The girl, we learn, followed Paul and his friends and gave loud testimony to their divine mission.

Probably she heard Paul's preaching and received an impression that resulted, owing to the peculiar condition of her mind, in an acute perception of the true character of the missionaries. Paul, however, had no desire to be introduced by any such medium as this. He cast out the evil spirit which possessed the damsel; that is, he freed the girl from the abnormal condition of mind which made her a soothsayer. (See Section I, "Searching Studies," "Lydia.")

NEREUS' SISTER

Nereus' sister (Rom. 16:15) was included in Paul's salutations to many in the Church at Rome. Addition of the phrase "and all the saints which are with them" indicated that she was a saintly woman.

THE UNMARRIED WOMAN

"The unmarried woman [I Cor. 7:34] careth for the things of the Lord, that she may be holy both in body and in spirit." The married woman (I Cor. 7:34) "careth for the things of the world, how she may please her husband." Paul was here saying that a woman undergoes a great change when she marries, and often strives harder to please her husband than she does to please God.

WOMEN IN THE CHURCHES

Women in the churches (I Cor. 14:34, 35) are admonished by Paul to keep silent. Because this is apparently a contradiction of what Christ had taught, that men and women are equal before God, there have been many interpretations of this phrase.

In this particular admonition, Paul was speaking to the church at Corinth, a Greek city where, for many generations, high-born women had lived in seclusion. Chloe was such a woman and may very well have been shocked by the loud-voiced railings of women of a lower station in life. Since all women were welcome in the new church, among these may have been many who had worshiped in pagan temples and had not yet had sufficient experience to assume leadership in the church. Rejoicing in their new-found faith, but undisciplined in it, these women probably required some silencing in Paul's time.

There had been dissensions in the church at Philippi, and it is easy to assume that one dissension might have centered around women's participation in public gatherings. We have an indication of this in the passage on Euodias and Syntyche in Philippians 4:2, in which Paul entreats these two women to be of the same mind in the Lord.

Paul, let us not forget, had grown up under the Law, which stated, "thy husband, . . . he shall rule over thee" (Gen. 3:16). He may have accepted the inequality without thought of injustice. But how could Paul deny women an active part in the church?

He showed no evidence that he did. Lydia was his first convert in Europe, and his first sermon in Europe had been addressed to women on the banks of the river at Philippi. If these women had kept silent, the Christian gospel would not have spread as fast as it did over Europe.

Paul found in Priscilla, too, a woman of great ability and intellect who became a leader in the church at Corinth and later at Ephesus. He did not silence her. Nor did he silence Phebe, who was a deaconess at Cenchrea.

Dr. Lee Anna Starr in her book *The Bible Status of Woman* has devoted sixty-two pages to the Pauline mandate. She quotes other scholars, who state that they regard these two verses as interpolations by a later hand. Dr. Starr also brings up the point that "great disorder prevailed in the religious services of this church at Corinth. Each one had a Psalm, a teaching, a tongue, an interpretation, and all endeavoring to participate in the service. The Apostle seeks to quell this disturbance; he commands silence. . . .

"The custom of interrupting the speaker prevailed throughout the Orient, but the practice was confined to men. . . . To have allowed a wife to instruct her husband in the public assembly in the capacity of a teacher would have outraged every prejudice of the age."

WOMEN PROFESSING GODLINESS

Women professing godliness (I Tim. 2:9, 10), says Paul to Timothy, should be judged by their good works, not by what they wear. Their adorning should come from the inside out. Their adorning was to be effected not by how they were clothed but by how they served. Works, not words, were what counted with such women.

SILLY WOMEN

Silly women (II Tim. 3:6, 7) are those "laden with sins, led away with divers lusts, Ever learning, and never able to come to the knowledge of the truth."

Here Paul, writing to Timothy, foretells of perilous times in the last days. These passages refer to women whose consciences are burdened with sins; thus they are ready prey to the false teachers who promise ease of conscience if they will follow them.

OTHER UNNAMED WOMEN

AGED WOMEN

Aged women (Titus 2:3, 4-5) are told that they should be holy in their behavior "that they may teach the young women to be sober, to love their husbands, to love their children, to be discreet, chaste, keepers at home, good, obedient to their husbands, that the word of God be not blasphemed."

HOLY WOMEN

Holy women (I Pet. 3:5) says this Scripture, are those who trust in God and whose adornment is a meek and quiet spirit.

THE LETTER TO THE ELECT LADY

The letter to the elect lady (Second Epistle of John) has been debated since ancient times and the identity of the "lady" is still unsolved. Whether the letter is to a real woman and her children or to a particular church and its members or spiritual children is still a question. Whether the John here is the same as the one who wrote the Fourth Gospel or John the elder of Ephesus is also a question.

The Order of the Eastern Star uses the name Electa in its ritual, along with those of other Bible women, Ruth, Esther, Martha and Jephthah's daughter. The latter is called Adah by this Order, though in the Bible she appears as one of the nameless women. These five women form this Order's five points in the star. To this Order Electa represents those women who have been pre-eminent in charity and heroic in the endurance of persecution.

The word "lady" occurs in the Bible only six times, and twice in this letter. It usually signifies a woman of the nobility; however, here it could mean a lady who in her very spirit is to the manner born. There is every evidence that the elect lady was one of the elect of God.

Though this epistle addressed to the elect lady is very brief, containing only thirteen verses, it says a great deal in these few words.

Key words we find here are "love" and "truth." The word "truth" occurs five times in the first four verses: "I love in the truth . . . have known the truth . . . for the truth's sake . . . the Son of the Father, in truth . . . walking in truth." The theme of the letter centers around this word, which here means Christ, His gospel, His commandments, His teaching.

In the fifth verse John continues, "And now I beseech thee, lady, not as though I wrote a new commandment unto thee, but that which we had from the beginning, that we love one another." In the next verse he goes on to say, "This is love, that we walk after his commandments."

The elect lady seems to be responsible for seeing that her children also walk in love and truth. We can imagine that she had made a Christian home for them and had thus taught each one.

If the woman of today wants to take the letter literally, there is a real challenge there for her individually. She sees what it means to walk in truth and to bring up her children in truth and love. In this epistle she is also enjoined to be ever watchful to obey the true Christ, who has a oneness with the Father. Strong warning appears against false teachers and evil associations. And we are assured that the elect lady has the spiritual perception to know the difference between what is false and evil.

WOMEN IN REVELATION

Women in Revelation represent apocalyptic symbolism, to which the key has been lost. In Revelation 12:1, we have "a woman clothed with the sun, and the moon under her feet, and upon her head a crown of twelve stars." The text continues, "And she being with child cried, travailing in birth, and pained to be delivered" (Rev. 12:2). In this same chapter, verses 13-17, there is more about how satan persecutes the woman.

In Revelation 17, reference is made to "the great whore that sitteth upon many waters . . . a woman upon a scarlet coloured beast . . . THE MOTHER OF HARLOTS . . . the woman drunken with the blood of saints . . . the mystery of the woman, and of the beast that carrieth her." All again represent apocalyptic symbolism and must be interpreted spiritually.

In Revelation 18:7-10, a queen is mentioned. This refers to the wicked city of Babylon and her destruction.

In Revelation 19:7-8, emphasis centers on "the Lamb is come, and his wife hath made herself ready. And to her was granted that she should be arrayed in fine linen, clean and white: for the fine linen is the righteousness of saints." Mention is made again in Revelation 21:9 of "the bride, the Lamb's wife." All of this imagery of the Lamb's bride, most scholars concede, centers around the ideal Church and its final glory. Other interpretations have been innumerable.

Bibliography

COMMENTARIES AND ENCYCLOPEDIAS

Buttrick, George Arthur. *The Interpreter's Bible,* 12 vols. (when complete). New York and Nashville: Abingdon Press, 1952.

Cobbin, Ingram. Edited by E. J. Goodspeed. *Commentary on the Bible.* Selmar Hess, 1876. Old but reliable.

Eiselen, Frederick Carl, Lewis, Edwin, and Downey, David G. (eds.). *The Abingdon Bible Commentary.* New York and Nashville: Abingdon Press, 1929.

Gore, Charles, Goudge, H. L., and Guillaume, A. (eds.). *A New Commentary on Holy Scripture.* London: Macmillan and Co., 1929.

Hall, Newton Marshall, and Wood, Irving Francis. *The Book of Life.* John Rudin and Co., 1952.

Hastings, James. *The Greater Men and Women of the Bible.* Edinburgh: T & T Clark, 1913.

Hertz, J. H. *The Pentateuch and Haftorahs,* 2 vols. Metzudah.

Jamieson, Robert, Fausset, A. R., and Brown, David. *Commentary on the Whole Bible.* Grand Rapids: Zondervan Publishing House.

Orr, James, Nuelsen, John L., and Mullins, Edgar Y. *The International Standard Bible Encyclopedia,* 5 vols. Grand Rapids: Wm. B. Eerdmans Publishing Co., 1941.

Peake, Arthur S., Grieve, A. J. (eds.). *A Commentary on the Bible.* New York: Thomas Nelson and Sons, 1920.

DICTIONARIES

Davis, John B., and Gehman, Henry Snyder. *The Westminster Dictionary of the Bible.* Philadelphia: The Westminster Press, 1944.

Hastings, James. *Dictionary of the Bible.* New York: Charles Scribner's Sons, 1948.

Hastings, James, Selbie, John A., and Lambert, John C. *A Dictionary of Christ and the Gospels.* Edinburgh: T & T Clark, 1906.

Mead, Frank S. *Who's Who in the Bible.* New York: Harper & Brothers, 1934.

Miller, Madeleine S. and J. Lane. *Harper's Bible Dictionary*. New York: Harper & Brothers, 1952.

CONCORDANCES

Eadie, John. *Cruden's Concordance*. Grand Rapids: Baker Book House, 1952.

Joy, Charles R. *Harper's Topical Concordance*. New York: Harper & Brothers, 1940.

Stevenson, Burton. *The Home Book of Bible Quotations*. New York: Harper & Brothers, 1949.

Strong, James. *Exhaustive Concordance of the Bible*. New York and Nashville: Abingdon Press, 1953.

Young, Robert. *Analytical Concordance to the Bible*. Grand Rapids: Wm. B. Eerdmans Company, 1936.

TOPICAL BIBLES

Hitchcock. *Topical Bible*. Grand Rapids: Baker Book House, 1952.

Nave, Orville J. *Topical Bible*. Chicago: Moody Press, 1921.

INTERPRETIVE BIBLES

Harper Annotated Bible Series. New York: Harper & Brothers, 1949 ff.

Masonic. *Holy Bible*. Chicago: John A. Hertel Company, 1949.

Thompson, Frank Charles. *The New Chain Reference*. Indianapolis: B. B. Kirkbride Bible Company, 1934.

Westminster Study Edition of the Holy Bible. Philadelphia: Westminster Press, 1948.

Williams, Thomas. *The Cottage Bible*, 2 vols. Hartford: A. Brainard, 1870.

OTHER SOURCE BOOKS

Gaer, Joseph. *The Lore of the Old and New Testaments*, 2 vols. Boston: Little, Brown & Company, 1951.

Josephus, Flavius. *Life and Works*. Philadelphia: John C. Winston Company.

Karraker, William A. *The Bible in Questions and Answers*. New York: The David McKay Company, 1953.

Latourette, Kenneth Scott. *A History of Christianity*. New York: Harper & Brothers, 1953.

Miller, Madeleine S. and J. Lane. *Encyclopedia of Bible Life*. New York: Harper & Brothers, 1944.

Parmelee, Alice. *A Guidebook to the Bible*. New York: Harper & Brothers, 1948.

Wright, George Ernest, and Filson, Floyd Vivian. *The Westminster Historical Atlas to the Bible*. Philadelphia: The Westminster Press, 1945.

BIBLIOGRAPHY

WOMEN OF THE BIBLE

Adams, Charles. *Women of the Bible.* New York: Lane & Scott, 1851.

Aguilar, Grace. *Women of Israel.* London: George Routledge and Sons, first published in the 1840's. The best of the old books on Women of the Old Testament.

Ashton, Mrs. S. G. *The Mothers of the Bible.* Boston: J. E. Tilton & Company, 1859.

Barnard, David. *Biblical Women.* Cincinnati: Hart & Company, 1863. A reliable and somewhat comprehensive work by an old Hebrew scholar.

Brown, Theron. *Nameless Women of the Bible.* Boston: The American Tract Society, 1905.

Buchanan, Isabella Reid. *The Women of the Bible.* New York: Appleton and Company, 1924. A 115-page book, includes a long list of women, but sketches are brief.

Chappell, Clovis G. *Feminine Faces.* New York and Nashville: Abingdon Press, 1942. Sixteen sketches.

Clement, Clara Erskine. *Heroines of the Bible.* Boston: L. C. Page and Company, 1900. Deals entirely with women of the Bible in art.

Cox, Francis Augustus. *Female Scripture Biography.* London: Gale & Fenner, 1817.

Davidson, Donald. *Mothers in the Bible.* London and Edinburgh: Marshall, Morgan and Scott, 1934. Twenty-six biographies.

Eminent Divines. *Women of the Bible.* New York: Harper & Brothers, 1900. Twelve biographies.

Harrison, Eveleen. *Little-Known Women of the Bible.* New York: Round Table Press, Inc., 1936.

Heaps, Isabel Warrington. *Five Marys.* New York and Nashville: Abingdon Press, 1942.

Hosie, Lady. *Jesus and Women.* London: Hodder and Stoughton, 1946. Inspiring.

Ketter, Peter. *Christ and Womankind.* Westminster, Md.: The Newman Press. Fundamental role of women in Christian scheme.

Kuyper, Abraham. *Women of the Old and New Testament,* 2 small vols. Grand Rapids: Zondervan Publishing House, 1934. Fifty character studies from Old Testament and thirty from New Testament.

Lofts, Norah. *Women in the Old Testament.* New York: The Macmillan Company, 1950. Twenty portraits.

Lord, Townley. *Great Women of the Bible.* New York: Harper & Brothers.

Lundholm, Algot Theodor. *Women of the Bible.* Atlanta: Augustana Book Concern, 1948. Thirty-one sketches, uplifting.

McAllister, Grace. *God Portrays Women.* Chicago: Moody Press, 1954. Sixteen sketches.

McCartney, Clarence Edward. *Great Women of the Bible.* New York and Nashville: Abingdon Press, 1952. Thirteen sketches.

Mace, David R. *Hebrew Marriage.* The Philosophical Library, 1953. A scholarly sociological study.

Mackay, Mackintosh. *Bible Types of Modern Women.* New York: Harper & Brothers. Twenty-two sketches.

Marble, Annie Russell. *Women of the Bible.* New York: The Century Company, 1923. More comprehensive than some, but not complete.

Martyn, Mrs. S. T. *Women of the Bible.* New York: American Tract Society, 1868. Twenty-seven sketches.

Matheson, George. *The Representative Women of the Bible.* New York: George Doran Company, 1907. Eleven inspiring sketches.

Miller, Basil. *Ten Famous Girls of the Bible.* Grand Rapids: Zondervan Publishing House. A 159-page study pamphlet for boys and girls.

Miller, Madeleine Sweeney. *New Testament Women and Problems of Today.* New York: The Methodist Book Concern, 1926. Discussion studies for young women.

Morton, H. V. *Women of the Bible.* New York: Dodd, Mead & Co., 1941. Twenty-three sketches.

Moss, Arthur Bruce. *Women of Scripture.* 145-page Methodist study pamphlet.

Murrell, Gladys. *Glimpses of Grace.* New York and Nashville: Abingdon Press. Devotionals based on lives of women of the Bible.

Nichol, C. R. *God's Woman, Her Sphere.* Clifton, Texas: The Nichol Publishing Company. A topic studybook.

Novotny, Louise Miller. *Women and the Church.* Cincinnati: Standard Publishing Company. A textbook and manual for women's organizations.

Ockenga, Harold John. *Have You Met These Women?* Grand Rapids: Zondervan Publishing House, 1940.

Oliver, French E. *Pilate's Wife and Others.* New York: Fleming H. Revell Company, 1932. Eight biographies.

O'Reilly, Bernard. *Illustrious Women.* New York: P. J. Kenedy, 1896. Twenty-eight women of the Bible.

Outlaw, Nell Warren. *And Certain Women.* Nashville: Broadman Press, 1947.

Overby, Coleman. *Bible Women.* Dallas: Coleman Overby, Publisher. A twelve months' study course.

Riley, ———. *Wives of the Bible.* Grand Rapids: Zondervan Publishing House, 1938. Eight studies.

BIBLIOGRAPHY

Sangster, Margaret. *The Women of the Bible.* New York: The Christian Herald Bible House, 1911. Forty-six sketches.

Sell, H. T. *Studies of Famous Bible Women.* New York: Fleming H. Revell Company, 1925. Twenty-one sketches.

Sprague, William B., ed. *Women of the Old and New Testament.* New York: D. Appleton and Company, 1849. Handsomely bound and illustrated with eighteen steel engravings, but outdated textually. Eighteen biographies.

Starr, Lee Anna. *The Bible Status of Woman.* New York: Fleming H. Revell Company, 1926. The most scholarly of all.

Steele, Eliza R. *Heroines of Sacred History.* New York: J. S. Taylor & Company, 1842.

Stowe, Harriet Beecher. *Women in Sacred History.* New York: J. B. Ford and Company, 1870. Nineteen biographies.

Sudlow, Elizabeth Williams. *Career Women of the Bible.* New York: Pageant Press, 1951. Twenty-two studies.

Sydenstricker, Hiram Mason. *Nameless Immortals.* Nashville and Dallas: Barbee & Smith, 1901.

Tinney, Ethel. *Women of the Bible in Verse.* New York: Pageant Press, 1953.

Wainwright, J. M. *Women of the Bible.* New York: Appleton and Company, 1849. Handsomely illustrated with eighteen steel engravings in color, but textually outdated. Eighteen biographies.

Weld, Hastings. *The Women of the Old and New Testament.* Philadelphia: Lindsay and Blakiston, 1848. Quaintly illustrated but outdated.

Williams, Isaac. *Female Characters of Scripture.* London: Rivington's, 1862. Thirty biographies.

Index

INDEX

INDEX

INDEX

INDEX

[391]

INDEX

INDEX

Horites; *see* Foreign women
Hosea
  daughter of, 277
  wife of, 263-64
Hospitality shown by women (*see also* **Food**)
  in Old Testament
    Abigail, 102
    Endor, woman of, 108
    Esther, 150
    Jael, 73, 269
    Jethro's daughters, 55
    Rahab, 66
    Rebekah, 23
    Sarah, 13
    Shunammite, the, 136
    Zarephath, woman of, 132-33
  in New Testament
    Apphia, 252
    Elisabeth, 170
    Lydia, 224 ff.
    Martha, 176 ff.
    Mary, mother of John Mark, 211-12
    Mary of Bethany, 176 ff.
    Phebe, 231-32
    Philip's daughters, 321
    Priscilla, 229-30
Huldah, 143-45, 269
Hur, 58
Hushim, 269
Hypocrisy in the Church, 217

Ibzan's daughters, 313
Ichabod's mother, 93-95, 341
Idolatry, 74, 301, 340; *see also* Goddesses; Gods; Idols
Idols
  household, 33-34
  Michal's, 98
Immaculate conception, dogma of the, 162
Immanuel, 366
Importunate widow, 354
Inheritance by daughters, instances of
  Barzillai's, 314
  Job's, 272, 276
  Laban's, 33-34
  Sheshan's, 313-14
  Zelophehad's, 62-64
Innkeeper; *see* Occupations
International relations, 124
International Standard Bible Encyclopedia, concerning
  Claudia, 258

International Standard Bible Encyclopedia, concerning—*continued*
  Queen of Sheba, 121
  Zeruiah, 301-2
Irenaeus, 257
Isaac, 9, 14 f., 22-27, 265
Isaiah
  daughters of Zion, prophecy concerning, 317
  reign of righteous king, prophecy of, 174
  virgin mother, prophecy of, 366
  wife of, 334, 345
Iscah, 269
Ishmael, 10, 13 f.
  daughter of, 280
  mother of, 10 f., 264-66
Israel
  founder of, 8
  twelve tribes of, mothers of, 28-36
Israel's heroic age, women of, 49-95
Israelite maid; *see* Hebrew maid
Issachar, 32

Jabal, 248, 284
Jabez' mother, 344
Jabin, 70
Jacob, 24-27
  birthright of, 25-26
  concubines of, 255, 303
  daughter of, 37-40
  daughter-in-law of, 253
  mother of, 21-27
  wives of, 28-36
Jael, 73, 269-70, 339
Jairus' daughter, 318-19
James, Epistle of, 211
James, son of Mary, 210 f.
James, son of Salome, 192 ff., 291, 319
Japheth, 323
Jared's daughters, 308
Jecholiah, 270
Jeconiah; *see* Jehoiachin
Jedidah, 144, 270
Jehoaddan, 271
Jehoahaz' mother, 267
Jehoiachin (Jeconiah), 286, 293
Jehoiada, 142
Jehoiakim, 286, 300
Jehoram (king of Israel), 129, 139
Jehoram (king of Judah), 130, 141
Jehosheba (Jehoshabeath), 142, 271-72
Jehozabad, 295
Jehu, 129 f., 141
Jehudijah, 272; *see also* Hodiah
Jemima, 272-73, 334

INDEX

INDEX